INTERNATIONAL ECONOMIC TREND ANALYSIS

INTERNATIONAL ECONOMIC TREND ANALYSIS

Howard G. Schaefer

Q

Quorum Books
Westport, Connecticut • London

Library of Congress Cataloging-in-Publication Data

Schaefer, Howard G.
    International economic trend analysis / Howard G. Schaefer.
      p. cm.
    Includes bibliographical references and index.
    ISBN 0–89930–956–9 (alk. paper)
    1. Business cycles.   2. International finance.   3. International
trade.   I. Title.
HF1359.S33   1995
337—dc20   94–40459

British Library Cataloguing in Publication Data is available.

Library of Congress Catalog Card Number: 94–40459

ISBN: 0–89930–956–9

3 2280 00518 5475

First published in 1995

Quorum Books, 88 Post Road West, Westport, CT 06881
An imprint of Greenwood Publishing Group, Inc.

Printed in the United States of America

The paper used in this book complies with the
Permanent Paper Standard issued by the National
Information Standards Organization (Z39.48—1984).

10 9 8 7 6 5 4 3 2

For my mother
Evelyn Schaefer

□ □ ■ □ □

Contents

Tables and Figures

TABLES

FIGURES

□　□　■　□　□

Preface

International economics is a complex subject made almost incomprehensible by the vast amounts of data and other information now available in quantities, accuracy, and real time unprecedented in human history. One of the most successful means of dealing with complex information is by using a systematic approach for accumulating and evaluating data. This approach is at the heart of most management information systems. Unfortunately, available systems for international economics were expensive and time consuming. Consequently, I began developing my own system utilizing the readily available data published in *The Economist*. It has proven remarkably helpful.

A successful analytical system also requires a basic analytical model. Law school had taught me that an important reason for written judicial opinions was as a discipline to force judges to reason logically about the facts and issues before them. Applying the same concept to the subject of international economics and finance, I found that writing this book forced me to think deeply about the subject matter and develop an overall understanding of the existing international economic system.

Although the subject matter may be laborious, patient attention to the material will make the diligent reader fully conversant with the complex ebbs and flows of international economic and financial events. We are entering an unprecedented period in international economic growth; yet there remain vast differences in economic theory, government policy, and data, causing national economies to move in divergent directions threatening to capsize trade and financial markets. The international matrix system presented here will improve the understanding of international economic events leading to better business and investment decisions.

This book could never have been accomplished without the love and support of my wife Debra and daughter Nicole whom I deeply love, and I appreciate the sacrifices they have made. I wish to give special thanks to Frank Thomas Murphy, C.P.A., of counsel to Coopers & Lybrand, for his diligent review of the manuscript and bringing to bear his long and active experience in international business affairs. I wish to also thank the wonderful people at John Beck Editing and Production Service for professional editorial guidance in bringing the manuscript to book form and Eric Valentine at Greenwood Publishing Group, Inc., for supporting this project. Appreciation is also given to *The Economist* and the International Monetary Fund for permission to use their published data and to Carol Howard, head of research (*The Economist*) for her patience in answering my questions.

CHAPTER 1

Perspective

Throughout history, those alert to international trade have considerably enhanced their individual and national wealth. In antiquity, the Egyptians, Greeks, and Phoenicians derived much of their wealth from flourishing Mediterranean trade; while in the Middle Ages, Arab traders exchanged European precious metals for the spices and silk of China. During the Industrial Revolution, Britain built its overseas empire on the international trade of its manufactured goods while following the Meiji restoration in 1868; Japan pursued cultural independence by commencing international trade to obtain natural resources and foreign technology to strengthen its domestic economy.

While increasing wealth has been the primary motivating force in international trade, astute leaders have recognized other important advantages. Companies that successfully compete in the international marketplace are less vulnerable to enterprising competitors invading the domestic market encouraged by consumers seeking better and cheaper replacements. Likewise, nations successfully competing in the international marketplace derive efficiencies and technologies that enhance their domestic economies, advance their citizens' standard of living, and enhance their ability to sustain the financial drain of a national defense apparatus.

International trade and investment is also a treacherous arena to the unwary, however. Extending beyond one's border is not a simple extension of existing business and investment practices. International commerce has its own unique characteristics increasing the risks of cross-border commerce. Cultural and religious differences, poor communications, incompatible business practices,

different legal systems, different financial systems, variations in utility infrastructure, and a political establishment anxious to protect domestic residents
are only some of the many differences facing the international venturer.

Overcoming these differences offers great rewards to those nimble and
skillful in navigating these unique characteristics. Europeans, Japanese, Chinese, and many other peoples who have accepted these additional difficulties
have also worked to reduce the risk by assiduously developing unique business practices and accumulating extensive experience dealing with these uncertain conditions.

Thus, for many people the term *global economy* means opportunity and
adventure. Yet for others, the term means uncertainty and depravation. Americans in the 1990s seem particularly distraught about this term as evidenced
by the public debate on adoption of the North American Free Trade Agreement (NAFTA). NAFTA eliminates many barriers to cross-border trade between Mexico and the United States which should be mutually beneficial. But
the decline in U.S. global economic hegemony and the rise of major global
competitors had created an uneasy feeling of impending decline in the national standard of living which threatened to block NAFTA's passage.

The term *global economy* signifies some massive economic transformation
that is profoundly altering the economies of all nations to the detriment of the
United States as large multinational corporations redistribute resources
around the globe to maximize profits, escape government regulation, and
minimize taxes. This transformation is said to cause vast capital flows to regions offering the highest return or stable financial conditions, thereby starv-
ing many nations of needed expansion capital while, in the meantime,
low-cost countries entice hard-pressed and overregulated manufacturing concerns with irresistible opportunities to relocate as employees of multinational
firms become a new class of stateless people developing their own cultural
values independent of local cultural values.

U.S. INTERNATIONAL ECONOMIC HERITAGE

Underlying American concern about global competition is a surprising lack
of understanding and sophistication in international commerce. It is surprising because American businesses have been formidable global competitors
skillfully exploiting the unique characteristics of the international marketplace. Americans traditionally demonstrated a keen knowledge of international business affairs. In fact, for most of American history, international
business has been an integral factor in economic growth and in the forefront
of American business and political strategy.

American global competitive skills and awareness of global economic opportunities began well before the founding of the great nation. During the
colonial period the colonists needed manufactured goods, and Britain was the
greatest and most advanced manufacturer in its day. However, the American

colonies had an unfavorable balance of trade and little specie or precious metals by which to pay for the trade deficit. A complex system of triangular trade was developed by the enterprising colonists. The agricultural products of the colonies were shipped to southern Europe and the West Indies in exchange for various products that were shipped to Britain and traded for the manufactured goods that could then be brought back to the Americas.[1]

After independence in 1789, the former colonists worked to reduce their dependence on foreign manufactured goods by developing their own manufacturing capability. To encourage domestic manufacturing, Alexander Hamilton spearheaded the drive for high tariffs on imported manufactured products.[2] In the early 1800s, this high-tariff policy triggered a national debate that highlighted not only the growing sectional disparity among the states eventually culminating in the Civil War but also the continuing impact of international commerce.[3]

Under tariff protection, the northern states built a flourishing and highly productive manufacturing sector that directed its output primarily to the growing domestic economy. The southern states, on the other hand, developed a thriving business exporting cotton to European textile mills. High tariffs not only made both imported and domestically produced manufactured goods expensive for the southern economy but also caused serious friction with foreign trading partners who threatened retaliatory tariffs on cotton exports.

An early demonstration of America's shrewd appreciation of global economic opportunity was Perry's opening of Japan in 1853 as its importance to economic growth became apparent. Whale oil was a principal source of illuminating oil, constituting at the time a major American industry. One of the principal whaling grounds was in the northern Pacific area where shipwrecked sailors occasionally washed upon the coast of Japan, whose government xenophobia impeded recovery of these unfortunate men. More important was the unfolding opportunity in international trade. The commercial success of ocean-going steamships indicated strong growth in Pacific shipping between the United States and the consumer market of China's vast population. However, successful steamship operation required coaling stations to supply coal for the passing steamships. Japan had commercially accessible coal deposits and controlled the Ryukyu Islands which offered an ideal location for a mid-ocean coaling station.[4]

Following the end of the Civil War in 1865, new opportunities in international commerce presented themselves. Enterprising commodity traders and banking houses built upon their overseas trading network to raise foreign capital for American railroad expansion. As the United States developed its intercontinental railroad system, the cheap transportation opened new opportunities for exploiting the vast natural resources and agricultural products of the interior for the expanding export business.[5] America's increased international trade and vibrant domestic economy led to an extensive expansion of international financial activity.

Then came the 1930s depression and World War II. American international trade declined and overseas investments suffered severe losses. American interest in international commercial affairs waned as attention turned to surviving the depression and rebuilding lost confidence. Economic recovery slowly returned, but international concentration was devoted to preparing for the coming war.[6]

The successful conclusion of World War II opened new opportunities for American business in overseas investment and trade. Rebuilding programs to replace the devastation visited on both victors and vanquished created great demand for American products and capital. The innovative Marshall Plan provided U.S. financial assistance to war-torn countries, while the defeat of Japan and Germany removed two major international competitors, enabling American businesses to become major suppliers of the rebuilding programs. Adoption of the Bretton Woods system of fixed exchange rates based on the gold exchange standard removed an important barrier to cross-border commerce threatened by the uncertainties of fluctuating international prices.

AMERICA IN THE POST–WORLD WAR II GLOBAL ECONOMY

While the new opportunities in international trade and investment reintroduced Americans to international commerce, it was, however, under a false understanding of the complexities. The great demand for American goods and capital combined with fixed exchange rates and limited global competition made it relatively easy for American business to effectively compete in the international marketplace. International commerce for many American businesses became merely an extension of existing domestic business practices as if a California company was simply doing business in a neighboring state.

As nations restored war-ravaged domestic economies, international economic conditions slowly returned to the more normal, tumultuous condition. Prices and currency values fluctuated, interest rate differentials affected capital availability, and above all else, intense and effective competition from rebuilt overseas economies steadily encroached upon American dominance. These pressures combined with the financial demands and inflation of the Vietnam War made it impossible to maintain the fixed exchange rate system of Bretton Woods. In 1973, this system collapsed replaced by floating and managed exchange rates fully confronting the U.S. economy with the complexities, uncertainties, and intensities of the dynamic international marketplace.[7]

Unfortunately, much of American business and political leadership was ill prepared to meet this challenge. Many of these leaders received their college education during the 1940s and 1950s when the United States was a dominant international economic force. A review of college texts used during this period indicates the contributing factor to this lack of preparedness. International economics and business was treated as a specialty rather than as an integral part of normal business practices. Textbooks on business, finance, law, and other subjects generally relegated international subjects to the last chapter. Time permitting, the professor would attempt interjecting some discussion on international commerce at the end of the course, a time when students were gearing up for final exams and could not devote much attention to the lectures. Even today, despite the renewed emphasis on the global economy, international matters are still usually found at the back of many publications; and the data are often limited and outdated.

To the rest of the world, the importance of international commerce was more evident. Through economic policies integrating international commercial strategies, Japan and Germany recovered from the devastation of World War II, achieving a standard of living and place in the world sought after but never gained through military domination and achieved at a fraction of the cost and dislocation that would otherwise have resulted using military means. A more recent dramatic lesson on the relation between economic strength and international influence was the end of the Cold War where the Soviet leadership recognized the inability of their economy to support both a global military presence and domestic standard of living comparable to the free world. To their credit, the Soviet leadership wisely chose to concede the military balance and concentrate on domestic economic and political reform.

Relieved of Cold War tensions and the cost of large military forces, many other countries are following the Soviet example and are reorganizing their domestic economies to become more competitive in the global marketplace. The competitive challenge to American innovative capability, management skills, and worker productivity is becoming intense and formidable.

PURPOSE OF THE BOOK

While there is expanding theoretical material on global economics, there is a lack of comprehensive discussion describing methods for comprehending the complexities of today's global economy. Economic resources are unevenly distributed among the nations so that basic economic rules such as supply and demand, capital formation, and the like are the same; but each nation organizes its unique resources, political structure, geographic location and other factors into a unique economic system designed to achieve the desired economic advancement. The global economic system and the policies pursued by governments are shaped based on this fact of unequal distribution. Any study of global economics is the study of competing economic systems confronting business cycle changes in response to altered domestic and international changes. The end of the Cold War is an example of a seminal global economic change causing many countries to experience wrenching business cycle modulations as they radically adjust their domestic economic systems to the new world system.

Understanding the magnitude of business cycle changes and anticipating such changes is essential to effective business and investment decision. This book presents an international matrix system that provides executives and investors with an immediate understanding of the business cycle of industrial countries, the international economic relationships, and the anticipated trend for major industrial economies. It is designed to use readily available data that are timely and inexpensively obtained to enable a noneconomist with limited time to understand international economic trends. This international matrix system is also useful in evaluating the economies of developing countries, although lack of timely and accurate data is a limiting factor.

To provide an analytical framework that fully utilizes the capability of the international matrix system, this book approaches the subject matter by segmenting the discussion into three principal parts. Part I discusses an overall model for understanding the domestic business cycle and international economic conditions in industrial countries. Part II discusses the nature of the global economy and the unique characteristics significant to industrial countries. Omitted from this discussion are unique characteristics of developing countries, although the discussion in Chapter 6 may be helpful. Part III presents the international matrix system and its application to economic trend analysis.

The international matrix system is similar to the matrix system described in the author's book, *Economic Trend Analysis for Executives and Investors*,[8] developed for understanding U.S. economic trends. Readers of the first book will find that this one uses a similar system of key indicators, benchmarks, and relationship analysis. However, there are several important departures. Dissemination of U.S. economic data by the American business news media is well developed and growing so that all key indicators can be timely obtained from a variety of sources. In contrast, dissemination of international economic and financial data is less developed. Most American business news publications provide immediate coverage of major international economic and financial events, but few provide the timely and systematic reporting of key economic and financial indicators so essential for informed business and investment decisions. While such data are available, the cost can be prohibitive.

An important solution to this problem is the key national indicators reported in *The Economist*, a weekly newspaper published in London and printed in a timely and inexpensive American edition. At the back of each week's edition, key economic and financial indicators are reported for fifteen major industrial nations; and beginning in 1994, this section was expanded to include key indicators for twenty-four developing nations. While *The Economist* does not publish all key indicators that may be desirable nor does it cover all countries, its key indicators do a good job for international economic trend analysis. The international matrix system discussed in this book is based upon these key indicators and can be expanded to include other data that focus on specific investments or other countries.

Historical context is a critical element to analyzing current economic indicators, and since 1864, *The Economist* has published key economic and financial data providing a rich source of historical data. An analysis of its key economic and financial indicators for the period 1978 to 1991 enabled development of benchmarks and other relationships specifically designed to interpret the most current data reported in the publication, providing a consistency and accuracy not available when using data from other sources. In addition, utilizing these data in the international matrix system enhances the usefulness of articles appearing in *The Economist*; and in turn, these articles provide better understanding of the economic trends indicated by the international matrix system.

There are several other reasons for utilizing *The Economist*. It is one of the premier international business publications devoting its resources to improving the understanding of international commerce. It has sponsored publication of many books providing extensive current and historical international economic and financial data useful in business and investment decisions. *The Economist* was founded in 1843 (celebrating its 150th anniversary in 1993), becoming prominent in the late nineteenth century through the direction of the gifted editor and writer Walter Bagehot (1826–1877). Bagehot had a keen interest in economic and business theory and worked to expand the general knowledge of these important subjects. He crafted a publication devoted to economic, business, and related news. Today, *The Economist* continues this high standard by extensively discussing current economic, finance, and business matters in terms understood by and useful to executives and investors.

NOTES

1. Harold Underwood Faulkner, *American Economic History* (New York: Harper & Brothers, 1943).

2. Richard B. Morris, *The Basic Ideas of Alexander Hamilton* (New York: Dial Press, 1957).

3. George Rogers Taylor, *The Great Tariff Debate, 1820-1830* (Boston: D.C. Heath & Company, 1953). A reading of the Congressional Debates shows that elected officials were well informed of overseas markets and had a good grasp of economic principles. These debates also summarize the basic pros and cons of protectionist policy that are heard today.

4. Peter Booth Wiley, *Yankees in the Land of the Gods* (New York: Penguin Books, 1990).

5. Roy C. Smith, *The Global Bankers* (New York: Truman Talley Books, 1989), Chapter 1.

6. Charles P. Kindleberger, *The World in Depression, 1929–1939* (Berkeley: University of California Press, 1973).

    7. John E. Floyd, *World Monetary Equilibrium* (Oxford: Philip Allan Publishers, 1985).
    8. Howard G. Schaefer, *Economic Trend Analysis for Executives and Investors* (Westport, Conn.: Quorum Books, 1993).

PART I
THE INTERNATIONAL
ECONOMIC MODEL

CHAPTER 2

Individual Country Business Cycles

International economic trend analysis is the study of a country's business cycle and its alteration in response to economic conditions transmitted by its principal trading partners. A dominant force in international economic trends is the *business cycle* continuum experienced by each country consisting of sustained economic growth followed by a period of stagnation or slower growth, occasionally transforming into a precipitous decline or recession, after which the economy recovers and resumes its growth. Some countries grow faster than others, sustain deeper economic downturns than others, or respond to economic adversity different from others; but the business cycle phases remain similar.

Businesses, investors, and governments survive and prosper by anticipating these business cycle phases. Accordingly, most governments prepare economic data by measuring economic activity associated with the business cycles of their respective countries; and the dissemination of such information receives widespread coverage in the local business news media, accompanied by useful and insightful commentary on the business cycle. However, the intense focus on local business conditions does not extend to other countries.

The international matrix system is designed to monitor an individual country's business cycle and those of its principal trading partners in the context of available economic and financial indicators. As a combination of domestic and international economic conditions, analyzing a nation's business cycle is a two-step process, beginning with (1) understanding the individual country business cycle and its unique domestic dynamics, followed by (2) studying the cross-border commercial relationship of principal trading partners that may significantly impact the particular country and evaluating the nature of the impact.

Presented in this chapter is a general behavior model of an individual industrial country business cycle to provide a context for understanding the economic and financial indicators used in the international matrix.[1] While every country's economy is unique, industrial countries manifest their business cycles in a similar manner. For readers familiar with the author's *Economic Trend Analysis for Executives and Investors*, the business cycle discussion in this chapter is essentially the same as the U.S. business cycle model discussed there. Such readers can briefly review this section as a refresher, moving on to the section on international transmission of the business cycle in Chapter 3.

CAUSES OF BUSINESS CYCLES

In the United States, causes of business cycles have generated substantial research, analysis, and debate. Despite the best-laid plans and economic forecasting techniques, a nation's economy periodically becomes unbalanced because of unexpected economic shocks such as new technology, "bad" business judgment, change in international trade patterns, change in government policy, weather conditions, war, and so on. If the economy quickly responds to the imbalance, people will little note any disturbance. On the other hand, the unbalancing may be of such magnitude or the economy be so incapable to quickly and effectively respond that the imbalance spreads into a general economic dislocation intensified by lost public confidence and a fall in consumption.

Post–World War II experiences with oil is one such example. Industrial countries have not responded well to dependence on foreign oil despite the best efforts of the oil industry and governments to manage this vulnerability. Major disruptions in oil supplies or rapid price increases have been quickly followed by declines in the industrial production of most industrial countries.

In other countries, business cycle analysis has received less attention as they view their economies' dependence on a major trading partner such as the United States or a major commodity such as copper or oil. Furthermore, many industrial country economies have been disrupted so often by war or political turmoil that cyclical patterns are less discernable. As the world recovered from World War II, it entered an extended period of prosperity in which business cycles reappeared, stimulating research in international business cycles.[2]

GENERAL DOMESTIC BUSINESS CYCLE

Recessionary or Contracting Period

To begin, assume an industrial country in the midst of a recession where unemployment is high and rising, industrial production is declining, interest rates are low relative to the prior year (but banks are reluctant to lend), and share prices are depressed. Bankruptcies are on the rise, often highlighted by several large and respected corporations seeking protection of the bankruptcy courts. Plant layoffs are being announced, and there is a general gloom pervading most business discussions. Office vacancies are high, and new commercial projects are unable to attract tenants. Consumers are cautious, preferring to pay down debts rather than increase purchases. No end to the contracting economy appears in sight.

Some industries are particularly hard hit because of overproduction. The normal response is to reduce production below normal needs, cut prices, reduce inventories, and cancel expansion plans. If the recession is mild, lost production is quickly restored so that vulnerable industries and individual firms will generally survive and eventually prosper. However, if overproduction is serious—requiring a long period to work off the excess inventory—the vulnerable industry and its firms will stagnate for an extended period contributing to a deepening recession. Marginal firms usually end up in bankruptcy.

Of course, the recession could rapidly develop into a repeat of the Great Depression. Since its founding, the United States has suffered three or four "great depressions" in which the depression of the 1930s may not have been the worst. Why the cyclical downturn of 1929 turned into a depression is one of the great debates in the business and economic community and need not be repeated here. The immediate concern is determining whether another depression is approaching. Some benchmarks of economic data derived from the depression period are discussed in Chapters 12 and 13 for evaluating current data to determine whether an individual country or the global economy is in serious trouble.

Beginning of Turnaround

Even in the midst of a recession, there are usually forces at work setting the stage for return to economic growth. A large and diversified economy, combined with a free market system that diversifies decision making, allows these forces to respond quickly and effectively to the imbalance. One of the important forces that sets the stage for the turnaround is that even as the downturn grows, income generally falls at a slower rate than production and inventory liquidation, thereby maintaining a certain level of continued expenditures. Firms are slow to commence layoffs; and when they do, there are often accompanying severance payments. Dividend and interest payments continue to help tide over many people. A key stabilizing force is a government safetynet system which slows the decline, permitting the other forces to take effect. Unemployment compensation maintains purchasing power of the hardest hit while farm price supports help the agricultural sector. National and local governments are slow to reduce expenditures, relying principally on increased deficit spending.

The rapid liquidation of inventories and wearing out of business equipment and consumer durables eventually create a pent-up demand for goods that cannot be met by depleted inventory levels. Eventually, firms diminish their inventory reductions and employee layoffs, causing the economic decline to moderate. Having struggled to survive the business contraction, most firms have reduced employment, inventory, accounts receivable, and debt, thereby improving their working capital position. As liquidity improves, firms expand equipment purchases to replace worn-out items, improve their competitive position, and prepare for the anticipated recovery.

Meanwhile, commercial banks, insurance companies, thrifts, and other financial institutions have also improved their liquidity positions and are in a position to expand loan activity. Financial institutions usually earn higher interest rates from lending activity rather than investing in government securities. Higher interest rates on loans also compensate for the higher default risk and lack of marketability. However, during a recession, the risk of loan default substantially increases, causing financial institutions to become cautious. They forego higher interest rates from higher-risk lending activity by limiting new loans to only their best customers and directing excess funds into prime liquid assets such as government securities. Liquid assets are further augmented as consumers and businesses pay down debts rather than increase borrowings. Meanwhile, earnings on assets of financial institutions decline commensurate with the decline in interest income and the decline in interest rates available from safer government securities. A slight pickup in business activity stirs the institutions to seek again new loans and their higher interest rates. Risk of loss from new loans is diminished by the improved business conditions and proved survivability of the borrowers.

A similar condition of diminishing decline begins unfolding in the construction industries. High interest rates and banks' caution at the beginning of the recession caused postponement of many construction projects. Buildings wear out and become obsolete, and the population continues to grow and relocate. Eventually, the inventory of office and residential space diminishes. With lower interest rates and stabilized construction costs, some building projects are resurrected and construction commences. Residential and commercial construction tend to have a multiplier effect on the economy because they are normally followed by increased furniture purchases to fill the new structures and infrastructure improvements to provide transportation, communication, and utility access to them.

If, on the other hand, a principal cause of the recession was overbuilding, the recession may linger, or the recovery may be retarded. Excess inventory of structures tends to liquidate more slowly than excess manufacturing inventory. Despite the diversity of many industrial countries, various regions within a country and various countries react differently to a recession because of a concentration of specific industries within a region or within a country. When recovery begins, manufacturers can move inventory to those regions or countries showing strongest recovery. In contrast, real estate developers must wait for their particular region or country to recover before unloading excess inventory.

One of the first sectors to sense the improved business conditions is the share market. Interest rates having fallen during the contraction, investors focus on the dividend-paying capacity of publicly traded companies. The possibilities of improved earnings and increased dividends make shares a bargain investment, and investors begin switching funds into the share market.

Prices and wage rates, which declined or leveled out during the recession, remain moderate. Prices on finished goods remain static as firms complete their inventory liquidation. There is little pressure for price increases because inventory levels of raw materials are still below normal levels. Foreign demand may expand to take advantage of better prices. Unemployment is still high, and there is little inflationary pressure on employees to seek cost-of-living adjustments. Improved employee productivity reduces pressure for further layoffs.

The impact of technology and innovation is still not well understood. It appears that if technology and innovation offer business and consumers cost savings or improved productivity, they may aid in the turnaround. Furthermore, if new products permit businesses and consumers to better survive a recession or better prepare for the upturn, there may be a greater willingness to accelerate purchases of the new products.

The Upswing

As the seeds of recovery take hold, the economy begins to move forward. Reacting to low interest rates and growing anticipation of a recovery, the share market has probably been rising—although slowly—for several months. Producer prices have begun to rise. Industrial production and employment begin steady improvement. The recovery appears confirmed when long-term investment begins to increase, especially in residential and commercial construction. Orders for equipment and durable goods show strong improvement. Improved consumer purchases are usually evidenced by increased purchases of durable goods such as automobiles and growth in consumer installment debt.

As public confidence grows, financial institutions reduce their overly cautious concern about risk and begin extending credit in accordance with more normal lending practices. The volume of share and bond public offerings increases significantly. Profits improve. Retail sales show improved growth and a sense of confidence begins returning. Residential and commercial construction shows increased activity, accompanied by mortgage growth.

Increased orders cause manufacturers to raise output and distributors to expand their inventories. As output and inventories expand, businesses increase their working capital by borrowing. Employment grows. Prices start to rise. Raw material prices are often the first to experience the pressure of demand exceeding available supply. Growth industries preoccupy many business discussions, causing a speculative increase in share prices of growth companies. Investment plans for enlarging existing facilities, developing new products, or expanding into new industries take on a bold and very optimistic character.

Over an extended period of time, the cautiousness developed during the recessionary period moves into healthy optimism. Lending terms become relaxed; real estate prices increase; the volume of new mortgages expands; venture capital is readily available; formation of new companies increases; industrial capacity is expanded; and share prices, especially in growth companies, move briskly upward.

At this stage, the healthy optimism often turns into speculation. Many individuals making business decisions were not in positions of authority when the last bust occurred and do not know the warning signals of economic imbalance. During the recession, the ranks of experienced workers are depleted as businesses reduce costs by eliminating the higher-salaried but more experienced senior executives through termination and early retirement. Furthermore, the struggle to survive the mergers and acquisitions that accompany recessions often disrupts the ranks of management, causing promotion of less-experienced personnel. As speculation develops, those now in authority have limited experience and judgment by which to properly evaluate projects. Because of a lack of experience, too much emphasis is placed on projections showing continuous upward trends.

Full Capacity

As the upswing gains full momentum, unemployment steadily declines. Product and raw material demands consistently exceed production capacity. Bottlenecks appear more and more frequently, causing rapid price increases. Demand for wage increases grows. In those regions experiencing high growth rates and expanded employment, real estate speculation becomes a major growth industry.

In reaction to the stresses resulting from full employment, the economy may from time to time experience minor dips. High interest rates and tightening bank credit may slow loan availability in certain industries. Rapid price increases may cause some businesses to become cautious out of concern that consumers will switch to less-expensive alternatives. Industry resistance to wage demands may result in strikes and work stoppages, thereby causing temporary industrial downturns. From time to time, some industries may experience a downturn; but resulting unemployment is rapidly absorbed by growth industries.

Seeds for Major Downturn

An economic locomotive moving uphill eventually runs out of steam. As consumers and businesses reach the limit of spendable income and available credit, incremental increases in purchases diminish. A period of rest is needed to prepare for the next major growth surge. At this point, the economy is most vulnerable to a major downturn caused by an unexpected maladjustment or an unexpected disruptive event. The unexpected force is most often a combination of excess production capacity and shortage of essential goods concentrated in a major industrial sector.

Economic imbalance caused by overproduction or shortages is a recurring leading cause of business cycle downturns. Under most economic theories, this situation should not occur—the pricing system is supposed to create an environment in which supply and demand always match at the market price. An important assumption in the price mechanism is that buyers and sellers have complete information by which to evaluate the market and set the price at which demand and supply meet. Such an assumption is often incorrect not only because complete information is not available but also because the information may not be fully understood.

According to economic theory, when demand exceeds supply—causing the price of a product to rise—new producers are encouraged to enter the market, causing an increase in supply that eventually causes a decline in the price. This portion of the theory is generally correct. The problem arises when many firms intend to enter the market and, unknown to one another, simultaneously undertake to build plants, train employees, and develop infrastructure. Because of the imperfect knowledge about the changing nature of the producers, an enormous increase in supply can suddenly flood the market, causing prices to fall below the ability of many firms to recoup manufacturing costs and pay debts.

Improper interpretation of available economic data signaling a downturn is another factor even for experienced business leaders. When the economy is at full capacity, certain industries become carried away with the prospects of unlimited growth as they expand production capacity to meet rising demand. At some point in time, supply and demand are balanced, but time elapses before companies recognize the situation. Meanwhile, production capacity continues to expand, and inventory levels build. At the first sign of overcapacity, companies have only limited information by which to evaluate the situation. Since most business operations tend always to experience fluctuating sales and cost pressures, they concentrate on immediate business problems—not realizing the severity of the overcapacity. With the inventory buildup, businesses attempt to liquidate inventory by extending payment terms and reducing prices. Inventory buildup soon becomes joined with accounts receivable buildup and narrowing profit margins. As cash flow becomes unable to support the inventory and accounts receivable buildups, companies respond by reducing production and laying off workers. If several large companies within a major industry begin contracting at the same time, it may trigger the economic downturn.

A variation on the overcapacity problem is associated with inflation. Some industries cannot expand fast enough to meet rising demand, causing a buildup of inflationary pressures. If the financial system accommodates the inflationary pressure by rapidly increasing money supply and credit, that step tends to fuel inflation. As demand for capital increases, interest rates rise. Investments are attracted to industries such as real estate that remain profitable during the inflation, causing an overexpansion in these industries. Industries less capable of adjusting to inflation become starved for capital, resulting in a major imbalance in the economy. Eventually, the overexpanded industries cannot obtain sufficient capital to finance the upward spiral of prices. Prices collapse, and the overexpanded industries liquidate excess inventories and excess fixed assets, resulting in further price reductions, employee layoffs, and the general downward spiral of the industry.

Another variation on the overcapacity problem is the overextension of bank credit. In many respects the banking industry is different from most other industries because it finances other businesses. However, it is prone to the same overexpansion tendencies that afflict all industries. In particular, from time to time, the banking industry tends to concentrate credit in certain perceived growth industries. If these industries get into trouble and default on their loans, the resulting losses are above normal, thus reducing current and subsequent bank earnings. To rebuild profits, banks curtail business loans, redeploy assets to safer investments, and lay off employees. All industries, even healthy ones, experience curtailment of credit. The banks' malaise spreads throughout the entire economy.

While overcapacity resulting from overexpansion is the most common cause of cyclical downturns, sudden shocks can have a similar effect. A sudden and unexpected curtailment of purchasing power can cause relatively healthy firms and industries to find themselves in a position of overcapacity. Historically, weather conditions, such as drought, have been one of the most common shocks. A resulting fall in agricultural production because of the weather causes a rise in farm prices. Consumers must allocate more money to food purchases and less to other products and services. Purchasing of manufactured and other products is curtailed, spreading economic malaise throughout the country. Fortunately, through better farm management, improved farming techniques, and geographic diversification of agriculture, weather has a less significant impact on the agricultural sector of most industrial countries other than the former Soviet Union.

However, economic shocks are still with us. More recently, oil embargoes and sudden rises in oil prices have caused dislocations similar to that caused by weather conditions. As industries and consumers dependent on foreign oil divert attention and resources to deal with the crisis, business in other industries declines. Firms react to declining demand caused by economic shock just as they would in a situation of overextension. They reduce prices, liquidate inventories, curtail purchases, and halt expansion plans.

Major industrial sectors affected by the overcapacity of production or nonavailability of credit are forced to lay off employees, spreading the malaise to consumers who become gloomy and fearful for their jobs. In response, consumers defer major purchases, reduce expenses, and pay down their debts. Reduced purchases place pressure on other industries to reduce production, thereby increasing employee layoffs. Banks begin experiencing loan defaults and become cautious in their lending practices. In particular, banks become unwilling to finance further consumer loans, further reducing consumer purchasing power. Public confidence in the economic future dwindles.

The inability of all sectors of the economy to respond rapidly to changing conditions caused by growing layoffs and reduced purchasing capacity begins taking on a momentum of its own. Banks become overly cautious, consumers become overly fearful, and businesses lay off the more skilled and capable employees. As the downturn continues, a general fear extends to the entire national economy. Share prices decline precipitously. Bank lending becomes frozen, and even the better businesses are unable to obtain loans for normal working capital and seasonal needs. If loan defaults reach unusually large proportions in certain industries or regional areas, the banking system itself may deteriorate seriously. If the credit system is threatened, a deflation in prices generally results. The economy now enters into the recessionary period, and the cycle begins anew.

MONEY SUPPLY, CREDIT, AND INTEREST RATES

Early indicators of domestic and international business cycle trends are domestic financial markets and money supply activity. These two essential economic activities are at the center of the process for allocating economic resources. Any imbalances in a domestic economy or among the trading nations are likely to be first indicated by changes in these two activities. To enhance the utilization of the international matrix system as a means of anticipating future economic trends, an expanded model of the money and credit segment of an industrial country's business cycle is important.[3]

Money Supply

Essential to the speedy and efficient movement of goods and services is an adequate supply of money. A growing supply of money is generally associated with an expanding economy, while a contracting supply of money is generally associated with a declining economy. However, in and of itself, a change in the money supply does not alter the economy's production capacity. It is the degree of change in relation to other domestic economic activity that is significant. A money supply that expands more rapidly than production can cause an increase in the price level with little or no improvement in production, especially if the economy is already producing at full capacity. A steady contraction of the money supply can cause a reduction in production with no reduction in prices. When an economy is contracting, firms tend to reduce production before reducing prices. Only after a reduction in production do firms begin reducing prices in response to a deteriorating economy.

While the significance of money supply is well understood, controlling its growth remains difficult. This difficulty stems primarily from two unstable conditions: a dual source of money and the shifting demand for it.

Dual Source of Money. A nation's money supply derives from a combination of two sources: (1) money created by the central government, either in currency—coin and paper money—or deposit accounts in a central bank, and (2) the far larger source of bank deposits in private-sector commercial banks and other depository institutions that are available for the writing of checks. By custom and, in some cases, by law, these two forms of money are legal tender to be accepted as payment of all public and private debts. Having both a government-created and privately created component of the money supply has evolved over centuries, providing a flexible money supply for expanding commerce. However, this dual source of money supply also has seeds of instability. The two sectors influence one another, but neither controls the other's actions.

Shifting Demand for Money. The other unstable condition is the shifting demand for money. Firms and consumers change their patterns of commercial transactions in reaction to a wide variety of developing circumstances. In a growing economy, the pattern of money demand is usually more predictable and can be accommodated by the financial institutions. However, as the economy approaches a speculative environment, firms and consumers use more credit as a money substitute without considering the need to eventually pay the debt. This behavior causes distortions in the relationship pattern between money supply and economic growth. In a weakening economy, the pattern is also distorted. Even though banks may be ready, willing, and able to lend and thereby increase the money supply, in a recession, firms and consumers remain cautious and unwilling to incur new debt.

Credit Supply and Interest Rates

Expanded use of credit instruments as a substitute for traditional forms of money makes changes in credit equally important to economic growth as changes in the money supply. However, by law and by the terms of most commercial contracts, credit instruments are not acceptable forms of payment. In a growing economy generating optimistic expectations, this rule is often fudged so that the growth in credit has a stimulative effect beyond the growth in money. When the economy declines and confidence deteriorates, the rules of payment are more strictly maintained. If the money supply does not grow sufficiently to offset the decline in credit, the economy will suffer further downturns. The interplay between changes in the money supply and changes in availability of credit has an enormous impact on the business cycle, especially because, in most countries, the organized credit market is larger than the money supply.

Unlike changes in money supply and demand, changes in credit supply and demand lag behind changes in the economy. As the economy moves out of a downturn, the demand for credit expands, as reflected by gradually increasing interest rates. When the economy approaches full capacity, credit supply tightens; but demand continues causing interest rates to reach the highest point in the business cycle. In fact, interest rates tend to remain high and perhaps rise even as the economy enters into a downward swing. This situation often occurs because some industries continue expanding and demanding credit. In addition, contracting industries also need credit because of the inability to effectively liquidate inventory and accounts receivables. As the recession unfolds and business conditions worsen, loan demand slackens and interest rates steadily decline. Interest rates tend to continue declining beyond the worst of the recession for two reasons: (1) at the trough of the business cycle, firms tend to be liquid and capable of financing the next growth stage out of existing working capital; and (2) financial institutions tend to remain cautious and are reluctant to increase lending until certain that economic growth is recurring.

Because changes in the supply and demand for credit follow rather than lead changes in the economy, the corresponding changes in interest rates also lag economic changes. This situation causes many experts to conclude that interest rates are not good leading economic indicators but are better lagging indicators. Using trend analysis techniques, this minimizing of the significance of interest rates is understandable. However, comparing interest rates to other economic factors with a historical relationship can make interest rates a helpful leading indicator.

For example, much of economic analysis treats all interest rates the same. No distinction is made between short-term and long-term interest rates. Yet, these interest rates react differently to the economic environment. Short-term capital consists of excess funds held primarily as a temporary investment for emergencies or until a more permanent investment is obtained. Supply and demand of liquid capital is the key factor in determining short-term interest rates. Since the investment is temporary, short-term capital tends to be less sensitive to interest rate trends, more concerned about liquidity, and willing to accept the prevailing interest rate. Because of rapid changes in supply and demand, short-term interest rates are more volatile. On the other hand, long-term capital tends to be more deliberate and responsive to interest rate changes relative to other investment opportunities. It weighs the risk and rewards of the investment with the understanding that long-term capital may not be as liquid as short-term. Long-term debt investments must compete with other investments such as stocks, collectibles, real estate, and the like. The risks of uncertainty, inflation, and economic expectations tend to influence long-term interest rates.

Both short- and long-term interest rates tend to follow a similar upward or downward trend depending on the particular stage of the business cycle. However, the spread between the two interest rates changes depending on the phase of the business cycle. As the economy grows, the spread between the two interest rates narrows. At full economic capacity, where credit is tight, short-term interest rates often exceed long-term interest rates. An economic downturn causes long-term investors to become cautious and place excess funds into temporary investments to ride out the decline. Hence, the increased supply of short-term capital causes short-term interest rates to fall faster than long-term interest rates. An economic recovery cannot begin unless there is a supply of short-term funds in excess of demand usually evidenced by short-term interest rates significantly below long-term interest rates.

The Credit Markets

In its widest form, *credit* is the supplying of cash, goods, or services from one person to another person with the expectation of payment in cash or kind sometime in the future. Probably the first form of credit, and one that is still very much with us, is when one individual performed a service for another expecting a payment when the service was completed. A similar early method of credit still very much with us is the providing of goods and services by firms to customers. This form of credit constitutes the accounts receivable and accounts payable that is such an integral part of business activity.

When firms and individuals accumulate excess money which they seek to invest, the process of deploying these funds for investment constitutes the financial system. The portion of the financial system that uses intermediaries to match suppliers with users of funds is generally referred to as the *credit markets* or the technically more correct *organized credit markets*. The stock, bond, and money markets are the principal components of the credit markets.

For much of modern economic history the financial system, credit market, and the banking system were almost synonymous terms. Today, there are a wide range of financial institutions that act as intermediaries and have gained public confidence in their safety and ability. Furthermore, various forms of credit instruments such as commercial paper and notes have become close substitutes for cash and checks, which are the more traditional forms of money used to transact business.

Operating the credit markets are two types of intermediary institutions. The names and functions of these intermediaries vary from country to country as do their importance within the respective domestic economies. However, the overall distinctions remain. *Financial intermediaries* are those institutions such as commercial banks, clearing banks, deposit banks, pension funds, or money market funds in which the depositor earns income or a service (a free checking account) from the financial institution but makes no further investment decision. *Agents* are those financial institutions acting solely to introduce the investor to the investee. The investor makes the ultimate investment decision. Investment banking houses, merchant banks, commercial paper dealers, and loan brokers constitute this type of intermediary.

Most people prefer intermediaries to prudently invest their funds, and the largest and most influential are the commercial banks. *Commercial banks* is the American term used to describe private institutions whose customer deposits are the principal component of the nation's money supply. Similar institutions in other countries are known by different terms—clearing banks in Britain, deposit banks in France, and chartered banks in Canada.[4] These banks are the linchpin of the domestic credit system and are, therefore, both regulated and protected by the national government to maintain the integrity of their financial system. Compared to total financial assets, the size of commercial banks varies from country to country, as is shown in Table 2.1, but in most countries constitutes the single largest financial intermediary.

Commercial banks have a unique influence on the domestic supply of both money and credit. To meet changing business conditions, commercial banks can expand or contract the deposit component of the money supply independent of the availability of currency from the government. This change in the money supply most often results from bank lending activity. A bank loan is, in essence, a new deposit of money in the account of the borrower. When the borrower writes checks on the new deposit, the transaction constitutes an addition to the existing money supply.

Monitoring the money supply and credit markets, in particular, the banking system, can provide the first glimpse of the direction of a country's business cycle. In addition, banks have developed expertise, abilities, and perceptions that uniquely influence the credit markets. As with the business cycle, developing a model of the typical reaction of the banking system to

Table 2.1
Bank Assets as Compared to Total Financial Assets, 1985

Country	Bank Assets as Percentage of Total Financial Assets
United States	30
Japan	47
West Germany	45
Britain	36
France	61

Source: World Bank, *World Development Report* (Washington, D.C.: World Bank, 1989).

different phases of the business cycle will aid in understanding the financial indicators used in the international matrix system.

Loans and Bank Liquidity

Commercial banks' ability to expand the money supply through their lending activity is subject to constraints having enormous economic consequences. Banks normally will not allow total deposits to exceed a certain ratio of liquid assets and currency. The banking system must always be in a position to satisfy normal deposit withdrawals, thereby maintaining depositors' confidence that their deposits can be quickly converted to currency. Central banks usually regulate the type of liquid assets and currency that a bank must maintain and the minimum ratio of reserves to total deposits. The reserves usually consist of vault cash, deposits with the central bank, and short-term marketable securities such as government debt with a maturity less than one year. Hence, banks will not expand loans beyond the mandatory reserve requirements.

Another major constraint is the demand for new loans. Borrowers are usually concerned about the ability to pay back loans and the trend in interest rates. Under normal economic conditions, loan demand may slacken as the costs of credit and repayment terms are not justified by projections for new projects. Particularly significant to the business cycle and banking system are customer reactions in a declining economy. Normally, individuals and businesses will reduce the demand for new loans until they believe the economy is in an upswing or that interest rates have ceased declining.

By far, the biggest constraints on bank lending activity are the credit risks associated with the business cycle. Banks are in the business of earning income from their lending and investment activities, and the highest income is normally from loans to firms and individuals. When the economy is declining and risks are increasing, banks curtail lending activity and accumulate liquid capital. While awaiting more profitable deployment, these excess funds are normally invested in government obligations. The resulting rise in the liquidity level of banks—the amount of funds invested in short-term instruments that are available for future lending—indicates both the general financial systems' reduction of current lending activity and its ability to finance economic growth sometime in the future.

Accordingly, interest rates on government obligations are a barometer of banks' liquidity and of their willingness to lend. Rising interest rates indicate that banks' liquidity levels are diminishing and that the banks are approaching the minimum safety ratio of liquid assets to total deposits. Sustained economic growth may be jeopardized as the banks approach their maximum lending capacity. Conversely, declining interest rates indicate that liquidity levels are rising. This increase in liquidity may stem from two sources. Because a slowing economy reduces the number of investment opportunities with reasonable risks, banks may be reducing lending activity. Lower returns on investments may induce consumers to pay down debt obligations incurred when interest rates were higher. While the economic environment is contracting, a pool of liquid capital nevertheless is accumulating and can be applied to finance economic growth sometime in the future.

CONCLUSION

The previously discussed model of a typical business cycle describes many of the elements that occurred in all the business cycles since World War II and many of the cycles that occurred before that period. No two business cycles are exactly alike, nor do they have the same magnitude of impact on overall economic growth and decline. Studying the economic data accumulated in the matrix system will provide the first outlines of an unfolding cyclical change.

NOTES

1. An extensive discussion of business cycles can be found in Philip A. Klein and Geoffrey H. Moore, *Monitoring Growth Cycles in Market-Oriented Countries*, National Bureau of Economic Research Studies in Business Cycles No. 26 (Cambridge, Mass.: Ballinger, 1985), and Robert Aaron Gordon, *Business Fluctuations* (New York: Harper & Brothers, 1952).

2. Pioneering work in American and international business cycles analysis is being conducted by several organizations such as the National Bureau of Economic Research (NBER) and the Columbia School of Business. Among other things, the NBER is the semiofficial determiner of American recessions and developed the leading economic indicator concept.

3. Friedrich A. Hayek, *Monetary Theory and the Trade Cycle* (New York: Augustus M. Kelley, 1966), originally published in 1937, is a classic analysis of the interaction between money, credit, and trade cycles. For a more contemporary discussion, see Martin J. Pring, *How to Forecast Interest Rates* (New York: McGraw Hill, 1981).

4. As Europe moves toward monetary union, it must grapple with the different banking systems in each country, which is extensively discussed in Jean Dermine, *European Banking in the 1990s* (Oxford: Blackwell, 1990).

CHAPTER 3

Cross-Border Transmission of Business Cycles

Business cycles of all the major industrial countries seem to follow a similar pattern, although the phases of these patterns are not necessarily concurrent with other countries' business cycle phases. Figures 3.1 and 3.2 plot the annual rate of change in real gross domestic product (GDP) for six key industrial countries demonstrating three important patterns regarding international business cycles. First, several economic downturns occurred at the same time by all the countries, indicating an economic interdependence among the national economies. On the other hand, some countries also experienced economic downturns independent of the other countries, indicating that domestic factors may have been the principal cause of these downturns. Finally, in some cases, all countries experienced economic downturns that appear related; but each country began the downturn at a different time with different lengths and severity, indicating some ability to cushion against international economic interdependence.

Accordingly, the cycle of growth, stagnation, recession, and upswing of an individual country is often mirrored in some form by principal trading partners except in situations where the trading partner has a much larger economy. A general understanding of the means by which economic conditions are transmitted between trading partners will be helpful in analyzing economic

Figure 3.1
Real GDP for the United States, Japan, and Germany, 1970–1992

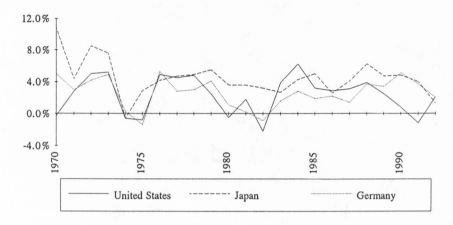

Source: *OECD Economic Outlook* (Paris: Organization for Economic Cooperation and Development, June 1993), p. 201.

Figure 3.2
Real GDP for Britain, France, and Canada, 1970–1992

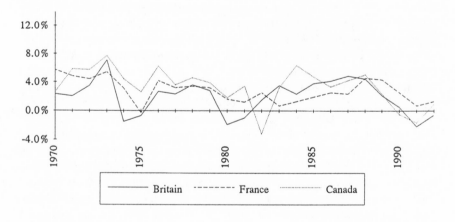

Source: *OECD Economic Outlook* (Paris: Organization for Economic Cooperation and Development, June 1993), p. 201.

and financial indicators. Theoretically, if trading partners' economic cycles are moving in tandem, nominal interest rates, prices, wage rates, and output should also be at the same level. As more often occurs, the levels are not the same, reflecting among other things variations in economic cycles, lags in transmission of economic conditions, economic size, and different economic policies.

GENERAL MEANS OF TRANSMISSION

Economic Expansion

The initial means by which economic conditions are transmitted is through the flow of trade among trading partners. A home country experiencing economic expansion increases income of its trading partners. Rising domestic income increases the demand for goods and services, which spills over into increased demand for cross-border goods and services. In satisfying this demand, trading partners increase their exports, resulting in rising income in their respective domestic economies. The degree of transmitted expansion depends on its strength in the home country, in the rising demand for imports, and in their volume. Likewise, the economic expansion in trading partners causes an increased demand for foreign goods and services which not only extends to other trading partners but also feeds back to the home country, further stimulating its economic expansion.

This cross-border transmission of economic expansion manifests itself in the trade balance and the current account of the countries. For the home country initiating the economic expansion, the increased demand for imports initially causes a deterioration in its balance of trade which subsequently reverses as the trading partner's economic expansion feeds back to increase home-country exports. In contrast, trading partners initially experience an improvement in their trade balance as exports increase to the home country; but then it reverses as expansion increases the demand for imports.

The degree of import and export volume between countries is also affected by imbalances in relative prices. The economic expansion in the home country is likely to increase domestic prices, which is a contributing factor to expansion spilling over to rising demand for relatively cheaper foreign goods and services. The resulting expansion in the trading partner's domestic economy also causes an increase in its domestic price level. If the price-level increases in both countries are unequal, the country experiencing a higher price increase will experience reduced demand for its exports and further increased demand for imports.

Some countries induce economic expansion by implementing policies to increase exports. An expansion by the home country solely for export purposes results in vulnerable dependency on a trading partner. If expanded trade also triggers expansion in plant facilities and other major capital projects, the new capacity may be beyond the normal needs of the home country's economy or the facilities may be unusable for domestic purposes. If these industries constitute a significant proportion of the domestic economy, the entire domestic economy is vulnerable to a major downturn. Trading partners eventually experience cyclical downturns, dragging down the export industries of the home country.

Economic Contraction

A home country experiencing an economic contraction also causes a contraction of the economy of major trading partners.[1] Declining home-country domestic income decreases the demand for goods and services which spills over to declining demand for foreign goods and services. Trading partners experience a decline in exports, resulting in a decline in their domestic income. The degree of the transmission of the contraction depends on its severity in the home country, on the decline in import demand, and on the volume of imports. The economic decline in the trading partners causes a decline in their demand for imports, which not only extends to other trading partners but also may feed back to the home country, further contracting its economy.

This cross-border transmission of economic contraction manifests itself in the trade balance and the current account of the countries. For the home country experiencing the economic contraction, the decline in imports initially causes an improvement in its balance of trade, which subsequently reverses as the trading partner economic decline feeds back to declining home-country exports. Trading partners initially experience a decline in their trade balance as exports to the home country decline, but then the situation subsequently reverses as contraction reduces the demand for imports.

Countries whose exports consist mostly of commodities or natural resources generally suffer more from cross-border economic contractions than those who are primary exporters of manufactured products. There are several contributing factors to this vulnerability. Commodities and natural-resource exports usually consist of items already fully absorbed in the domestic economy so that only the surplus is exported. Hence, when the export market suffers, there is no domestic capacity to absorb the excess and no imports that can be substituted by reorientation of production facilities. Furthermore, commodities and natural resources tend to be fungible items and, therefore, indistinguishable in the international marketplace, making them highly price sensitive. In contrast, manufactured products are distinguished by a variety of factors, thereby making it difficult for substitution by competitors and more resistant to price competition. In the event of loss of export markets, many manufactured products and their facilities can be redirected to the domestic market, often replacing imported manufactured products.

Trading partners suffering economic decline often attempt to transmit their domestic economic problem to the home country by expanding their exports to absorb unused domestic capacity. In this situation, the home country often experiences both increased import volume and lower prices. However, the import expansion can create significant price and other competitive pressures in the home-country economy—even to the point of threatening the extinction of certain home-country industries and causing a severe decline in the home economy.

The ability of the home country to absorb expanded imports without suffering domestic economic disruption is primarily a function of the strength and size of its domestic economy in relation to the trading partner. If the home country's economy is growing, the increased domestic demand can generally absorb the increase in imports; but if the economy is declining, the increased import pressure can be quite harmful. If the home country has difficulty surviving the import onslaught, it will often restrict imports by high tariffs, nontariff trade barriers, or quotas to blunt the transmission of the domestic economic decline.

Monetary Conditions

Changes in a country's monetary policy often transmit to major trading partners in a manner similar to that of exports and imports of goods and services.[2] A home-country monetary expansion provides more money and credit to domestic residents, fueling their demand for more products including more imports. As the trading partner expands domestic production to meet export demand, it creates a demand for increased money and credit within its own country. If its domestic financial system obliges with such increase, the monetary expansion in the home country has transmitted itself to the trading partner's economy.

As full capacity is reached, inflationary concerns increase domestic interest rates in both countries. If the expansion causes deterioration in the home country's current account, the exchange rate may depreciate unless short-term interest rates are increased to stimulate cross-border demand for home-country financial assets, causing the trading partner's financial markets to respond by also raising interest rates. A home-country economic expansion accompanied by a restrictive monetary policy raises both short- and long-term interest rates, which may cause an appreciation of the exchange rate attracting substantial imports from trading partners.

In contrast, if the home country adopts a restrictive monetary policy that retards domestic economic growth, the slowdown spills over into reduced demand for imports. As the trading partner's export industries suffer a decline, demand for money and credit falls, causing its monetary authorities to curtail growth in domestic money and credit. A trading partner's economic contraction curtails domestic economic activity, especially if accompanied by a restrictive domestic monetary policy. On the other hand, an economic contraction accompanied by a monetary expansion may maintain a stable domestic economic environment.

However, cross-border transmission of monetary conditions differs in several important respects from transmission through expansion or contraction of economic output. In the model of economic output, it is assumed that both the home country and its trading partners have excess production capacity so that the transmission of economic conditions is through normal cross-border commercial activity. Often such conditions do not exist because countries may be at different stages in a business cycle, have different domestic economic characteristics, or have adopted different economic policies. Accordingly, trading partners may adopt monetary policies different from the home country, thereby negating or complicating home-country monetary policy.

For example, a home country combating inflation may adopt a restrictive monetary policy intended to reduce domestic money and credit to dampen domestic demand. A trading partner, concerned about a subsequent export decline, may attempt financing exports to the home country by pursuing a contrary expansionist monetary policy, causing an expansion of the home country's demand to be met by increased imports as the trading partner accepts home-country financial assets as payment for its exports. Consequently, rather than causing a reduction in demand the diverging monetary policies satisfy rising domestic demand while creating a major shift in the home-country economy as domestic manufactured products are replaced with foreign manufactured products.

Exchange Rates

Exchange rates are the pricing mechanism's means of adjusting the currency supply and demand forces caused by cross-border transmission of economic conditions. However, a country's policy regarding exchange rate management is an important influence on the transmission of cross-border economic conditions.[3] In a fixed exchange rate regime, countries follow similar economic policies to maintain the exchange rate parities, thereby facilitating the transmission of cross-border economic conditions. Thus, their respective domestic economies are tied to similar business cycle modulations. Smaller countries experiencing a trade deficit have limited financial markets to finance such trade deficit and may be compelled to use foreign reserves to pay for such deficit to maintain the exchange rate parities.

On the other hand, exchange rates under a flexible regime fluctuate to cushion the transmission of cross-border economic conditions. A decline in home-country exports deteriorates the trade balance, causing a decline in its exchange rate. While falling exchange rates will not overcome the resulting home-country economic decline, it increases import prices, causing domestic demand to shift to price competitive domestic substitutes and thereby partially offsetting the disruptive consequences in the export industries. The success of this substitution depends on the ability to replace imported products with similar domestic production and the speed by which it occurs. However, the decline of import demand causes the economic contraction to spread to other trading partners and feed back to the home country. Thus, flexible exchange rates do not stop the transmission of economic conditions but do permit a smoother transition, allowing time for the domestic economy to adjust.

However, exchange rate policies are conducted in the framework of an overall economic policy. For example, some countries prefer the competitive advantage and certainty of fixed exchange rates but nevertheless wish the economic benefit of declining imports otherwise achieved under a depreciating exchange rate. To achieve this goal, a fixed exchange rate policy may be conducted in tandem with an active means of restricting imports, which many countries pursued during the gold standard. In an economic contraction where countries following a fixed exchange rate regime cannot reduce imports by a depreciating exchange rate, import reduction is accomplished by higher tariffs or nontariff barriers.

Transmission of monetary conditions between trading partners is also a function of the exchange rate regimes. Under a fixed exchange rate regime where countries cannot adopt monetary policies that would change exchange rate levels, all participating countries must consequently follow similar monetary policies to maintain the established parities. Under a free-floating or managed exchange rate regime, trading partners can pursue different monetary policies.

However, the effect of independent monetary policy may not be as intended as trading partners pursue their own independent monetary policy which feeds back to the home country, disrupting its domestic monetary policy. For example, if a home-country monetary expansion increases demand for imports while the trading partner's economy is at full capacity, the trading partner's monetary authorities may adopt a restrictive monetary policy to fight inflation, causing an increase in its exchange rate. The resulting import price increase to the home country may cause its manufacturers to increase domestic prices to the level of imports rather than increase output so that the home-country expansionary monetary policy causes domestic inflation rather than expansion of production.

Fiscal Policy

Fiscal policy covers a broad range of central government activity, including trade policy, antitrust policy, subsidies, taxation, regulation, and the like. While these activities have some impact on cross-border commerce, the economic activity of greatest impact is generally the central government budget balance. For most industrial countries, central government receipts and expenditures exceed 20 percent of their respective nominal GDP, making them the single largest participants in the domestic economy. Government debt is the least risky and most marketable of credit investments and is ideal for international capital markets facilitating government budget deficit financing. Accordingly, fiscal policy, as represented by budget deficits, has enormous impact on cross-border as well as domestic economic conditions.

The cross-border economic impact of fiscal policy is similar to the economic expansion or contraction and monetary policy previously discussed.[4] However, exchange rate policy can play a significant role in altering the domestic economy's response to such fiscal expansion. A budget deficit has the initial impact of an economic expansion. Government purchases of goods and services in excess of receipts are financed by increased government debt that causes a rising interest rate. Under a flexible exchange rate regime, the increased interest rates cause an appreciation of the exchange rate that makes imports cheaper relative to domestic goods. Consequently, the increased demand in both public and private sectors arising from the fiscal policy expansion is satisfied by growing imports while deferring the economic consequences of debt payment to later periods.

On the other hand, under a fixed exchange rate regime, attracting additional foreign capital is difficult because the potential rise in domestic interest rates would cause a rise in the exchange rate. To maintain exchange rate equilibrium with the trading partners, the fiscal expansion must cause a reallocation of existing domestic resources from private to public use. This reallocation is accomplished either by (1) increasing domestic taxes or, as a more politically achievable alternative, (2) expanding the money supply. Monetary expansion creates inflation that limits private purchasing power but causes higher interest rates to maintain exchange rate equilibrium.

OTHER CHARACTERISTICS OF TRANSMISSION

In analyzing the impact of the cross-border transmission of economic conditions, two characteristics of economic data are important.

Exchange Rate Changes and the J-Curve Effect

There is a delayed effect in the transmission process usually described by the *J-curve effect*. The J-curve effect is a model of the impact on a country's trade balance caused by a depreciating exchange rate. The trade balance initially worsens as the cost of imported goods rises in terms of domestic currency. Eventually, higher import prices reduce import demand while improving the price competitiveness of exports, thereby improving the overall balance of trade. Thus, in a depreciating exchange rate, the trade balance moves in a manner that corresponds to the letter *J*. Because of contractual commitments, orders already made, negotiation of new trade terms, and other lags, the upward movement in the trade balance often occurs after a six- to nine-month lag following the exchange rate depreciation.

Differences in Interest Rates, Prices, and Output

In the growing unrestricted cross-border movement of goods, services, and capital it would seem that, in the absence of political instability, interest rates and prices should remain generally the same. Any divergences will quickly cause a change in trade and capital flows. In practice, divergence in interest rates, prices, and output are the more common condition reflecting differences in business cycles, economic policies, and lags in transmission of economic conditions. In addition, though interest rates and other opportunities may be better elsewhere, the risks and uncertainties of cross-border commerce make most domestic residents satisfied to maintain local business and investment activity. Consequently, for most industrial countries, cross-border commerce constitutes less than 25 percent of overall economic activity, giving domestic economic conditions the principal influence on financial and economic factors. Exploiting differences in nominal interest rates and prices is further inhibited by the uncertainty created as trading partners experience different business cycle phases and diverging consumer and financial markets. Consequently, differences in nominal interest rates and rates of change in price indexes are normal, becoming more prominent by diverging business cycles. Comparing nominal interest rate levels is of only limited help in understanding economic conditions.

NOTES

1. For a more extensive discussion of cross-border transmission of economic conditions, see Francisco L. Rivera-Batiz and Luis Rivera-Batiz, *International Finance and Open Economy Macroeconomics* (New York: Macmillan, 1985).

2. A good theoretical discussion of the complex monetary relationship between trading partners is John E. Floyd, *World Monetary Equilibrium* (Oxford: Philip Allan Publishers, 1985).

3. A more in-depth discussion of exchange rate economics is Nick Douch, *The Economics of Foreign Exchange* (Westport, Conn.: Quorum Books, 1989).

4. Under Keynesian analysis, fiscal policy has a more extensive impact on cross-border transmission of economic conditions, as seen in Rivera-Batiz and Rivera-Batiz, *International Finance*, and Warwick J. McKibbin and Jeffrey D. Sachs, *Global Linkages* (Washington, D.C.: The Brookings Institution, 1991); and little consideration is given to the implications of exchange rate regimes. Under a monetary approach, monetary policy and exchange rate regimes have more significance in this transmission process.

CHAPTER 4

Exchange Rate Regimes

In the model for transmitting cross-border economic conditions, exchange rates were discussed principally as a function of domestic economic conditions. Notwithstanding this general model, in order to achieve economic growth and price stability, governments attempt to influence economic conditions by managing the exchange rate through monetary and fiscal policies. The effect of such management policies is not limited to exports, imports, and related commerce but ultimately impacts the entire domestic economy, thereby contributing to modulations in the business cycle. For example, a falling exchange rate triggers fear of rising inflation from higher import prices. This causes monetary authorities to institute a tight monetary policy that stabilizes the exchange rate but also makes interest rates rise for all domestic residents. Likewise, a rising exchange rate that adversely impacts export industries may cause institution of an easy monetary policy to lower interest rates, thereby increasing general domestic credit and triggering a surge of domestic inflation.

GOVERNMENT EXCHANGE RATE CONCERNS

Government desire to manage exchange rates arises from a combination of economic and political concerns. Exchange rates can be a major catalyst for changing economic conditions and are a critical factor to attracting foreign capital.[1] However, exchange rate changes have a complicated and mixed impact on domestic economic conditions and foreign investment so that the consequences vary from country to country depending on a variety of economic conditions. Politically, exchange rates are an aspect of national prestige that can have great impact on a country's foreign policy as well as the morale of its people. Declining exchange rates are often viewed by the domestic population and other governments as indicators of declining economic strength.

Cross-Border Commerce

An example of the mixed economic impact of exchange rate changes is illustrated by examining the ramifications of such change. Under the government's desire to expand exports, declining exchange rates cause home-country export prices to fall, thereby improving their international competitiveness. However, home-country consumers pay more for imports, although home-country manufacturers may benefit by the price advantage achieved against competitive imports. Under a falling exchange rate, foreign investment income denominated in foreign currency increases in value, but obligations payable in foreign currency become more expensive and crippling to countries carrying heavy foreign debt obligations.

In contrast, rising exchange rates cause home-country exports to become more expensive and less internationally competitive, thereby reducing export purchases. On the other hand, imports are cheaper, benefiting consumers and those home-country manufacturers dependent on foreign raw materials. However, cheaper imports can allow foreign companies to compete more effectively against domestic firms, thereby dislocating domestic employment. An appreciating currency also reduces the cost of paying obligations denominated in a depreciating foreign currency, although income from foreign investments decline as repatriated foreign income is converted to domestic currency.

Dislocation in Financial Markets

Concerns over the harmful financial dislocations from exchange rate volatility stems from fears that foreigners will "take money out of the country," which was the harmful experiences of the gold standard. Under the rules of the gold standard, a declining exchange rate caused foreigners to convert their currency into gold at the fixed rate of exchange, shipping the gold out of the country and causing a contraction of the domestic money supply, which, in turn, resulted in a rapid and serious deflation in financial markets, curtailment in production, and massive unemployment. A country fearing a depreciating exchange rate stemmed the gold outflow by raising interest rates, creating a tight monetary condition and economic consequence almost as severe as the loss of gold.

Today, countries no longer follow the gold standard, and domestic monetary systems provide a flexible domestic money supply less impacted by outside forces. Nevertheless, exchange rate changes can severely impact economies dependent on cross-border investment activity. A falling exchange rate can cause a selloff of financial assets by international investors that not only exacerbates the exchange rate decline but discourages future international investment or raises the price of future financing. Unless the home country undertakes steps to restore international investor confidence, the home-country government and businesses will find it difficult to obtain cross-border capital.

Restoring confidence may require economic policies that can worsen the domestic economy. Increasing domestic interest rates to arrest expectations of further exchange rate declines raises domestic interest rates, increasing the cost of capital to all domestic residents. Issuing debt obligations denominated in foreign currency also gives confidence to cross-border investors but defers to a later period the cost of earning the necessary foreign currency for making the debt payment.

MEASURING INTERNATIONAL ECONOMIC DEPENDENCE

In managing exchange rates, governments are guided by the dependence of their domestic economies on cross-border commerce. Measuring international dependency is accomplished by a number of methods. A commonly used method is calculating the ratio of a country's commercial exports to GDP and commercial imports to GDP, as more fully discussed in Chapter 8. This analysis can be extended to include more specific activities such as merchandise trade, types of products, and trading partners. If exchange rates change gradually over an extended time period, economic activity will adjust so that price changes will have negligible impact. On the other hand, if exchange rates change dramatically within a short time period, economic activity can become severely impacted.

Another measure of international dependency is the ratio of cross-border claims and liabilities to GDP, as is shown in Table 4.1 for selected countries in 1992. With U.S. short-term foreign liabilities representing only 11 percent of its GDP, a significant fall in the dollar's value caused by a rapid and concerted sale of cross-border money market instruments would have a negligible impact on the domestic economy. Japan and Germany are in a similar situation with liability to GDP ratios of 19 percent and 10 percent, respectively. On the other hand, countries with relatively large international financial industries—such as Britain, Belgium/Luxembourg, and Switzerland—are vulnerable to wide fluctuations in the currency value, as indicated by the bank liability to GDP ratio of 76 percent, 187 percent, and 40 percent, respectively.

Table 4.1
Cross-Border Claims and Liabilities, Ratio to GDP, 1992

Country	Billions of Dollars			Ratio to GDP	
	Claims	Liabilities	Balance	Claims	Liabilities
United States	537	663	-126	9%	11%
Japan	679	691	-12	19%	19%
Germany	252	184	68	14%	10%
Britain	728	804	-76	69%	76%
Canada	35	46	-11	6%	8%
France	354	348	6	28%	27%
Belgium/Luxembourg	319	319	0	187%	187%
Switzerland	345	97	248	142%	40%
Netherlands	137	105	32	55%	42%

Source: International Financial Statistics (Washington, D.C.: International Monetary Fund, January 1994).

TYPES OF EXCHANGE RATE REGIMES

Government exchange rate management usually revolves around three basic regimes: fixed or pegged, floating, and managed.

Fixed Exchange Rate Regime

In a *fixed exchange rate regime*, the central government maintains the exchange rate at a fixed rate in relation to some other clearly identifiable standard. This regime is accomplished by appropriate domestic economic policies, including changes in interest rates, changes in government budget balances, export and import controls, and currency market intervention. These economic policies are designed to achieve levels of interest rates, prices, wage rates, output, and money supply growth similar to all participating countries in the fixed exchange rate regime and result in common monetary and fiscal policies. Consequently, participating country business cycles move in tandem, forcing the burden of any divergences to fall on domestic economic activity through changes in domestic wages, prices, and interest rates until the common level is in conformity with the other participating countries and the fixed exchange rate is maintained.

Critical to an effective fixed exchange rate system is choice of the identifiable standard around which the exchange rate will be fixed. In most cases, the identifiable standard is some monetary item in common with a country's principal trading partner or partners. During the nineteenth and early twentieth centuries, most industrial countries maintained fixed exchange rate regimes by a fixed purchase price of gold. These policy decisions were independently made but pursuant to a common desire to protect commercial relationships with the principal industrial power, Britain. By pegging exchange rates to gold, countries also fixed their exchange rates in relation to all other countries participating in the same regime, thereby creating what came to be called the gold standard. Other metallic standards have also been used, such as silver by China and Mexico or a bimetallic standard combining silver and gold.

As a variation of the gold standard, the Bretton Woods system was created in 1944 by a formal multilateral agreement establishing a global fixed rate regime by pegging exchange rates to the U.S. dollar, which was, in turn, fixed at $35 to an ounce of gold. When established, the United States dominated the global economy, was a principal trading partner for most countries, and held substantial quantities of gold. War reconstruction required a more flexible supply of international reserves better achieved by expansion of dollar-denominated financial assets rather than expanded quantities of gold. Under this fixed exchange rate regime, countries were allowed to unilaterally adjust their exchange rate by no more than 1 percent in relation to the dollar. Larger changes required approval of the International Monetary Fund (IMF), established to monitor the Bretton Woods system.

Following the demise of the Bretton Woods system, many countries reestablished fixed rate regimes by substituting as their identifiable standard the exchange rate of a major trading partner or a trade-weighted exchange rate composed of principal trading partners. Today, the bilateral exchange rate with the dollar is retained by some countries, but in many cases, a variety of bilateral and multilateral exchange rates are used as the identifiable standard. These fixed rate regimes are established either as a unilateral policy that is publicly announced or inferred by continuously stable exchange rates or through a multilateral agreement such as Bretton Woods or the European Monetary System (EMS).

While the fixed rate regime has been abandoned, the Bretton Woods infrastructure created to monitor the system remains. The IMF provides a critical apparatus and staff support for coordinating exchange rate management and assisting countries in stabilizing exchange rate levels. Through the more informal consultive process of the Group of Seven (G-7) meetings, the United States has provided leadership in coordinating monetary and economic policies to achieve exchange rate stability.

As with many economic policies, a fixed rate regime has both advantages and disadvantages. Where participating countries have common economic goals of stable growth and stable price levels, a fixed rate regime imposes a common discipline ideal for dealing with monetary shocks, such as unusual credit expansion; global economic disturbances, such as an oil price rise; or economic disturbances from countries outside the exchange rate regime. Generally, such discipline also contributes to domestic economic efficiency and stable price levels, making such countries effective international competitors.

On the other hand, fixed rate regimes do not work well when one or several participating countries have widely different domestic economic characteristics, pursue conflicting economic policies, or embark upon conflicting economic objectives. Where one country has a large domestic agricultural sector compared to other participating countries with large manufacturing or financial sectors, different economic conditions make it difficult to pursue similar economic policies. Similarly, participants with political constituencies with different views of economic policy, such as the importance of full employment versus inflation, may limit the ability to pursue common economic policies. In many cases, major events occur that compel a country to pursue a separate economic policy, such as war, internal instability, or unusual political events such as the large German budget deficits incurred to speed East German unification.

For example, fighting inflation is roundly condemned for its disruptive effect on economic growth, and its containment is a principal benefit of a fixed exchange rate regime. However, a country may be unable to resolve internal social or economic policies, making it difficult to maintain fiscal policies consistent with trading partners. Furthermore, governments resort to inflation as a means of spreading the burden of fiscal expansion while avoiding the painful political decision of specific burden allocation necessitated by tax increases.

Implementing a fixed exchange rate regime creates almost as many difficulties as a floating regime. Because it ties a country to the economic conditions of other participants, choosing the identifiable standard to peg exchange rates and the level at which the exchange rate will be maintained are critical to an effective fixed exchange rate regime. Errors will cause the burden of readjustment to fall on the domestic economy with possible severe consequences to domestic wage and price levels. For example, a country that exports and imports principally from one country usually sets a fixed exchange rate regime according to the bilateral exchange rate between the two countries. In contrast, a country with different principal trading partners for exports and imports has a more complex task in maintaining a fixed exchange rate. One of the principal benefits of the gold standard and the Bretton Woods system was the adherence to one identified standard that all countries followed.

Establishing the appropriate exchange rate level is the most difficult aspect of fixed exchange rate regimes because of the ever-changing global economy. Because business cycles have different phases and long-range growth patterns, it is difficult to determine the appropriate exchange rate level, and a country can never be confident that the chosen level is the correct one. Should the exchange rate level be set at (1) current market rates, (2) long-term equilibrium rates based on purchasing power parity methods, (3) the desired level for long-term growth, (4) the desired level to contain inflation, (5) the desired level for exports, or (6) some other level? The period following World War I has many examples of economic upheavals as countries attempted to reestablish a fixed rate regime under the gold standard based on exchange rate levels that did not reflect changed economic conditions following the war. The exchange rate mechanism (ERM) of the EMS established a fixed exchange rate regime for its member countries that nevertheless required eleven realignments of exchange rate levels from time of inception in 1979 through 1987.

Subsequent to the establishment of a fixed rate regime, a country may determine that its economy is so out of balance with its trading partners that the exchange rate level must be permanently realigned to reflect changed economic conditions or correct an overoptimistic peg of the exchange rate parity. A weakness of many fixed exchange rate regimes is the lack of a formula or a mechanism by which to make such adjustment because of the assumption that exchange rate pressures are due solely to controllable domestic economic conditions, with no consideration for uncontrollable outside conditions or policy mistakes. Accordingly, to correct a growing economic imbalance, a country may be forced to abandon outright the fixed rate regime and adopt a free-floating or managed exchange rate regime or realign its exchange rate to a new level. The ERM fixed exchange rate regime required eleven realignments of exchange rate levels, while the dramatic economic changes in Germany following unification forced Britain and several other countries to temporarily abandon the ERM.

A realignment of the exchange rate level within the fixed exchange rate regime is usually described as a revaluation or devaluation of the exchange rate. These terms distinguish this purely government activity from the market characteristic of a floating or managed exchange rate regime where exchange rate changes are referred to as an appreciation or depreciation of the exchange rate.

Floating Exchange Rate Regime

In contrast to a fixed rate regime a *floating* or *free market exchange rate regime* allows exchange rate fluctuations according to market forces free of government intervention. Thus, a country is free to adopt independent domestic monetary and fiscal policies, which will cause interest rate, wage, output, and money supply levels to digress from the levels of the principal trading partner, ultimately causing the economy to embark on a separate business cycle. Unlike the fixed rate regime, the burden of adjusting for different cross-border economic conditions falls initially on the exchange rate, which eventually causes a change in domestic economic activity affected by the cross-border activity.

The principal advantage of a floating exchange rate system is that participating countries have greater flexibility in pursuing domestic economic policies while confining the disruptive consequences of exchange rate
fluctuations to those economic sections primarily engaged in cross-border
economic activity. This advantage is particularly important to countries not
dependent on cross-border commerce and countries with unique domestic
economic strengths such as sustained economic growth. Under standard price
theory, the floating exchange rate system provides an efficient means of adjusting cross-border commercial relationships allowing the market to adjust
for the many complex factors influencing economic conditions.[2]

In practice, a free-floating exchange rate regime presents a country with
several problems, of which one is the principal dilemma of the pricing mechanism. Fluctuating exchange rates allow adjustment for current economic conditions at the expense of long-term investment, while stable exchange rates
encourage long-range planning and investment while masking current economic imbalances. Daily volatility of the exchange rates that inhibit business
and investment decisions can be partially overcome by hedging and other
derivative devices. However, such strategies add to the cost of cross-border
commercial activity and may outweigh the benefits. On the other hand, derivative devices are still in their infancy and unable to provide the exchange
rate stability necessary for long-range planning and investment.

A country adopting a floating exchange rate regime faces another problem.
Trading partners may wish to manipulate the exchange rate in their favor by
intervening in currency markets, changing domestic monetary policies, or
adopting protectionist trade policies. Consequently, an effective floating exchange rate system requires agreement among trading partners not to intervene in the currency markets or engage in protectionist trade policies.
However, truly free-floating exchange rates tend to be volatile, creating uncertainty among businesses and governments. Most economic policymakers
believe that maintaining orderly currency markets permit gradual exchange
rate changes giving participant countries opportunity to adjust domestic economic activity also in an orderly fashion. Accordingly, it is virtually impossible to obtain international agreements on a truly free-market exchange rate
regime.

Nevertheless, during times of unusual economic disturbances, governments
occasionally accede to a floating exchange rate regime for short periods of
time. War, depression, oil price hikes, and other economic disturbances may
be of such magnitude that monetary authorities are prevented from maintaining orderly currency markets or determining the appropriate exchange rate
level. Monetary authorities may then withdraw from the currency markets,
allowing market forces to determine exchange rate levels reflecting changes
in underlying economic conditions. When exchange rate levels appear to begin to firm at a new appropriate level, the monetary authorities may reenter
the currency markets to maintain orderly exchange rates at the new levels.

Countries with low levels of cross-border commercial activity often pursue independent economic policies while maintaining fixed exchange rates because the smaller costs permit them to easily maintain the exchange rate level. Such countries can also quickly change exchange rate regimes, suffering only minimum domestic economic disruption. On the other hand, countries heavily dependent on cross-border commerce may have the benefits of an independent economic policy offset by the lost export markets as a result of differences in price levels, interest rates, wage rates, output, and business cycles which occur when pursuing independent monetary and fiscal polices in floating exchange rate regimes. Furthermore, exchange rate volatility and conflicting economic policies of trading partners may undermine monetary policy, reducing the ability to maintain independent policies.

Managed Exchange Rate Regime

With the demise of the Bretton Woods system in 1971, many countries adopted a *managed exchange rate regime* in which a variety of monetary policies such as interest rate changes and currency market intervention are implemented to achieve a desired exchange rate level. For countries following this regime, the exchange rate policy consists of moderating wide swings in exchange rates while permitting gradual exchange rate adjustments to reflect differences in economic conditions between trading partners such as price levels, current account balances, and interest rates. Thus, countries following a managed regime pursue the best of the other two exchange rate regimes, including relative exchange rate stability and more efficient cross-border commercial activity.

In some cases, managed exchange rate policy may provide domestic industries with a competitive international advantage such as a lower exchange rate to reduce the price of domestic products in the international marketplace. However, such "beggar thy neighbor" attempts to transmit economic problems to trading partners may be countered by competitive devaluations, creating instability in exchange rates.

Most managed exchange rate regimes are conducted in a manner similar to fixed rate regimes except that greater tolerance is given to exchange rate fluctuations. Like fixed rate regimes, countries following a managed regime must determine the identifiable standard or standards around which the exchange rate will be managed. Then the countries must determine the degree of acceptable fluctuation before implementation of interventionist policies. In most cases, the identifiable standard or standards are chosen according to the same criteria used in fixed rate regimes. Thus, the standard may be a currency basket of principal trading partners or the currency of one principal trading partner. Canada manages its exchange rate in relation to the U.S. dollar, and in 1993, the ERM was modified to permit exchange rates of member countries to move 15 percent above or below the basket of member currencies.

To maintain the orderly adjustment of the exchange rate to market forces, the exchange rate is normally managed within a certain band width in relation to the identified standard, allowing flexibility by monetary authorities in dealing with domestic economic issues. Normally, the band will be from 2.5 percent to 5 percent and will be adjusted to allow the exchange rate to move in the general direction indicated by market forces. However, if the band width is a narrow one, the exchange rate regime resembles a fixed regime with attendant economic consequences.

Managed regimes are often conducted without formal international agreements. Monetary authorities have a strong mutual desire to avoid disorderly markets caused by competitive devaluations and are willing to engage in informal arrangements to manage exchange rates. Global communications and frequent meetings through international organizations such as the G-7, IMF, and the Bank for International Settlement (BIS) permit a wide array of consultation by central banks to coordinate their exchange rate management.

Choice of Regime

The choice of exchange rate regime is a function of government policy goals.[3] A fixed exchange rate regime offers a number of advantages to countries desiring stable prices through stable exchange rates. An exporting country with a positive trading balance usually desires a fixed exchange rate to preserve its international competitive advantage while minimizing the costs and risks to its exporters of a fluctuating exchange rate. Countries heavily dependent on international trade want stable domestic employment, prices, and output undisturbed by disruptive economic conditions of trading partners. A country importing goods critical to the domestic economy will also desire a fixed exchange rate to avoid price dislocations to the domestic economy caused by uncertain or fluctuating prices in the key imports. Countries experiencing unstable domestic monetary conditions may achieve stability by pegging their exchange rates to an economically stable trading partner, thereby enhancing creditability with foreign investors. Many European countries adopted this policy by pegging their exchange rates to the Deutsche mark via the ERM.

While countries best protect their international economic position by adopting a fixed rate or a managed rate regime, implementing such a regime may impose unacceptable costs as the domestic economy is aligned with economic conditions of trading partners. In addition, determining the appropriate standard and exchange rate level is difficult, and the cost of error may be too great. Exchange rate studies based on historical data are like economic forecasts and often not up to date with dynamic forces. Another major issue is this: Who bears the cost of maintaining the exchange rate regime? In a bilateral relationship, one country is more interested in maintaining a stable exchange rate level. A smaller country dependent on the market of a larger trading partner prefers a stable exchange rate such as Canada in relation to the United States.

Furthermore, not all countries have sufficiently resolved domestic economic imbalances that would accommodate a fixed exchange rate regime. Countries with deficit trade balances often wish to improve the competitive price of exports and may prefer a floating or managed regime to allow depreciation of the domestic exchange rate. Countries not dependent on foreign commerce likewise prefer the flexibility of managed or floating exchange rates to pursue independent international and domestic programs.

Whichever regime is chosen, implementation must be in conjunction with other monetary and fiscal policies affecting domestic and international commerce, in particular, interest rate levels, budget deficits, and trade policy. Table 4.2 provides an analysis of exchange rate regimes for 152 countries as of 1991. Two-thirds of the countries followed fixed rate regimes, and one-third followed managed exchange rates, indicating that stable exchange rates

Table 4.2
Exchange Rate Regime Analysis, 1991

	Number of Countries
Fixed Rate Regimes	
Pegged to Single Currency	
U.S. dollar	30
French Franc	14
Other Single Currencies	5
Total Single Currency Peg	49
Pegged to Currency Basket	
ERM Currency Basket	11
Other Currency Baskets	44
Total Currency Basket Peg	55
Total Fixed Rate Regimes	104
Managed Floats	48

Source: The Economist, *Guide to Economic Indicators* (London: Century Business, 1992), p. 145.

and alignment with principal trading partners is a desire of most countries. However, the independent standard around which the fixed exchange rate regimes are managed varies widely ranging from bilateral exchange rates such as the dollar and the French franc to currency baskets such as the ERM. Such a variety of exchange rate regimes adds to the complexity of exchange rate management, indicating continuing divergence in cross-border economic conditions.

IMPLEMENTATION OF EXCHANGE RATE REGIMES

Whichever exchange rate regime is adopted by a country, key factors in the choice are the methods and procedures for managing the regime and the country providing the anchor currency.[4] There are two principal systems governing this choice: the key currency system and the monetary union.

Key Currency System

In practice, the choice of regime and related exchange rate decisions are thrust upon most countries by economic circumstances. To maintain export markets with trading partners, access to their financial markets, and foreign investment, most countries align themselves around the currency and exchange rate regime of the dominant trading partner, creating what is called a *key currency system*, in which the trading partners maintain a fixed or managed exchange rate regime in relation to the exchange rate of the key currency country.[5]

The distinguishing feature of a key currency system is that maintaining a stable exchange rate is more important to the trading-partner countries than to the key currency country. Consequently, the trading partners are burdened with maintaining stable exchange rates including any adversity from aligning domestic monetary policy to that of the key currency country. The economic dominance of the key currency country makes its currency readily acceptable in the surrounding countries, permitting them to hold as foreign currency reserves monetary instruments or bonds denominated in the key currency country. Such key currency also becomes the principal medium for cross-border transactions.

A key currency system usually incorporates a fixed or managed exchange rate regime with the identifiable standard being the exchange rate of the key currency. However, to protect their access to key currency trade and financial markets, trading partners assume the burden of maintaining a stable exchange rate. Thus, the key currency country determines monetary policy, price level, interest rate levels, and business cycles of all countries in the key currency system, allowing it to pursue independent economic policies the trading partners must follow.

Trading partners that attempt to follow economic or monetary policies independent of the key currency country risk significant economic dislocation. Uncoupling from the key currency country will cause a change in the bilateral exchange rate, which may cause loss of market share in the key currency country, reduced access to key currency financial markets, and dislocation in a trading partner's financial markets as foreign investors readjust their investment portfolios. Countries less ambitious in their goal of complete independence may achieve more limited economic objectives and reduce economic dislocation by realigning exchange rate parities to more appropriate levels.

For more than two hundred years, Britain in the nineteenth century and the United States in the twentieth century have been dominant trading partners for most countries, creating a global key currency system revolving around their currency and economic policies. The consumer market offered by these two countries combined with financial markets willing to invest overseas was a magnet drawing surrounding countries to organize their domestic economies to take advantage of these opportunities. The Bretton Woods system was both a fixed rate regime and a key currency system established by formal multilateral agreement pegging exchange rates to the U.S. dollar, which was, in turn, pegged to the price of gold. With dollars in plentiful supply to meet the demand for a principal vehicle currency for international transactions, the system was also a key currency system with the United States as the key currency and the burden for maintaining the stable exchange rate falling on the surrounding countries.

As Europe, Japan, and the rest of the world recovered from World War II, trade and financial patterns changed, reducing many countries' dependence on the U.S. market while increasing dependence on newer industrial countries. Abandonment of the Bretton Woods system in 1971 was not only an abandonment of a fixed rate regime but also a realignment of the key currency system to reflect changes in global trade and financial relationships. The resulting realignment created a multiplicity of new key currency systems revolving around the currency reserves and exchange rate of several large industrial countries such as Germany, France, and Japan, which had become critical export markets and capital sources for many countries. Germany is the principal trading partner of most European countries, while Japan is an important market to Asian countries. France is an unusual situation since it simultaneously is an important member of the EMS key currency system while a key currency country for several African countries that were former colonies.

The largest of the new key currency systems is Europe, where the success of the European Economic Community (EEC) made its member economies more interdependent and strongly in favor of fixed exchange rates to preserve economic stability. Following the demise of the Bretton Woods fixed exchange rate system and the unwillingness of the United States to establish some other fixed rate regime, Europe embarked upon its own fixed exchange rate system. In 1979, the EMS was adopted, which created the ERM key currency system based upon the Deutsche mark and a fixed exchange rate regime based on a weighted average of member currencies with the Deutsche mark constituting about 30 percent of the currency basket. A currency unit that could act as a vehicle currency for cross-border transactions, the ecu, was also introduced. Coordination of monetary and economic policies was also a part of EMS but was dropped in favor of movement toward full monetary union approved in 1991 by the Maastricht Treaty.

However, under the current global economic environment, these new key currency systems are fragile as the United States remains an important trade and financial market for most countries and is the key currency for much of the global economy. The EMS is a good example of the difficulty experienced in uncoupling from the U.S. key currency system. The European key currency system is based on the dominant economy of Germany. Germany, in turn, has a major export market in the United States and needs access to international financial markets because of the underdevelopment of its own capital markets. Accordingly, after adjusting its relationship with the United States to account for its postwar economic resurgence and embarking on its new role as a key currency for Europe, Germany nevertheless continued to align much of its economic policy to that of the United States.

When unification forced Germany to follow an economic policy diametrically different from the United States and other members of the European key currency system, the weakness of the system became fully apparent. Many European countries had domestic economies whose business cycle had markedly diverged from Germany's while maintaining significant trading and financial relationships with the United States and Japan. These countries were forced to choose between the two key currency systems. Several countries withdrew or significantly changed their exchange rate relationship with the ERM causing a modification of its permitted band width to resemble more of a managed exchange rate regime.

Monetary Union

A *monetary union* is an alignment of countries to maintain a fixed or managed exchange rate regime by delegating responsibility to a central organization to coordinate monetary policy. Normally, the economic size and stability of one or two member countries permits the monetary union to base the exchange rate levels in relation to the exchange rate of these dominate countries, giving them the status as the *anchor currency*. While a monetary union has many characteristics similar to a key currency system, it is distinguished by two important features: (1) the economically dominant country surrenders control over domestic monetary policy in favor of the monetary union, and (2) an organization is established to act as a central bank for the monetary union.

In 1979, Europe established a key currency system based on the Deutsche mark as the key currency, relying on the Bundesbank to maintain a stable exchange rate through the ERM. Although the ERM has been bumpy and experienced many exchange rate realignments, member countries believe they have developed sufficient coordination of their domestic economies to move toward European Monetary Union (EMU). In 1991 at Maastricht, the member countries agreed to movement toward full monetary union. Membership criteria were established to achieve economic cohesion through converging economic conditions while a monetary commission was instituted to coordinate the convergence and lay the foundation for a European central bank—at which time monetary policy will be transferred to it.

EXCHANGE CONTROLS

To maintain exchange rate regimes and exchange rate levels, a wide array of economic and monetary policies are available and have been discussed. However, such policies may not achieve desired exchange rate objectives because they aim primarily at influencing the exchange rate level through policies often at variance with domestic economic or political needs while relying on the cooperation of independent financial markets and trading partners which may be pursuing other objectives. Furthermore, countries may need to preserve limited international reserves to pay for critical imports, restore international confidence, or reduce foreign currency–denominated debt.

Accordingly, countries may implement an exchange rate regime by direct controls consisting of two broad programs: currency control and capital control. Currency controls are the most direct and effective means encompassing a wide variety of methods restricting payment on items associated with a country's current account such as trade, services, and debt payments. The most comprehensive currency control method is prohibiting conversion of domestic currency into foreign currency and often referred to as lack of *convertability*. Under this method, domestic residents are not allowed to sell domestic currency or purchase foreign currency without prior approval of government authorities. Countries needing international reserves may also require that all existing domestically owned foreign currency be transferred to the government. To further discourage foreign currency ownership, banks may be ordered to maintain high reserves against foreign liabilities. A method widely used by less-developed countries are official exchange rates, whereby all domestic residents are required to conduct currency transactions at the official exchange rate. Protectionist trade policies can also be incorporated to control specific cross-border trade to achieve a targeted trade balance, thereby manipulating the supply of available currency.

Investment outflows threaten exchange rate depreciation, inhibiting future foreign investment, while large investment inflows threaten appreciation of the exchange rate, disrupting the competitiveness of the country's exports and causing speculation in financial markets. Currency controls can regulate cross-border investment activity, but the government machinery necessary for such regulation is sometimes too pervasive and cumbersome, interfering with normal trading relationships. Capital controls are generally more selective and are usually in the form of government approval for use of currency in any capital transaction; government approval for foreign ownership and participation in domestic investments; or more subtle means such as taxes on ownership transfers, special levies on investments, or high withholding taxes on interest and dividends repatriated to foreigners.

Extensive currency and capital controls were developed by most industrial countries to cope with the Great Depression and the economic consequences during and after World War II. Much of post–World War II economic policy of the industrial countries has dealt with advantages and disadvantages of such controls with the ultimate conclusion to dismantle most of these controls in favor of a free-flowing global capital market. Britain in 1979 abolished its remaining foreign exchange controls, followed by Japan in 1980. France and Italy dismantled capital controls in 1990; however, many countries have informal arrangements or social biases toward foreign participation in domestic financial markets contributing to distortions in exchange rate levels similar to currency and capital controls.

NOTES

1. For the deep concerns about exchange rate policy, read the discussion by former chairman of the Federal Reserve, Paul Volcker, in his book coauthored with Toyoo Gyohten, *Changing Fortunes* (New York: Times Books, 1992).

2. For the classic discussion of the advantages of a free-floating exchange rate system, see the discussion by Milton Friedman, *Essays in Positive Economics* (Chicago: University of Chicago Press, 1953).

3. There is growing debate over developing an international exchange rate regime to replace the current ad hoc system. The costs and benefits of exchange rate regimes are discussed in Peter Newman, *The New Palgrave Dictionary of Money and Finance*, Vol. 2 (London: Macmillan, 1992), pp. 467–469.

4. Federal Reserve methods for implementing U.S. exchange rate policy are intensively discussed in B. Dianne Pauls, "U.S. Exchange Rate Policy: Bretton Woods to Present," *Federal Reserve Bulletin*, Washington, D.C., November 1990, pp. 891–908.

5. See John E. Floyd, *World Monetary Equilibrium* (Oxford: Philip Allan Publishers, 1985), for an in-depth discussion of the economic model of a key currency system.

CHAPTER 5

Measuring Exchange
Rate Changes

Exchange rates are not only an important means for adjusting differences in cross-border economic conditions but also an indication of a country's basic economic policy toward the global economic system. A stable exchange rate arises from a desire to coordinate domestic economic conditions among principal trading partners by placing the burden of adjustment upon domestic wages and prices. In contrast, a free-floating exchange rate indicates pursuit of an independent domestic economic policy in which differences with trading-partner economies are adjusted through exchange rate changes. Accordingly, monitoring exchange rate movements is critical to international economic analyses.

EXCHANGE RATES DEFINED

Currency is a country's national unit of account, while the exchange rate measures the relation of currency units between countries. While exchange rate movements are often discussed in general terms, effective international economic trend analysis requires a more precise measurement of exchange rate changes. The complex web of international commercial relationships and currency markets has spawned a variety of methods to measure exchange rate movements, and some of the more useful and widely used methods are discussed in the sections that follow.

Bilateral Exchange Rates

A *bilateral exchange rate* is the exchange rate of the home currency in relation to the currency of another nation and is usually quoted in terms of one home-currency unit in relation to the number of units of a foreign currency. Hence, a U.S. dollar's exchange rate for a British pound may be quoted as $/£.65 while from the British point of view, the pound's exchange rate is £/$1.45. Bilateral exchange rates are most commonly used and are the basis for most other methods. Bilateral exchange rates are quoted daily based on trading activity in the international currency markets by major commercial banks that are the leading international currency traders.

In discussing exchange rates, confusion often occurs as to which side of the bilateral exchange rate is being examined. For example, if the dollar's rate of exchange to the pound moves from $/£.65 to $/£.60, is this a rise or fall in the exchange rate? The fall in the dollar can also be reported as a rise in the pound from £/$1.538 to £/$1.667. The confusion is made worse when exchange rate quotes depart from a uniform practice. Because of historical precedent, American financial news often quotes the exchange rates for the British pound and the Canadian dollar in terms of U.S. dollars rather than the customary method of units of foreign currencies. To avoid confusion, this book uses the exchange rate in terms of one U.S. dollar unless otherwise indicated.

Official Rate of Exchange

Notwithstanding the supply and demand forces determining market exchange rates, some countries attempt controlling exchange rates by fixing an *official exchange rate* at which its official institutions and residents will conduct business. Official exchange rates are distinguished from a pegged exchange rate in that the rate is fixed by law or government decree—irrespective of market forces—and is enforced by government sanctions. In a pegged exchange rate, monetary authorities undertake policies and conduct currency trades to influence the market toward the desired exchange rate. Most industrial countries do not have official exchange rates, although they have been implemented in times of extreme emergencies such as war.

Because of the lack of extraterritorial jurisdiction or enforcement capability, official exchange rates apply only to activities within the control of government authorities. Inability of governments to control all commercial activity or to control markets outside government jurisdiction usually results in market exchange rates that differ from official exchange rates, creating a sizable currency black market to exploit the difference. Prior to its collapse, a sizable currency black market existed in the Soviet Union, indicating significant imbalances in its domestic economy.

Effective or Multicurrency Exchange Rate

To obtain an overall picture of a country's exchange rate vis-à-vis its major trading partners, an average of the nominal exchange rates is compiled to create an *effective* or *multicurrency exchange rate*. Usually, such effective exchange rates are weighted to create an index by which to measure overall rate changes as discussed more fully in the following sections.

Real Effective Exchange Rates

To determine the relative price of foreign products in relation to domestic products and the competitiveness of a country's products in the global economy, the nominal effective exchange rate is adjusted by a ratio of foreign to domestic prices arriving at the *real effective exchange rate*.

Trade-Weighted Exchange Rates

One of the principal effective exchange rate index methods is based on a basket of bilateral exchange rates weighted according to participation in global trade and generally referred to as *trade-weighted exchange rates*. There are four widely used indexes using this method:

- The Federal Reserve Trade-Weighted Multilateral Dollar Exchange Rate
- J. P. Morgan U.S. dollar index
- The Bank of England Trade-Weighted Multilateral Exchange Rate
- The International Monetary Fund Multilateral Exchange Rate

These trade-weighted exchange rate indexes began with different methodologies to determine the weight assigned to each bilateral exchange rate. However, the J. P. Morgan U.S. dollar index was revised in 1993; and the IMF and Bank of England indexes were revised in 1988 so that, along with the Federal Reserve index, the methodology is similar. The weights are based on cross-border trade in manufactures which represents more than 70 percent of the cross-border trade of most industrial countries. Consequently, trade in commodities are excluded from the weighting process. The volume of cross-border trade that is the basis of the weights is not only the bilateral trade between principal trading partners but also the trade with third countries where the trading partners are significant competitors. Despite similar methodologies, the evaluation and interpretation of economic data result in the assignment of different weights so that each index retains its unique characteristic.

For international economic trend analysis, the Bank of England and IMF multilateral exchange rates are particularly useful because they use a uniform weighting formula helpful for comparing exchange rate movements of many countries. Table 5.1 shows the distribution of weights used in the IMF trade-weighted index developed for each of the matrix countries in 1988.[1] For the U.S. trade-weighted index, the Canadian dollar and Japanese yen represent, in the aggregate, 43 percent of the index. On the other hand, the U.S. dollar constitutes 21 percent of all currencies included in the Japanese index and 49 percent of all currencies included in the Canadian index. Currencies are more evenly spread among the British and German indexes.

In most cases, these weights parallel the ratio of cross-border trade of the respective principal trading partners contained in Table 8.5. However, in several notable cases such as Canada and U.S. trade, there was a major difference in weights indicating the significance of commodity or natural resource trade which is not included in the IMF trade-weighted exchange rate method based on manufacturing trade.

The international matrix system uses the Bank of England trade-weighted indexes for each of the matrix countries because they are quoted daily in London's leading financial paper, *The Financial Times*, and weekly in *The Economist*. This index is derived from the IMF trade-weighted index methodology. For following only the U.S. dollar, the J. P. Morgan index in its revised methodology beginning in 1994 not only parallels the accuracy of the Bank of England and IMF trade-weighted dollar index but also has the addi-

Table 5.1
Distribution of Weights Derived from Trade in Manufacturing, Bank of England Trade-Weighted Exchange Rate Indexes, 1988

	U.S.	*Japan*	*Germany*	*Britain*	*Canada*
United States	-	21.2%	4.1%	6.1%	49.2%
Japan	16.0%	-	4.4%	4.6%	8.5%
Germany	4.8%	6.9%	-	5.5%	2.5%
Britain	7.4%	7.2%	5.6%	-	5.0%
Canada	26.7%	6.1%	1.1%	2.3%	-
Subtotal	54.9%	41.5%	15.3%	18.5%	65.3%
France	4.4%	5.3%	7.7%	5.2%	2.7%
Italy	4.2%	5.2%	7.8%	4.8%	2.2%
Netherlands	3.7%	4.1%	8.7%	5.5%	2.3%
Switzerland	4.2%	5.4%	8.1%	8.0%	1.8%
Subtotal	16.5%	20.0%	32.3%	23.4%	9.0%
Other	28.7%	38.5%	52.4%	58.1%	25.8%
Total	100.0%	100.0%	100.0%	100.0%	100.0%

Source: Bank of England, *Quarterly Bulletin* (London: Bank of England, November 1988).

tional advantage of being quoted daily in *The Wall Street Journal*. The Federal Reserve trade-weighted dollar index is not as widely used.

Trade-weighted indexes are attempts to measure complex cross-border commercial relationship, and the above four indexes suffer one major weakness. They all measure exchange rates based on manufacturing trade activity and do not include weights for the growing cross-border activity in services and investment. Accordingly, though trade-weighted indexes are the most accurate measure of aggregate exchange rate changes currently available, careful attention should be given to the bilateral exchange rates between countries having a significant service or investment relationship.

DETERMINATION OF MARKET EXCHANGE RATES

In accordance with basic price theory, exchange rates are determined by the forces of supply and demand caused by a wide array of other economic conditions such as interest rates, current account balances, status of economic growth, currency speculation, and inflation. In uncertain times, political stability, military tensions, and civil unrest also affect exchange rates. However, these market forces are often distorted by direct government intervention in the currency markets and by government economic policies designed to maintain a fixed or managed exchange rate regime or achieve a specific exchange rate level.

Short-Term Market Exchange Rates

Which economic conditions have the greatest impact on exchange rates has been the subject of intense study. Most studies have been unable to develop a dependable means of predicting future exchange rate changes. The supply-and-demand forces differ widely for each currency and are often reoriented by government exchange rate policies.

A study of the international matrix of historical data indicates that in situations other than war or political turmoil, the exchange rate changes for major industrial countries is a function of three economic conditions measured by the following indicators:

1. Current account balance
2. Real long-term interest rate
3. The spread between nominal short-term and nominal long-term interest rates

Cross-border commercial activity is the principal source of currency entering the international currency market and is best indicated by the current account balance. A current account deficit indicates a rising flow of home-country currency into the international currency market, causing an exchange rate depreciation. A current account surplus causes a restriction in supply of home currency, leading to an exchange rate appreciation as foreign firms scramble to pay for their purchases.

Almost as significant as currency supply-and-demand forces is cross-border investment activity. For industrial countries with large liquid financial markets, demand for currency is stimulated by attractive rates of return on investments; and the most important indicator of investment opportunity is real long-term interest rates defined as nominal long-term interest rates less the expected rate of inflation. A country offering higher real long-term interest rates compared to others can often attract sufficient capital flow to increase the demand for its currency and drive up the exchange rate. Hence, the downward pressure on exchange rates caused by the home country's chronic current account deficit can be countered by high-interest-rate securities to attract foreign demand. A rising current account surplus, on the other hand, can make home-country investments even more attractive than the interest rate offered by home-country investments due to gain from an appreciating exchange rate. A country experiencing current account surpluses will receive a rush of foreign investors, allowing domestic interest rates to decline and thereby further stimulating the domestic economy.

Where the home-country current account deficit is sizable, real long-term interest rates may not attract sufficient cross-border investment demand to counter downward pressure on the home-country exchange rate. Exchange rate stabilization may become an important economic goal and monetary authorities have a number of available options. Intervention in the currency market to purchasing home currency is usually the first action undertaken. However, intervention is difficult to detect—except by currency traders sensitive to the market—and has limited success where current account deficits are sizable and recurring. The more effective measure is raising short-term interest rates above nominal long-term interest rates to attract sufficient foreign investment demand to offset the downward exchange rate pressure. However, raising short-term interest rates has negative implications for the home-country economy, which may prevent the high short-term interest rate policy from being maintained for any length of time. In this situation, speculation in the home-country currency becomes rife, triggering extensive shortselling of the currency and adding further downward pressure in the exchange rate.

Studying current economic conditions, government policy, and the above three factors are important indicators of exchange rate trends which are more fully discussed in Chapter 13. Conversely, government economic policy can be derived by studying exchange rate movements to determine exchange rate regime policy and anticipating the necessary economic policies that will be followed to maintain the regime.

Long-Term Equilibrium Exchange Rates

At any given moment in time, the market rate of exchange is determined by immediate supply-and-demand forces. However, many economists believe

that long-run supply-and-demand forces move exchange rates toward an equilibrium level that more accurately reflects the overall economic relationship
between trading partners rather than the short-term market forces. For long-
range planning and investment strategies, businesses, investors, and governments often attempt forecasting the equilibrium exchange rates. Identifying
the complex economic relationships between countries that determine equilibrium exchange rates is a difficult task occupying the attention of many
economists.

In theory there may be, in fact, an equilibrium exchange rate; but current methods have been unable to develop realistic figures. Many studies undertaken to
identify such equilibrium exchange rates have been incorporated into economic
policies designed to fix or manage exchange rates at the designated equilibrium
level. In most cases, the results have been excruciating economic dislocation
leading to embarrassing abandonment of the policy. Pegging the "true" or equilibrium exchange rate is still a very difficult and imprecise process.

Nevertheless, equilibrium exchange rate analysis provides important economic insights into structural conditions in the global economy. One of the
principal methods used to develop equilibrium exchange rates is based on the
real purchasing power of countries. Under the *purchase power parity* (PPP)
method, the equilibrium exchange rate between two currencies should be determined by differences in relative price levels. To the extent the actual prices
converted at market exchange rate differs, there is a price disequilibrium which is
assumed to adjust in time to the equilibrium rate. The equilibrium exchange rates
are derived from price ratios for similar products found among the countries.[2]

An example of the application of the PPP is the study of the local price of
Big Mac hamburgers conducted annually by *The Economist.* Originally begun in 1986 as a tongue-in-cheek presentation of PPP methods, the annual
study has since been viewed as a rough indicator of market exchange rate
variations from long-term equilibrium. From various parts of the world, *The
Economist* assembles the retail price in local currency of the Big Mac ham-
burger sold by the McDonald's chain. The local currency is then converted to
dollars at the market exchange rate. Big Macs were chosen because they are
sold throughout the world using similar ingredients and similar sizes, making
them ideal for PPP purposes. The dollar prices for this universally desirable
commodity are then compared to the U.S. price. The deviation from the U.S.
price indicates the deviation of the market exchange rate from the equilibrium
rate.

Table 5.2 shows the PPP analysis of Big Mac hamburgers given by *The
Economist* in April 1993.[3] The local average retail price in the United States
was $2.28, making it similar in price in Mexico where the average local retail
price was P7.09 (new pesos) which is converted to $2.29. In contrast, the
Swiss Big Mac at Swfr5.7 was an expensive $3.93. Assuming that the Big
Mac should have sold at the same dollar price in all the countries, the difference between the $2.28 price in the United States and the local price con-
verted at the dollar exchange rate indicates the difference to the equilibrium

Table 5.2
Purchashing Power Parity and the Big Mac, 1993

Country	Price in Local Currency	Exchange Rate April 13, 1993	Price in Dollars	Implied Difference	Implied PPP Exchange Rate
United States	2.28	1.00	2.28		
Japan	391.00	113.00	3.46	52%	171.49
Germany	4.60	1.58	2.91	28%	2.02
Britain	1.79	0.64	2.80	23%	0.79
Switzerland	5.70	1.45	3.93	72%	2.50
Canada	2.76	1.26	2.19	-4%	1.21
Mexico	7.09	3.10	2.29	0%	3.11
China	8.50	5.68	1.50	-34%	3.73
Russia	780.00	686.00	1.14	-50%	342.11
South Korea	2,300.00	796.00	2.89	27%	1,008.77
Brazil	77,000.00	27,521.00	2.80	23%	33,771.93

Source: "Big Mac Currencies," The Economist, April 17, 1993, p. 79.

rate which some economists believe indicates the degree a currency is over- or undervalued.

Utilizing this PPP method explains some of the criticism of conventional GDP analysis using market rates of exchange. As an example, Table 7.1 shows that under conventional GDP calculations, the 1990 Swiss GDP per person of $32,230 was the highest of all the countries. However, at $3.93 the Swiss are also paying one of the highest prices for a Big Mac, indicating that under conventional GDP calculations, Swiss buying power is overstated. Table 7.2 shows the 1992 Swiss GDP per person calculated using a PPP method resulting in a GDP per person below that of the United States because the high prices for internationally traded goods limits Swiss purchasing power. On the other hand, a Big Mac in China costs only $1.50, which is 34 percent below the U.S. price. Hence, at market exchange rates, Chinese residents have understated purchasing power. This calculation illustrates that the purchasing power of many developing countries is understated causing the World Bank to use PPP methods in a recent GDP analysis of those countries.[4]

PPP analysis is helpful in understanding structural economic forces that are occurring in the global economy but, in practice, has a number of disadvantages preventing its use for economic trend analysis. PPP is difficult to measure with any degree of accuracy. Domestic price levels for internationally traded products vary reflecting conditions unique in each domestic market such as differences in transportation costs, taxes, labor rates, consumer legislation, consumer tastes, and so on. For example, the PPP based on the Big Mac constitutes primarily a commodity-based measurement. With manufacturing being the more important component for economic growth, PPP should be based on similar manufactured products sold throughout the world. However, the many product distinctions made by manufacturers make a manufacturing-based PPP much more difficult to apply. In addition, PPP calculations are effective only to goods and services that are internationally traded. Measuring the impact on purchasing power of unique domestic products and services is much more difficult. In fact, other than commodities, most internationally traded manufactured goods are dissimilar to meet the specific needs of trading partners.

Another primary weakness of PPP is that it assumes that exchange rate equilibrium is a function of international merchandise trade and does not take into account the effect on prices by subsequent monetary policy. Domestic prices do not determine trade flows but are a consequence of domestic economic conditions including monetary policy. Exchange rates are adjustments to reconcile different cross-border economic conditions.

While equilibrium exchange rates can be a helpful indicator of future exchange rate trends, the short-term market forces are so important to economic activity and have such an enormous influence that they often prevent exchange rates from ever reaching the equilibrium point. Market exchange rates and not equilibrium exchange rates are the real dominant force in the global economy.

EXCHANGE RATE EXPERIENCE

Experience indicates that changes in exchange rates reflect fundamental economic conditions as discussed in Chapter 3 rather than causing economic changes as discussed in Chapter 4. From 1982 to 1992, the dollar-to-yen value has fallen 54 percent from $/¥270 to $/¥125, while in the same period the pound has fallen 42 percent from £/DM4.3 to £/DM2.5. These large currency declines should have devastated the export trade of Japan and Germany while tremendously boosting the competitive advantage of American and British exports. During this period, many exchange rates have fluctuated as much as 15 percent within a three-month period and on several occasions have been as high as 30 percent, which should have dislocated cross-border commerce. However, international commerce did not stop or for that matter significantly slow down.

Trade Experience with Fluctuating Exchange Rates

When internationally traded products consisted primarily of commodities or simple manufactured items, the similarities made prices a key competitive factor; and exchange rates therefore had a critical impact. Today, international trade consists of a wide variety of complex manufactured goods and services where the cost of exchange rate changes is dissipated among other costs. Many imports are components of domestically manufactured products so that exchange rate fluctuations have a mixed impact on producer prices, while the complex distribution system necessary to support many imported manufactured items makes the import costs only a part of the overall retail price to consumers. Manufactured products also require replacements parts, servicing, and upgrades, creating an ongoing relationship between consumers and foreign suppliers that is resistant to exchange rate changes. Furthermore, while exchange rate changes may effect the price of these items, price is only one of several other factors influencing buying decisions such as quality and technology.[5]

An example illustrates the dissipating effect of exchange rate changes. Assume that a Japanese manufacturer exports a manufactured product to the United States and that the yen appreciates a hefty 20 percent. Does this yen appreciation mean that the U.S. retail price in dollars must be increased 20 percent in order for the Japanese manufacturer to avoid losses from the change in the exchange rate? To begin, a 20-percent rise in the yen value does not necessarily mean that the Japanese manufacturer's price in dollars rises by the same 20 percent. The rise in the yen-to-dollar exchange rate would normally be paralleled by increases in the yen exchange rate with other currencies enabling the Japanese manufacturer to purchase imported raw materials at a yen price 20-percent lower. If raw materials constitute 40 percent of the cost of the manufactured item, the Japanese manufacturer's costs fall by 8 percent. Hence, the Japanese manufacturer need only raise the dollar price of the product 12 percent.

When the product comes to the U.S. end user, it will have passed through a domestic marketing chain of wholesalers, dealers, and retailers who provide valuable services in warehousing, support, repair, advertising, convenience and other functions that are not affected by the yen-to-dollar exchange rate. Thus, the cost of the Japanese-manufactured product may only constitute 50 percent of the retail purchase price. To cover the price increase in dollars sought by the Japanese manufacturer, the retail price of the product need only be increased 6 percent. Hence, in this hypothetical example, a 20-percent rise in the yen-to-dollar exchange rate translated into only a 6-percent rise in the retail price.

Compared to the competition, a 6-percent price increase could be an important disadvantage. However, like many countries before it, the Japanese worked on other means to overcome the price disadvantage of the rising exchange rate. The 1980s indicated that American consumers were willing to pay higher prices for Japanese products because of better quality, more efficient usability, higher resale value, and other benefits. In the modern industrial economy, price is only one of many factors considered in the purchase of goods and services. Japan also pioneered several manufacturing and cost-containment techniques to reduce manufacturing costs, thus offsetting the disadvantage of the rising yen.

Another factor limiting the impact of exchange rate changes is the pricing to market response of domestic competitors. If the exchange rate decline causes import prices to rise, will domestic competitors maintain lower price levels to regain market share or raise prices to the import level to reap greater profits or cover the higher expenses of an inefficient industry? Business and economic strategy is a far more complex process than mere price advantage.

The struggle for the American automobile market is a fascinating example of the complex impact and competitive response of exchange rate changes. Despite a 40-percent decline in the dollar-to-yen exchange rate during the 1980s, Japan expanded auto exports to the United States because U.S. auto companies raised prices rather than compete for market share. While in the short run the decision to raise U.S. auto prices was arguably a poor business decision, there is another side to the analysis. The criticism assumes that even at lower prices, U.S. auto companies would have effectively competed against higher-priced Japanese models. Considering the quality and design of U.S. auto products at the time, lower prices may not have been sufficient competitive advantage to maintain market share. U.S. auto companies needed time to revamp their operations and corporate culture to provide products that were not only cheaper but also of better quality. Higher prices may have been necessary to offset losses from declining market share, thereby gaining time for the companies to restructure themselves.

There are many reasons for the limited impact of exchange rate changes, but the most significant are the dominance of cross-border trade in manufactured products and the growing internationalization of financial markets. A strong economy that produces products desirable in the international marketplace will achieve a trade surplus, causing a rising exchange rate, while a less competitive country will suffer a trade deficit triggering a falling exchange rate. Attempts to manipulate exchange rates will only temporarily mask more fundamental domestic economic conditions. Gradual changes in exchange rates indicate reorientation of fundamental economic conditions.

Nevertheless, sudden and dramatic changes in a country's exchange rate can have a major dislocating economic impact. Economies are resilient and can adjust to changed conditions if given sufficient time. A change in an exchange rate of 10 percent or more within a nine-month period appears to have a dislocating effect. An exchange rate decline of such a magnitude worsens the trade balance as higher prices must be paid for the same volume of imports while exporters receive less foreign exchange. In time, the J-curve effect kicks in as demand declines for the higher-priced imports while domestic industrial production begins improving as lower export prices improve the competitive advantage in foreign markets.

Conversely, an exchange rate increase of such a magnitude improves the trade balance as exporters earn higher prices and imports are cheaper. However, the higher price eventually makes exports less competitive in foreign markets so that export volume declines, causing a decline in domestic industrial production within nine months. Increased volume of import purchases exacerbates the domestic industrial decline as imports replace higher-priced domestic products.

Financial Experience with Fluctuating Exchange Rates

Fluctuating exchange rates would seem to have a devastating impact on cross-border investments, but even here, experience indicates the mixed effect of such fluctuations. Managing exchange rate fluctuations is easier because cross-border claims and liabilities are concentrated among only a few large industrial countries that have working relationships to coordinate exchange rate policies. Some 73 percent of these cross-border claims are between industrial countries with extensive currency markets and international institutions that have considerable expertise in dealing with cross-border claims. Most of the other claims are held by offshore banking centers composed primarily of branches and wholly owned subsidiaries of industrial countries' financial institutions.

For countries dependent on large cross-border currency trading, exposure to exchange rate fluctuations is minimized by a number of methods. One of the oldest methods is maintaining equal amounts of claims and liabilities so that a loss on one side of the ledger is likely to be offset by a gain on the other side. While the claims and liabilities with respect to specific countries usually do not balance, managing exchange rate risks is now an important element in international finance and the international financial centers provide considerable expertise in managing the risks of currency fluctuations. As indicated in Table 4.1, this method is followed by some countries, while others are developing a disturbing imbalance in their claims and liabilities that could destabilize their exchange rates. Other methods to protect investments from the vagaries of exchange rate fluctuations include hedging, options, and futures commonly called *derivatives*. The cost of these strategies are an additional cost of international investment, requiring higher returns to entice foreign investors.

Probably the most important factor limiting the impact of exchange rate changes on portfolio investments are the other changes occurring in financial markets that offset the exchange rate fluctuations. For example, a depreciation of the currency can cause a decline in the value of investments held by foreign investors, causing them to become reluctant to make further investments in the home country. On the other hand, the cheaper prices may attract foreign investors, especially if the exchange rate decline is caused by falling interest rates, causing a rising stock and bond market. Many investors consider safety of investment far more important than the rate of return so that industrial countries such as the United States may experience falling exchange and interest rates but nevertheless attract significant foreign investors because of the safety and liquidity offered by its financial system.

Economic Policy Dilemma

Fluctuating exchange rates have an economic impact that is far more complex than the mere cost of exports and imports, creating a dilemma for economic policy. While exchange rate stability is just as desirable as stable prices, such stability is contrary to one of the principal functions of the pricing mechanism: to efficiently match supply and demand. Economic activity is a dynamic and ever-changing force contributing to ongoing differences between trading partner domestic prices, output levels, and other economic factors that place pressures on exchange rates to adjust for these differences. While many benefits could be achieved through stable exchange rates, such a system requires trading partners to maintain similar economic conditions. Many countries are unwilling to adjust domestic price, wage, and output levels to maintain stable exchange rates because the economic and political dislocation of imposing a rigid system to harness domestic market forces often outweighs the benefits of stable exchange rates.

NOTES

1. Bank of England, *Quarterly Bulletin* (London: Bank of England, November 1988).

2. A good discussion of methods for calculating purchasing power parity is found in Peter Newman, *The New Palgrave Dictionary of Money and Finance*, Vol. 3 (London: Macmillan, 1992), pp. 236–238.

3. "Big Mac Currencies," *The Economist*, April 17, 1993, p. 79.

4. International Monetary Fund, "World Economic Outlook" (Washington, D.C.: International Monetary Fund, May 1993).

5. An in-depth analysis of the impact on imports from the dollar's decline during the period 1985 to 1992 was made by Thomas Klitgaard and reported in "The Dollar and U.S. Imports after 1985," *Quarterly Review*, Autumn 1993, Federal Reserve Bank of New York. The author concluded that the declining dollar slowed import growth for certain product groups, while the computer product group was unaffected.

CHAPTER 6

Structural Change

In developing an economic model, it is helpful to distinguish between business cycles and structural changes. Business cycles refer to the economy's alternating movements between growth and stagnation, assuming that the overall economic structure remains little changed. Structural changes are the more fundamental and permanent economic changes that occur over a long period of time and extend over several business cycles.

Structural changes are the key factors causing a general growth or decline in a nation's standard of living or a general growth rate that is faster or slower in comparison to other nations. Such changes are slow but have a more permanent impact on economic growth. A nation truly prospers when, over the course of several business cycles, there is an upward spiral in economic growth. Structural changes are also more difficult to measure because existing methods of data collection usually are not adjusted until the structural changes become readily apparent. Occasionally, structural changes contribute to imbalances that make the economy vulnerable to business cycles.

There are numerous examples of the economic consequences of major structural changes. Movement from an agrarian- to a manufacturing-based economy was a major structural change. Some economists believe that one of the contributing factors to the depression of the 1930s was the inability to understand the influence of manufacturing and inventory buildup on economic dislocation. Over several post–World War II business cycles, Japan has experienced the fastest rate of economic growth of all major industrial countries; and the structural causes of the consistent growth is still not well understood. The more current movement to women working away from home and computer-based information systems appears to be another momentous structural change.

Substantial research and analysis have been undertaken to identify factors causing structural economic changes leading an agrarian-based country to become a successful industrial-based country. The clear distinction between the two economic types makes it easier to identify the significant structural factors causing the change. The effect of structural changes on industrial economic growth has been more difficult. Such changes are often gradual and imperceptible until well under way.

In contrast to Keynesian and monetary models for evaluating business cycles, there is a lack of a well-developed theoretical models for evaluating structural changes.[1] Consequently, also lacking are regularly published comprehensive data by which to track structural factors, although such data are scattered among an array of reports prepared by a wide assortment of government and private organizations.

The international matrix system described in this book focuses on the business cycle of industrial countries and includes only some structural factor information. Nevertheless, the ability of industrial countries to successfully adjust to structural changes or make improvements in existing structural factors is an important element in economic growth. Concern about structural change and related economic policies shapes a nation's reaction to business cycle developments. As global competition intensifies, monitoring structural changes will become as important as monitoring the business cycle.

Some of the more significant structural factors in industrial economies that should be monitored are

- Population growth and demographics
- Size and composition of labor force
- Educational system conducive to economic production
- Changes in amount of investment
- Changes in management techniques and industrial organization
- Capacity to make technological discoveries and adaptations
- Political and social stability
- Natural resources
- Physical infrastructure
- Energy

POPULATION GROWTH AND DEMOGRAPHICS

Probably the most significant factor impacting a nation's economic structure is population growth, but the consequences are often conflicting.[2] Rapid population growth creates strong demand for a wide variety of products and services that can spur economic growth. On the other hand, countries with underdeveloped infrastructure and centralized economic management can be overwhelmed by rapid population growth undermining attempts at economic growth.

As the twentieth century draws to a close, uneven population growth among countries and regions is having a great impact on the global economy. Large increases in a youthful population increase the labor force, which leads to either higher unemployment or the opening of opportunities for new businesses. Table 6.1 provides population growth rates for the period 1990 to 2000 for selected countries.

An example of the economic problems caused by uneven population growth is a comparison of Mexico and the United States. Table 6.1 projects Mexican population growth at 2.1 percent per year compared to the U.S. growth rate of 0.7 percent. During its rise to industrial preeminence in the late nineteenth century, U.S. population growth rates were similar to the projection for Mexico, although it was caused by immigration rather than high birth rate. This population growth created social tensions, but the high U.S. economic growth provided jobs for most immigrants. In contrast, Mexico's economy has not grown sufficiently to provide jobs so that its high population growth is contributing to U.S. social problems because of illegal immigration and competition with low-cost labor. In response, the United States and Mexico have promoted NAFTA as a means of shifting commercial emphasis to the new employment and consumer opportunities presented by Mexico's growing population.

Table 6.1
Projected Annual Population Growth Rate for Selected Countries

Country	Projected Annual Population Growth Rate, 1990-2000
World	1.6%
United States	0.7%
Japan	0.4%
Germany	0.3%
Britain	0.2%
Canada	1.0%
China	1.4%
Mexico	2.1%
Russia	0.3%

Source: U.S. Department of Commerce, Statistical Abstract of the United States: 1992 (Washington, D.C.: U.S. Government Printing Office, 1992), p. 820.

For industrial nations, stable population growth has created a new set of economic issues arising from demographic changes as reflected in the projections to the year 2000 for selected countries contained in Table 6.2. Age patterns have become a significant factor as the longer life span requires a restructuring of industrial economies. On the one hand, great strain is being placed on a wide variety of old-age programs such as pension plans, health care, senior housing, and mandatory retirement. One of the consequences of such strain is a growing desire to increase retirement savings, opening up new opportunities for the financial services industry. On the other hand, increased productivity may result from utilization of the growing pool of experienced workers that do not have the financial demands of supporting a young family.

In response to this demographic change, countries are moving in different directions. Japan is greatly concerned about the growing bulge of people over age 65, which, according to Table 6.2, is projected to exceed 16 percent of its population by the year 2000. In an innovative response, Japan is developing the robotics industry to enable increased productivity by the working population to support the aging population. However, concern for adequate savings to finance old-age programs inhibited implementation of a deficit spending package to counter the 1991–1992 recession. In contrast, Germany, facing a similar problem, developed an extensive guest-worker program which was economically effective but created a social problem as the guests took roots in the country. Mexico's projected population expansion of children less than fifteen years of age is presenting its economy with an enormous challenge to provide sufficient employment in their adulthood.

Table 6.2
Projected Age Distribution for Selected Countries, 2000

| Country | Age Group | | | |
	Under 5 Years	5 to 14 Yrs.	15 to 64 Yrs.	65 Yrs. and Over
World	10.9%	20.2%	62.1%	6.8%
United States	6.3%	13.9%	66.8%	13.0%
Japan	5.5%	10.2%	67.6%	16.7%
Germany	5.2%	11.1%	67.1%	16.7%
Britain	6.1%	13.1%	64.7%	16.0%
Canada	6.0%	13.0%	67.9%	13.1%
China	9.0%	18.3%	65.7%	7.0%
Mexico	11.9%	22.5%	61.1%	4.6%

Source: U.S. Department of Commerce, *Statistical Abstract of the United States: 1992* (Washington, D.C.: U.S. Government Printing Office, 1992), p. 823.

SIZE AND COMPOSITION OF LABOR FORCE

Labor force size and composition is a balance between those involved directly in manufacturing and agriculture production compared to those involved in child rearing, training, education, medicine, criminal justice, military defense, and government service. In a competitive labor market, market forces usually achieve the necessary balance so that, except in war time, little attention is given to this structural factor. Nineteenth- and twentieth-century warfare imposed enormous manpower demands, requiring combatant nations to balance their armed-forces needs with an adequate supply of labor to manufacture and transport arms and equipment.

Distribution of the labor force is an important indicator of domestic economic strength and capability. Table 6.3 presents the distribution of the labor force in

Table 6.3
Labor Force Distribution of Selected Countries, 1987

Country	Manufacturing	Other Industry	Total Industry	Services	Agriculture
OECD	20%	9%	29%	58%	9%
United States	18%	9%	27%	68%	3%
Japan	23%	10%	33%	56%	8%
Germany	31%	8%	39%	54%	5%
France	19%	8%	27%	55%	7%
Britain	19%	8%	27%	60%	2%
Switzerland	30%	7%	37%	55%	6%
Italy	19%	9%	28%	51%	9%
Mexico	12%	9%	21%	24%	26%
Canada	17%	9%	26%	69%	5%
China	12%	4%	16%	10%	74%
India	10%	3%	13%	16%	63%
Indonesia	8%	0%	8%	36%	54%
Brazil	16%	8%	24%	46%	25%
USSR			39%	41%	20%
Iran			33%	31%	36%
South Korea	26%	7%	33%	43%	21%
Nigeria			12%	20%	68%
Saudi Arabia			14%	37%	49%
South Africa	16%	16%	32%	42%	14%
Thailand	6%	2%	8%	17%	72%

Source: The Economist, *The Economist Book of Vital World Statistics* (New York: Times Books, 1990), pp. 194–195.

1987 for selected countries. More-advanced countries such as the United States, Japan, and Germany have larger labor force participation in the industrial sector, with 27 percent, 33 percent, and 39 percent, respectively. Less-advanced countries such as China, India, and Nigeria have higher labor force participation in agriculture, with 74 percent, 63 percent, and 68 percent, respectively. Some countries not understanding the complexity of modern-day economic systems have neglected the important service and distribution sector. The Organization for Economic Cooperation and Development (OECD) countries actually have a larger share of their labor force in services and distribution (58%) than in industry (29%). In contrast, the former Soviet Union had only 41 percent of its labor force in services and distribution, causing a misallocation of labor that contributed to the inability to move goods from the farm and factory to the consumers.

EDUCATIONAL SYSTEM CONDUCIVE TO ECONOMIC PRODUCTION

Education has always been an important structural factor clearly indicated by the education levels achieved by the population of industrial countries compared to developing countries. As technological development offers greater opportunity for a better standard of living, education will become even more vital for economic growth.

However, among industrial countries engaged in global competition, evaluating education systems is more complex. Despite virtually universal education, economic growth rates among industrial countries have varied. This disconcerting situation raises questions about the type rather than the level of education needed to support economic growth and the effectiveness of the education system to deliver the necessary instruction.[3] Some economists attribute the decline in British international competitiveness during the first half of the twentieth century to an educational system that emphasized the study of classical literature rather than science and business.

Today, there is growing concern that the educational curriculum of the United States and several other industrial countries is the same as it was sixty years ago despite the enormous changes in industry and society. A disciplined semiskilled work force educated in fundamental communication skills and national values was considered the principal educational needs for both social cohesion and economic growth. Today, technology and rapid global change require expanded education in applied sciences and logical reasoning. Unfortunately, the U.S. educational system has expanded its role in social cohesion, diluting its ability to focus limited resources to provide a labor force capable of achieving high economic growth.

CHANGES IN INVESTMENT

It is well understood that a nation must devote a portion of its income to investment in infrastructure, research, training, plant, equipment, and other capital improvements. However, a more difficult question is the right mix between investment and consumption. Too little investment deprives the economy of the tools necessary for state-of-art manufacturing, thereby retarding economic growth. On the other hand, too much investment creates overcapacity, resulting in stagnation, as the economy must make up for deficiencies caused by the poor allocation of investment capital.

Another question is the type of investments. Many centralized economic systems invested in expanded production capacity without also investing in necessary infrastructure such as transportation systems and utilities to support the expansion. During the late 1980s, Japan overinvested in export-related industries, resulting in overcapacity in the early 1990s. In the meantime, the United States has suffered from both a lack of investment in industrial infrastructure and an overinvestment in unusable commercial real estate.

CHANGES IN THE ART OF MANAGEMENT
AND INDUSTRIAL ORGANIZATION

Improved management and organizational techniques is a structural factor often overlooked in economic analysis. This factor was probably one of the most important contributions to the great economic growth of the United States in the late nineteenth and early twentieth century. While many countries have abundant natural resources and pioneered new inventions, the United States systematically developed new management and organizational techniques that enabled the molding of technology and natural resources into a low-cost, large-scale production system. Some of the many techniques pioneered by American business were interchangeable parts, assembly line systems, large-scale stock and bond financing, and the large but effective corporate organizational structure.

Developing new management techniques continue to be the mark of dynamic economies. Japan pioneered just-in-time inventory control and worker participation, which has been effective in managing high-technology manufacturing where high-quality and low-cost products are so important. U.S. companies are integrating the computer, telecommunications, and the video into flexible management structures that allow firms to diversify into regional office clusters to be closer to customers and markets.

TECHNOLOGICAL DISCOVERIES AND ADAPTATIONS

A legal and social environment that promotes technological discoveries and adaptations such as a well-defined patent and copyright system is the basic necessity for technological advancement and was considered so important as to be included in the Constitution of the United States. The complexity of modern-day science and the wide range of technology now requires a system that enables companies to assemble the extensive teams of researchers, equipment, and funding to support commercially viable technological advances.

Technological development is well understood to be one of the most important factors in economic growth, but the economic consequences are difficult to measure because of the long lead time from development, to commercial viability, to supporting infrastructure. Table 6.4 provides a comparison of research and development (R&D) expenditures to GDP for selected countries in 1989. Because of subjective judgments in determining what constitutes R&D, the figures used to develop this table are suspect. Nevertheless, serious questions are being raised regarding the capacity of the U.S. economy to provide the technological development necessary in an increasingly global competitive environment under conditions of a shrinking defense budget.

POLITICAL AND SOCIAL STABILITY

Political and social stability is such an essential prerequisite to sustained economic growth that it would seem that nothing more need be discussed because all the major industrial countries meet this condition. Nevertheless, in today's intense international competition, the real question is the degree by which the political and social stability of an industrial country is superior to that of its competitors. For example, the ethnic homogeneity of Japan and Germany makes it easier to integrate individuals into the work force as compared to the United States with its diverse population. America's difficulty is that while the diversity of the population give its tremendous vitality, workers from several ethnic groups are not being fully integrated into the labor force, indicating a fundamental weakness in the entire system by which all citizens are incorporated into the work force that is causing higher unemployment and social unrest. Furthermore, while the United States and Europe are certainly considered politically stable countries, the enormous growth in government laws and regulation combined with expanded judicial theories on tort and criminal liability are creating uncertainty and frustration, which, in the

Table 6.4
R&D Expenditures as a Percentage of GDP

Country	Total R&D	Nondefense R&D
United States	2.7%	1.9%
Japan	3.0%	3.0%
Germany	2.9%	2.8%
Britain	2.0%	1.6%
France	2.3%	1.8%

Source: U.S. Department of Commerce, *Statistical Abstract of the United States: 1992* (Washington, D.C.: U.S. Government Printing Office, 1992), p. 588

aggregate, is retarding economic growth and increasing inflation in a manner similar to that of political instability.

NATURAL RESOURCES

Traditionally, an abundance of natural resources has been a significant factor in economic growth. Japan, South Korea, and to some extent, Germany are examples that natural resources may no longer be as significant as they once were because of gradual changes in economic structures. These countries developed a sophisticated manufacturing sector to produce unique products that could be traded for necessary natural resources and an extensive network of dependable foreign suppliers.

PHYSICAL INFRASTRUCTURE

Historically, physical infrastructure has been an important element in economic growth and a means of more efficiently integrating diverse economic resources. Roads, bridges, harbors, railroads, telephone systems, sewage disposal, and the like have enabled countries to take advantage of whatever resources were available in the country.

ENERGY

Cheap and abundant energy has been the basis of a successful industrial sector. Hydroelectric power, coal, and oil are the significant energy sources of the modern industrial economy. Japan is an example of a country lacking significant cheap domestic energy that nevertheless developed successful export industries to earn the necessary foreign exchange to pay for energy imports.

NOTES

1. A major step toward formulating a comprehensive theory is found in Sumner H. Slichter, *Economic Growth in the United States* (New York: The Free Press, 1961). Professor Slichter was an authority on the subject, and the book is one of the best on the subject of structural economic growth factors. Unfortunately, the book was based on his lectures and never integrated into a complete text. Another authority that devoted considerable research to structural factors was W. Arthur Lewis. His book, *Growth and Fluctuations, 1870–1913* (London: George Allen & Unwin, 1978), is an extensive comparative economic analysis of Germany, France, Britain, and the United States during the 1870–1913 period to distill those factors contributing to their industrial growth.

2. Projected world population increase from the present 5.5 billion to 8 billion in ten years is expected to cause unprecedented economic and political turbulence, as fully analyzed in Paul Kennedy, *Preparing for the Twenty-First Century* (New York: Random House, 1993).

3. An extensive analysis of the school to work transition is found in Kaori Okano, *School to Work Transition in Japan* (Philadelphia: Multilingual Matters, Ltd., 1993).

PART II

THE EXISTING INTERNATIONAL ECONOMIC SYSTEM

CHAPTER 7

Key Global Economies

Although the term *global economy* may convey the idea of one giant market-place, the diversity in national economies manifests itself in a complex array of cross-border economic relationships. International economic trends are very much a function of the strength, size, and cross-border economic activity of key countries or groups of countries. International economic trend analysis requires an integration of the general economic models discussed in Part I with a broad understanding of the global economic system as it exists at any given period of time.

THE MATRIX COUNTRIES

With more than 150 countries in the global economic system, and the number constantly changing, a complete model for international economic analysis is an expensive and time-consuming undertaking. A distinguishing feature of the global economy is that no two countries are alike or for that matter even similar. Through geographic happenstance, natural resource endowment, historical experience, population size, recurring weather conditions, and many other factors, every country confronts a host of complex economic conditions. In response, each country has developed private and public institutions, social norms, and a legal environment to utilize its resources, educate and train the population, and mobilize the will to succeed, creating within each country a unique economic system and cross-border commercial relationships.

For most countries, internal economic conditions are influenced by their principal trading partners so that an international matrix system should be based on economic data of the home country and its principal trading partners. The international matrix system presented in this book is composed of those industrial countries that are the principal commercial partners of most other countries and, therefore, have the greatest influence on the global economy. The system is based on a historical analysis of key economic and financial indicators for the following five industrial countries, referred to in this book as the *matrix countries*:

• United States
• Japan
• Germany
• Britain
• Canada

Through the volume of cross-border commercial activity and the wide range of trading partners, the United States and Japan dominate both the present global trading and financial system and will continue to do so for the foreseeable future. Germany is also one of the largest global trading countries dominating its European neighbors, although its cross-border financial activity is less developed. In contrast, although Britain's cross-border trade has been superseded by other countries, it has maintained extensive international financial activity. In addition, Britain's inclusion in the international matrix system expands the insights gained from *The Economist* articles that incorporate its economic and financial indicators when covering the British economy. An understanding of international economic theory and practice is greatly enhanced by the many articles discussing British economic issues.

Although Canada does not have significant global economic influence, it is included in the international matrix for two reasons. First, Canada is a country that must pursue economic policies in the shadow of a large giant, a situation shared by many countries in the global economy. Application of the analytical techniques to Canadian economic and financial data exemplifies the international matrix system as a useful tool in understanding the economies of a wide range of smaller industrial and semi-industrial countries. Second, as a principal trading partner, Canadian economic conditions influence a wide range of American business and investment decisions receiving extensive coverage in American business news media.

As the global economy adjusts to the end of the Cold War and the financial press expands coverage of worldwide economic and financial data, the international matrix system will require modification to include other countries achieving significance in the global economy and influence on trading-partner business cycles. Three countries, in particular, are candidates for future inclusion in the international matrix system but, for reasons discussed in the following paragraphs, are not included at this time.

France is a large industrial country and indeed has a technological and financial base to support greater international economic involvement. However, for a number of historical reasons, France has refrained from extensive international economic involvement, preferring to play a regional role in Europe, the Mediterranean, and northwest Africa. To avoid the rivalries that historically have plagued Europe, France has also boldly chosen to follow the economic lead of its neighbor, Germany. Accordingly, a discussion on French economic activity would have duplicated much of the discussion on German economic conditions. Nevertheless, in the event European economic unification stalls, France may capitalize on its regional relationships and develop an economic bloc of nations influential in the global economy.

Mexico is a major trading partner of the United States and a gateway to Latin America. Unfortunately, *The Economist* only began the systematic reporting of key Mexican economic and financial indicators along with those of twenty-nine other developing nations in 1994. Consequently, limited historical experience prevents effective evaluation of current and historical economic indicators which are not readily comparable to the matrix-country economic and financial indicators. Converting data to the matrix system would have required an extensive discussion, detracting from the principal focus on understanding the basic international matrix system.

China is another country of which *The Economist* began in 1994 to systematically report key economic and financial indicators. China is the most populace economic system in the global economy and is finally overcoming the internal disarray that has plagued it for more than 300 years. If its economy continues to expand at the same rate as the previous ten years, it will become a major participant in international commerce, requiring inclusion in the international matrix. China is also shedding its isolation from international commercial activity in which amalgamation of Hong Kong (scheduled for 1997) will be a major advancement in its international economic activity. It will be fascinating to follow this process, including the impact on Chinese financial and economic growth and the reaction of the global economic community. Unfortunately, as with Mexico, lack of extensive historical economic and financial indicators comparable to the matrix-country indicators prohibits its current inclusion in the international matrix system.

Many other countries could also have been included in the international matrix system. However, doing so would have made this book and the related economic data cumbersome, unwieldy, and difficult to understand. By concentrating on the matrix countries, the methodology of the international matrix system and its trend analysis interpretation is better understood. Applying the basic methodology of the international matrix system to economic and financial data of other countries will be an important means of determining their economic trends.

GLOBAL ECONOMIC OVERVIEW

Evaluating the cross-border economic influence of countries begins with an overview of each country's economic resources in relation to both its neighbors and the overall global economy measured by the following three factors:

• Gross domestic product

• Population

• Cross-border economic activity

When performing economic trend analysis for an individual country, cognizance must always be made of the above factors both for the country being studied and for its principal trading partners. Comparing the matrix-country factors to those of others indicates the extent to which industrial countries excel in combining these factors, giving them influence in the economic activities of their neighbors. It also illustrates the reasons for choosing the particular countries included in the international matrix system.

Gross Domestic Product

Economic strength is a relative term measured by many different methods. The most widely used method is comparing the *gross domestic product* of each country to the other. GDP is the sum of four broad economic activities—consumption, investment, government purchases, and net exports—which in the aggregate represent all the goods and services produced by a country's domestic economy and sometimes referred to as output. GDP is distinguished from the old gross national product (GNP) measurement which included income earned abroad by domestic citizens while excluding domestic income earned by nonresidents. For most current and historical economic analysis, the distinction between GDP and GNP is generally not material for industrial countries.

A country with a large GDP exerts its influence on the global economy through several activities. If its economy is open to international commerce, the size of its domestic market attracts many countries and its capacity to absorb significant imports and capital inflow gives it a market power to influence the behavior of trading partners. It can also use its financial resources to influence the international economic system. More directly, it can support a military force larger than other nations but commanding a proportionately smaller share of domestic economic resources. Foreign aid and other economic assistance can also be provided in support of desired policies.

An understanding of the strength of selected domestic economies is derived from the nominal 1990 GDP figures shown in Table 7.1. With a $5.4-trillion GDP, the United States has the largest national GDP and is considered the strongest domestic economy in the global system. In addition, it dwarfs al-

Table 7.1
Economic Size of Selected Countries, 1990

Country	Popu-lation (Millions)	GDP per Person	Nominal GDP (Billions)	Trade		Exports as % of GDP	Imports as % of GDP
				Exports (Billions)	Imports (Billions)		
United States	250	$21,790	$5,392	$390	$498	7%	9%
Western Europe	359	16,337	5,865	367	376	6%	6%
Japan	124	25,890	2,943	280	217	10%	7%
Germany	80	22,360	1,484	392	320	26%	22%
France	56	19,521	1,189	207	221	17%	19%
Britain	57	16,060	981	182	215	19%	22%
Switzerland	7	32,230	225	77	84	34%	37%
Italy	58	16,860	1,091	170	169	16%	15%
Mexico	86	2,490	238	27	30	11%	13%
Canada	27	20,370	569	129	119	23%	21%
China	1,134	370	365	62	49	17%	13%
India	850	350	284	18	27	6%	10%
Indonesia	178	570	107	27	21	25%	20%
Brazil	150	2,680	474	31	20	7%	4%
Russia	148			24	20		
Iran	56	2,490	119	18	16	15%	13%
South Korea	43	5,400	236	63	65	27%	28%
Nigeria	115	290	35	14	7	40%	20%
Saudi Arabia	15	7,060	101	44	21	44%	21%
South Africa	36	2,530	101	23	17	23%	17%
Thailand	56	1,420	80	23	30	29%	38%
Taiwan	20	7,150	143	66	52	46%	36%

Source: World Bank, *World Tables 1992* (Baltimore: Johns Hopkins University Press, 1992).

most all other countries, including Japan's $2.9-trillion GDP and Germany's $1.5-trillion GDP, and is clearly the reason for its enormous international influence.

GDP per person is a measure of the standard of living achieved for a country's residents. Based on this measure, the people of Switzerland with a $32,230 GDP per person have achieved the highest economic standard of living. However, with a population of only seven million, this accomplishment cannot be translated into economic strength to match several other industrial countries with much larger populations. The U.S. GDP per person of $21,790 combined with its large population gives it the economic muscle to be the major industrial global power.

Growth in GDP is another measure of sustained economic viability. GDP is usually reported in both nominal and real figures. *Nominal* GDP is calculated using current prices, while *real* GDP is adjusted for price changes. In calculating annual quarterly rates of change in GDP, the real GDP figures are the more useful for measuring economic growth and are the ones reported by *The Economist*. For most industrial countries, annual growth in real GDP of 2.5 percent or more indicates a growing economy. A decline in real GDP in any one quarter is an indication of a weak economy, and a decline in two successive quarters is considered a recession.

Compiling GDP figures is a monumental task requiring extensive use of estimates and sampling techniques, resulting in figures that should be considered as only rough approximations. Each country compiles its GDP figures according to its own domestic currency, which, for international comparative purposes, is converted to a common currency such as the U.S. dollar using a market exchange rate. Because of the immense undertaking required for assembly, GDP is reported quarterly thereby limiting its use for economic trend analysis.

Considering the immense difficulty in obtaining current and accurate data by which to prepare GDP figures, it is surprising to see the effort made to forecast its rate of change. Most executives and investors need more specific economic information, finding that GDP is such a broad measure that it is not helpful in economic trend analysis except when used as a ratio to other economic figures. Rather than adjusting all economic data to account for price changes, use of such data as a ratio to GDP provides better understanding of economic conditions.

While GDP is a good approximation of the economic strength of industrial countries, it is a less-accurate measure for many developing nations. The methodology used for calculating GDP does not adequately measure the effects of government price regulation or unrecorded barter exchanges that form a larger share of the economy of lesser-developed countries. Comparing GDP figures also requires that national accounts calculated in home-country currency figures be converted to a single currency such as the U.S. dollar. Since virtually all countries attempt to manage the exchange rates of their respective currencies, the conversion rate may not accurately reflect the domestic economy. Furthermore, some experts contend that developing countries deliberately underreport their GDP figures in order to obtain grants and other economic favors from the industrial countries.

In search for better methods to measure national economies, some studies have begun calculating GDP using a long-term equilibrium exchange rate such as the PPP method discussed in Chapter 5. PPP attempts to measure domestic economic activity by calculating an equilibrium exchange rate based on the price of similar products used throughout the world. This equilibrium exchange rate is then used to convert country data rather than the conventional method of converting such figures at market exchange rates.

Using the PPP method, the World Bank released a report in 1993 that showed the economies of many developing countries to be much larger than originally thought. Table 7.2 shows the GDP calculated using a PPP method. China is shown to have a per-person GDP of $2,870, which is four times larger than that calculated using conventional GDP methods as used in Table 7.1, and a national GDP of $2.9 trillion, which is larger than Japan. This World Bank economic report using PPP has been a shock to the international economic community, resulting in significantly more attention being given to China and other developing Asian nations.

While there are many weaknesses with the PPP method which may cause the World Bank's GDP calculation to be overstated, conventional GDP numbers have likewise understated the economies of the developing countries, underscoring the difficulty in international economic analysis. However, this book's primary focus is on the economic trends for industrial countries in which conventional GDP numbers are comparable and are sufficiently accurate for the stated purpose. In an analysis of the more widely diverse developing countries, consideration should be given to using GDP figures prepared on the basis of PPP exchange rates. It is likely that the dynamic changes oc-

Table 7.2
Economic Size of Selected Countries Using Purchasing Power Parity, 1992

	Population (Millions)	GDP per Person	GDP (Billions)
United States	250	$21,760	$5,440
Japan	124	17,240	2,138
Germany	80	16,500	1,320
Britain	57	14,298	815
Switzerland	7	18,857	132
Mexico	86	6,590	590
Canada	27	18,778	507
China	1,134	2,460	2,870
India	850	1,256	1,105
Indonesia	178	2,770	510
Brazil	150	4,940	770
South Korea	43	8,635	380
Nigeria	115	1,560	190

Sources: World Bank, *World Tables 1992* (Baltimore: Johns Hopkins University Press, 1992); *OECD Economic Outlook* (Paris: Organization for Economic Cooperation and Development, June 1993); "Chinese Puzzles," *The Economist*, May 15, 1993, p. 83.

curring in the global economy will produce volatile or manipulated exchange rates requiring more objective procedures for uniform measurement of national economies.

Population

Analyzing GDP figures along with population statistics provides an even better indication of overall economic strength. The United States is powerful because its large $5.4-trillion GDP is supported by an equally large population of 250 million people. Japan is the second largest economy with a $2.9-trillion GDP and, following World War II, has grown faster than the United States. However, with a population of 124 million people, Japan is half the size of the United States and is unlikely to continue the same accelerated growth rate necessary to achieve a GDP greater than the United States. Nevertheless, if the U.S. economy should falter, a dynamic domestic economy could propel Japan to becoming the largest GDP in the global economic system.

In contrast, China's population of 1.1 billion people is the largest in the global economy and four times larger than that of the United States. However, with a GDP of $0.4 billion, in conventional numbers, its present global economic influence is limited. Nevertheless, China's real GDP is growing rapidly, averaging 8 percent per year compared to U.S. average annual real GDP growth of 2.5 percent. If this accelerated pace continues, China's economy, combined with its large population, will make it a major global economic influence within twenty-five years with the possibility of attaining a GDP greater than that of the United States in sixty years.

Cross-Border Economic Activity

Although a country may have a large domestic GDP and a large domestic population, limited cross-border commercial activity diminishes its global economic influence. The classic example is the former Soviet Union, which carefully restricted its cross-border interrelationships.

The most widely used means of evaluating cross-border economic relationships is by a country's exports and imports of tangible products, commonly referred to as merchandise trade or trade in goods. These tangible products generally consist of commodities, natural resources, and manufactured products sold cross-border. Table 7.1 shows 1990 trade exports and imports (in billions of dollars) for selected countries. In terms of overall trade volume, the global influence of the United States is indicated by its $390-billion trade exports, the second largest trade exporter in the world, and the $498-billion trade imports, the largest trade importer in the world.

However, trade figures must be carefully evaluated to determine the nature of the cross-border economic influence. An analysis of the trading-partner relationships reported in Table 8.5 provides further information on global economic influence. About one-fifth of U.S. exports and imports constitute trade in automobiles and automobile parts to plants in Canada owned by U.S. auto manufacturers. This trade consists primarily of shipment of parts to Canada for assembly and manufacturing into finished automobiles shipped back to the United States for retail sales. These transactions are an unusual captive arrangement that may not constitute trade activity comparable to other trading nations.

If Canadian trade data were excluded from the U.S. trade figures, Germany would appear to be the dominant trading influence. However, Germany's trade figures should also be carefully evaluated. Compare Germany's trade figures to the trade figures for Western Europe as a whole (see Table 7.1). While Germany's 1990 trade exports constitute 26 percent of its nominal GDP, the 1990 trade exports of Western Europe as a whole constitute only 6 percent of Western European nominal GDP. Much of Germany's trade is with its European neighbors, resulting in the country becoming a dominant European economic influence. However, such economic influence does not extend beyond this region.

Merchandise trade figures are used to evaluate a country's dependence on cross-border commercial activity by calculating the ratio of trade exports to nominal GDP and trade imports to nominal GDP as shown for selected countries in Table 7.1. Under this analysis, U.S. trade exports are only 7 percent of GDP; and Japanese trade exports are only 10 percent of GDP, indicating that international trade does not constitute a large part of the domestic economies of these two countries. International trade is far more significant to the European countries but only among themselves. The high trade export and trade import ratios for the European countries explain the driving force behind the formation of the EEC and the desire for economic unification—or at least economic cooperation.

Some economists prefer measuring international trade significance or *openness* by aggregating exports and imports into one combined figure and then calculating the ratio to nominal GDP. For example, the ratio of combined exports and imports of Germany to its GDP is 48 percent compared with a similar calculation for the United States which is 16 percent. Hence, Germany is considered an economy more open to international trade than that of the United States. However, maintaining separate GDP ratios for exports and imports is more useful. For some countries, imports constitute raw materials used in exports, and thus a combined figure overstates the dependence on international trade. Separate ratios identify trading relationships where dependency on export markets differs from dependency on import sources.

WORLD BUSINESS CYCLES

An analysis of GDP, population, and cross-border commerce shows the enormous economic activity of industrial countries led by the United States,

Japan, and Germany compared to the rest of the world. As major trading partners to most other countries, following these three plus Britain through the
international matrix system provides a general understanding of global economic trends influencing individual countries.

Nevertheless, an often repeated expression is that when the United States
sneezes, economies of the rest of the world catch cold. While perhaps at one
time a true statement, the world has recovered from the devastation of World
War II so that its validity is diminished. The economic growth and self-sufficiency of most industrial nations combined with the adoption of flexible exchange rate regimes have enabled industrial countries to better insulate their
domestic economies from adverse disruptions from the American economy.
Japan and Europe have been particularly active to insulate their economies
from the cyclical effect of the U.S. economy, albeit with only limited success.

With a population of 250 million people and one of the largest if not the
largest capital markets, the United States still dominates the globe. Foreign
exporters and investors want to do business in the United States, make it a
leading trading partner for their respective home countries, and use its currency for conducting international commercial activity. Supported by a policy
favoring free trade and open markets, the United States trades around the
world, giving it a wider range of economic influence than Japan or Germany.
Any change in the American business cycle or any change in its economic
policy spreads around the world like ripples in a pond. Dependent on the key
currency system developed by the United States, many countries anticipate
that their business cycle and other economic conditions will mirror that of the
United States after only a few months' lag. Therefore, the economic business
cycle of the United States still influences other countries. As the global
economy expands and other nations develop larger and more diversified domestic economies, the cyclical impact of the United States will undoubtedly
diminish.

An intriguing question is whether there is a global business cycle. Historically there have been periods of worldwide inflation caused from new gold
discoveries, general economic decline caused by worldwide weather conditions, and more recently, worldwide recession caused by disruptions in oil
supply and increased prices that occurred in 1973–1974. To develop a matrix
system to monitor a worldwide business cycle is an ambitious undertaking
that could require inclusion of many more countries. Obviously, executives
and investors will probably not devote time and resources for such a study.

INTERPRETING ECONOMIC DATA

In utilizing economic and financial data from many countries and a variety
of other sources, certain reservations should be kept in mind. International
economic analysis requires large amounts of economic and financial data for
all countries that is both current and comparable. While great strides have

been made toward this goal, it is nevertheless a continuing problem in economic trend analysis. Most international economic data are first developed by the national governments of each country, which have their own internal methods and criteria for collecting the data and their own priorities as to significance. These national data must then be converted to a common standard. Economic data for a single country often differ according to the preparing statistical agency and the year the data are developed.[1]

Consequently, it is not unusual for cross-border transactions between two countries to be reported differently by each country. For example, the United States regularly reports one figure for Canadian trade imports which differs from the trade export figure reported by Canadian authorities. Representatives from the two countries periodically review these statistics and make adjustments to obtain greater accuracy.[2] In fact, some of the data presented in this book are not symmetric because of the reliance on data from the specific country. A comparison of partnership trade data in Table 8.5 highlights the different trade numbers compiled for each country such as French exports to Germany of $40 billion compared to Germany reporting imports from France of $48 billion in the same year. This discrepancy is attributable in part to differences in exchange rates and interpretation of data. Nevertheless, a 20-percent variation in statistics intended to measure the same activity is disturbing. Economics is not an exact science, and international economic data should be viewed simply as approximations or estimates of economic activity.

The global economic system is continuously evolving; and to understand its most current configuration, several years' data must be accumulated and analyzed, which is cumbersome to present in the body of this book. Balance of payments and GDP are the principal sources of economic data by which to analyze international economic relationships and are incorporated in the discussions contained in this and subsequent chapters. Appendix C contains historical balance of payments data for several key countries for 1988 to 1992, which can be subsequently reviewed. More current information should be obtained from available sources.

NOTES

1. International Monetary Fund, "Report on the Measurement of International Capital Flows" (Washington, D.C.: International Monetary Fund, December 1992); Rodney H. Mills, "Foreign Lending by Banks: A Guide to International and U.S. Statistics," *Federal Reserve Bulletin*, Washington, D.C., October 1986, pp. 683–694.

2. The results of a recent review are found in "Reconciliation of the U.S.–Canadian Current Account," *Survey of Current Business*, October 1993, pp. 67–78.

CHAPTER 8

International
Commercial
Relationships

With the bulk of international economic data and theory concentrated on international trade, transmission of cross-border economic conditions is usually understood in terms of trade exports and imports. However, the dynamic worldwide growth in services and financial markets makes the interrelationships between countries and avenues of transmitting cross-border economic conditions more complex. This changing global economic activity requires a broader analytical framework achieved by expanding cross-border economic activity into two broad categories:

- *Commercial activity*: primarily consisting of the trade in both goods and services as well as the receipt and payment of investment items
- *Capital flow*: consisting of the disposition of investment assets and commonly referred to as capital flow

In practice, these two broad categories are intertwined activities difficult to separate. The distinction is arbitrary and made to expedite the discussion and presentation of data. International commercial activity is discussed in this chapter, and capital flow—more accurately described as international investment activity—is discussed in the next chapter.

THE NATURE OF COMMERCIAL ACTIVITY

In the preceding discussion, evaluation of international economic relationships was based on the traditional method of analyzing the cross-border trade in merchandise. Technological and financial advances combined with elimination of currency and capital controls have expanded the global orientation of many economies, making the trade balance only one of several significant aspects of international business. Balance-of-payments accounting divides international commerce into the following segments:

• Merchandise trade
• Services
• Investments

Table 8.1 presents the dollar amount of these segments included in the 1992 current account reported for each of the selected countries, and Table 8.2 presents the ratio of these figures to nominal GDP for each of the selected countries.

While trade in goods still remains the largest single segment of cross-border commercial activity, services and investment are significant and rapidly growing factors. Outside the United States and in many international publications, these two cross-border commercial activities are lumped together under the term *invisibles*, distinguishing them from the visible trade in goods. However, these two activities are so different, arising from different commercial activities, that they should be treated separately and distinctly. Accordingly, the terms *services* and *investment* are used here.

Merchandise Trade

Merchandise trade is the cross-border purchase and sale of tangible products ranging from natural resources, crops, and animal products to manufactured finished goods and assembled component items, constituting the most important international commercial relationship and a major source for domestic employment. As discussed in Chapter 5, the importance of international trade to a country's economy is best understood by calculating the ratio of both trade exports and trade imports to nominal GDP. Specific industries may also be dependent on international trade, which is usually well known and discussed in trade journals so that extensive research is generally not necessary.

Economic history indicates that manufactured exports contribute more to a nation's growth than exports of commodity or natural resources where product similarities cause competition to be based primarily on price and shipping costs. Manufactured products, on the other hand, are more distinctly differentiated, allowing competition on a wide range of factors other than price and allowing manufacturers to earn higher profits, thereby enhancing the nation's

Table 8.1
Current Account Components for Selected Countries, 1992 (Billions of Dollars)

	U.S.	Japan	Germany	Britain	Canada
Trade Exports	440	331	407	187	133
Trade Imports	-536	-198	-374	-212	-125
Trade Balance	*-96*	*133*	*33*	*-25*	*8*
Service Exports	159	48	74	55	17
Service Imports	-117	-90	-107	-49	-29
Service Balance	*42*	*-42*	*-33*	*6*	*-12*
Investment Receipts	131	146	83	121	7
Investment Payments	-111	-115	-76	-114	-27
Investment Balance	*20*	*31*	*7*	*7*	*-20*
Private Transfers	-14	-1	-8	-1	1
Official Transfers	-18	-3	-24	-8	-1
Transfer Balance	*-32*	*-4*	*-32*	*-9*	*0*
Current Account	*-66*	*118*	*-25*	*-21*	*-24*
Commercial Exports	730	525	564	363	157
Commercial Imports	-764	-403	-557	-375	-181
Commercial Balance	*-34*	*122*	*7*	*-12*	*-24*

	France	Italy	Switzer-land	Mexico	China
Trade Exports	225	177	79	27	69
Trade Imports	-223	-175	-79	-48	-64
Trade Balance	*2*	*2*	*0*	*-21*	*5*
Service Exports	99	61	19	14	9
Service Imports	-79	-61	-12	-11	-9
Service Balance	*20*	*0*	*7*	*3*	*0*
Investment Receipts	82	29	28	3	5
Investment Payments	-92	-50	-19	-10	-5
Investment Balance	*-10*	*-21*	*9*	*-7*	*0*
Private Transfers	-3	-2	-2	2	1
Official Transfers	-6	-4	-1	0	0
Transfer Balance	*-9*	*-6*	*-3*	*2*	*1*
Current Account	*3*	*-25*	*13*	*-23*	*6*
Commercial Exports	406	267	126	44	83
Commercial Imports	-394	-286	-110	-69	-78
Commercial Balance	*12*	*-19*	*16*	*-25*	*5*

Source: International Financial Statistics (Washington, D.C.: International Monetary Fund, January 1994).

Table 8.2
Current Account Components as a Percentage of GDP for Selected Countries, 1992 (GDP Figures in Billions of Dollars)

	U.S.	Japan	Germany	Britain	Canada
Nominal GDP	5,961	3,670	1,775	1,051	569
Trade Exports	7%	9%	23%	18%	23%
Trade Imports	-9%	-5%	-21%	-20%	-22%
Trade Balance	*-2%*	*4%*	*2%*	*-2%*	*1%*
Service Exports	3%	1%	4%	5%	3%
Service Imports	-2%	-2%	-6%	-5%	-5%
Service Balance	*1%*	*-1%*	*-2%*	*1%*	*-2%*
Investment Receipts	2%	4%	5%	12%	1%
Investment Payments	-2%	-3%	-4%	-11%	-5%
Investment Balance	*0%*	*1%*	*0%*	*1%*	*-4%*
Private Transfers	0%	0%	0%	0%	0%
Official Transfers	0%	0%	-1%	-1%	0%
Transfer Balance	*-1%*	*0%*	*-2%*	*-1%*	*0%*
Current Account	*-1%*	*3%*	*-1%*	*-2%*	*-4%*
Commercial Exports	12%	14%	32%	35%	28%
Commercial Imports	-13%	-11%	-31%	-36%	-32%
Commercial Balance	*-1%*	*3%*	*0%*	*-1%*	*-4%*

	France	Italy	Switzer-land	Mexico	China
Nominal GDP	1,323	1,223	241	334	417
Trade Exports	17%	14%	33%	8%	17%
Trade Imports	-17%	-14%	-33%	-14%	-15%
Trade Balance	*0%*	*0%*	*0%*	*-6%*	*1%*
Service Exports	7%	5%	8%	4%	2%
Service Imports	-6%	-5%	-5%	-3%	-2%
Service Balance	*2%*	*0%*	*3%*	*1%*	*0%*
Investment Receipts	6%	2%	12%	1%	1%
Investment Payments	-7%	-4%	-8%	-3%	-1%
Investment Balance	*-1%*	*-2%*	*4%*	*-2%*	*0%*
Private Transfers	0%	0%	-1%	1%	0%
Official Transfers	0%	0%	0%	0%	0%
Transfer Balance	*-1%*	*0%*	*-1%*	*1%*	*0%*
Current Account	*0%*	*-2%*	*5%*	*-7%*	*1%*
Commercial Exports	31%	22%	52%	13%	20%
Commercial Imports	-30%	-23%	-46%	-21%	-19%
Commercial Balance	*1%*	*-2%*	*7%*	*-7%*	*1%*

Source: International Financial Statistics (Washington, D.C.: International Monetary Fund, January 1994).

domestic wealth. In addition, manufactured products result in an ongoing commercial relationship for parts, repair services, and upgrades which is resistant to competitive pressures and changes in exchange rates.

An analysis of the foreign trade component of selected countries in Table 8.3 graphically illustrates the importance of manufactured products. Japan and Germany have maintained trade surpluses by extensively exporting manufactured goods, achieving a share of total exports of 98 percent and 90 percent, respectively. On the other hand, the United States, Britain, Canada, and Mexico have achieved manufacturing share of total trade exports of 78 percent, 81 percent, 63 percent, and 44 percent, respectively. Furthermore, all these countries incurred deficits in their balance of trade in manufactured goods.

In the United States, the lower proportion of manufactured exports causes the U.S. government to focus on international agricultural trade issues even though export of manufactured products is growing faster than agricultural

Table 8.3
Foreign Trade Analysis (Customs Basis) for Selected Countries, 1990

Trade Components	U.S.	Japan	Germany	Britain	Canada	Mexico
	In Billions of Dollars					
Trade Exports						
Nonfuel Primary Products	69	6	34	21	33	5
Fuels	12	1	5	14	13	10
Manufacturers	290	279	359	151	79	12
Total Trade Exports	371	286	398	186	125	27
Trade Imports						
Nonfuel Primary Products	55	70	61	38	12	6
Fuels	68	57	28	14	7	1
Manufacturers	393	104	253	173	96	21
Total Trade Imports	516	231	342	225	115	28
	Distribution					
Trade Exports						
Nonfuel Primary Products	19%	2%	9%	11%	26%	19%
Fuels	3%	0%	1%	8%	10%	37%
Manufacturers	78%	98%	90%	81%	63%	44%
Trade Imports						
Nonfuel Primary Products	11%	30%	18%	17%	10%	21%
Fuels	13%	25%	8%	6%	6%	4%
Manufacturers	76%	45%	74%	77%	83%	75%

Source: World Bank, *World Tables 1992* (Baltimore: Johns Hopkins University Press, 1992).

exports and is a more important source of national wealth. With nonfuel primary products comprising only 19 percent of trade exports—the same proportionate share of total trade exports for Mexico—American trade policy should give more attention to the manufacturing sector.

Because of the wide-ranging impact of cross-border trade to some countries, national governments have assumed responsibility in this area hoping to solve domestic economic problems by adopting policies which encourage export-led economic growth. Historically, export-led growth is more a consequence rather than a cause of dynamic growth. An economy unable to produce better-quality or lower-cost products for its own population is unlikely to be any more successful in the global marketplace.

Services

Services generally consist of revenue and payments arising from travel; tourism; licensing; royalties; and professional services such as engineering, consulting, finance, insurance, and advertising. Indeed, the general movement of many industrial countries into a more technologically based environment is making the distinction between goods and services both more difficult and at the same time less significant. Computer programming, software upgrading, specialized consulting, and other support services are growing aspects of international business, requiring an ongoing relationship between suppliers and users that were not feasible when international communication was so difficult.

For most industrial countries, the dollar volume of services is not as great as that of trade; but the net service balance for some countries is almost as large as the balance of trade in goods as indicated in Table 8.1. The United States and Britain were able to substantially reduce their 1992 trade deficits of –$96 and –$25 billion, respectively, by a healthy surplus in the net service balance of $42 and $6 billion, respectively. Japan on the other hand experienced a sizable deficit in its 1992 international service activity of –$42 billion that reduced the adverse cross-border economic impact of its sizable 1992 $133-billion trade surplus.

Investments

Investment has always been a significant part of the international economy but traditionally has been treated as a separate and distinct segment of international trade. As is more fully discussed later, the relationship between trade in goods and services and trade in investment assets is more complex and intertwined so that it can no longer be treated as separate and distinct but a segment of the overall global trading relationship.

There are two types of cross-border investment activities: portfolio and direct. *Portfolio investment* consists of marketable stocks, bonds, notes, savings accounts, and a host of other income earning assets in which the investor does not control the source of the investment. In contrast, *direct investment* is the ownership of stock and obligations of the investment entity that is directly owned or controlled by the investor. The definition and degree of ownership constituting direct investment varies, but the most widely used definition is that of the United States which defines direct investment as ownership or control of 10 percent or more of a business entity.

Table 8.1 illustrates the importance of analyzing a country's commercial relationships as a whole. For Britain, international investment receipts in 1992 were $121 billion, which is two-thirds of its trade exports for that year of $187 billion. In fact, the dollar size of British international investment activity is one of the largest and is comparable to the two other major international investment participants—the United States, with $131 billion in investment receipts, and Japan, with $146 billion in investment receipts. This extensive international financial activity requires that Britain be included in the international matrix, although its domestic economy is no longer a sizable influence on global trade. The size of Britain's international financial activity is also a major element contributing to the difficulty integrating its economy with continental Europe where British investment receipts in 1992 of $121 billion (shown in Table 8.1) exceed Germany's $83 billion, France's $82 billion, and Switzerland's $28 billion.

Canada's international investment activity presents a situation different from most industrial countries and more akin to developing countries. While in 1992 Canada enjoyed a trade surplus of $8 billion, Table 8.1 shows that it incurred a sizable –$12-billion net service deficit and a –$20-billion deficit in its net investment balance causing a significant current account deficit of –$24 billion and constituting 4 percent of its GDP. If this situation persists, Canada may suffer steady decline in its currency value, higher domestic interest, and perhaps even defaults on its foreign-held debt.

The Commercial Balance

As the preceding discussion indicates, focusing strictly on trade in goods provides an incomplete understanding of international trade relationships. A better understanding is achieved by aggregating all three segments into what is sometimes called the balance in goods, services, and investment income, or the balance of trade in goods and factor income. To shorten the phraseology and facilitate comprehension, the aggregate of all three segments is referred to in this book as the *commercial balance*. Hence, the total exports receipts from goods, services, and income is referred to as commercial exports and the imported items as commercial imports. The current account is the commercial balance discussed here less government transfers such as grants and military assistance, which can also be a large number. For most industrial countries, the balance on current account arrives at a number similar to the commercial balance, making it more significant in international economic analysis.

Unfortunately, most discussions on international commerce focus on the balance of trade and do not consider the other important commercial activities. An analysis of cross-border commercial activity both in dollar terms and as a percentage of GDP provides some striking information. In dollar terms, the significance of the United States in international economics is clearly shown in Table 8.1. Its commercial exports of $730 billion are larger than Japan's $525 billion and Germany's $564 billion. The combined commercial exports of these three countries give them even greater dominance in international commercial activity. With $363 billion in commercial exports, Britain also becomes a more significant international economic player, particularly in Europe. On the other hand, at 12 percent of GDP, international commercial exports comprise only a small part of the U.S. economy. At the other end of the scale is Switzerland, where commercial exports constitute 52 percent of its GDP.

There is yet another and more compelling reason for utilizing commercial export and import figures as the basis for evaluating cross-border commercial relationships. Direct investments in other countries are significant aspects of international business that are blurring the distinction between goods, services, and investment income. Many goods and services reported in international trade data are being sold to owned or controlled affiliates of foreign parent companies. The existing tax and legal framework surrounding international transactions use traditional distinctions between goods and investment which are exploited by enterprising companies. The most significant exploitations are the customs duties on goods sold to affiliates compared to withholding tax on interest or dividends earned from foreign affiliates. If a withholding tax on interest income is 30 percent but the customs duty on products sold to the affiliate is 6 percent, it is not unusual for the parent company to invoice goods sold to the affiliate at a higher price while the interest or dividends paid by the same affiliate are made as low as possible. Thus, remittances to pay for the goods and services are disguised payments for parent-company financing. Furthermore, both customs duties and income taxes can be reduced by billing foreign affiliates for management services ostensibly rendered by the parent company.

An analysis of U.S. balance-of-trade data contained in Table 8.4 suggests that many foreign companies are engaging in the above practice with their U.S. affiliates. In the United States, $406 billion of foreign direct investments is as large as U.S. investment abroad. Yet Table 8.4 shows that in 1992 there was only $1 billion of profit repatriated to foreign direct investors, whereas U.S. companies repatriated $50 billion from their foreign direct investments.

Before claiming unfair business practices, bear in mind that many practices designed to exploit these distinctions were first pioneered by U.S. multinational

Table 8.4
Selected Geographic Analysis of U.S. Current Account, 1992

	Total	Japan	Western Europe	Canada	Latin America	Other Asian & African Countries	Eastern Europe
Trade							
Exports	*440*	*47*	*114*	*91*	*75*	*98*	*5*
Imports	*-536*	*-97*	*-111*	*-100*	*-69*	*-152*	*-2*
Trade Balance	*-96*	*-50*	*3*	*-9*	*6*	*-54*	*3*
Services							
Service Exports							
Travel	94	17	31	10	19	13	1
Military	11	0	3	0	0	7	0
Royalty	20	3	11	1	1	2	0
Other	54	6	19	6	6	13	0
Total Service Exports	*179*	*26*	*64*	*17*	*26*	*35*	*1*
Service Imports							
Travel	-74	-8	-26	-4	-17	-14	-1
Military	-14	-1	-10	0	0	-2	0
Royalty	-5	-1	-3	0	0	0	0
Other	-30	-3	-13	-4	-5	-4	0
Total Service Imports	*-123*	*-13*	*-52*	*-8*	*-22*	*-20*	*-1*
Service Balance	*56*	*13*	*12*	*9*	*4*	*15*	*0*
Investments							
Receipts							
Portfolio	53	5	20	6	12	3	0
U.S. Government	7	1	3	0	1	2	0
Direct Investment	50	2	22	3	12	9	0
Total Receipts	*110*	*8*	*45*	*9*	*25*	*14*	*0*
Payments							
Portfolio	-62	-6	-32	-3	-14	-5	0
U.S. Government	-41	-9	-17	-1	-4	-9	0
Direct Investment	-1	1	-5	0	0	1	0
Total Payments	*-104*	*-14*	*-54*	*-4*	*-18*	*-13*	*0*
Investment Balance	*6*	*-6*	*-9*	*5*	*7*	*1*	*0*
Unilateral Transfers	*-33*	*0*	*0*	*0*	*-9*	*-14*	*-1*
Current Account	*-67*	*-43*	*6*	*5*	*8*	*-52*	*2*

Source: U.S. Department of Commerce, *Survey of Current Business,* June 1993.

companies to minimize taxation. Countries with sizable multinational corporate investment responded by developing a number of ingenious methods to overcome these practices. U.S. government tax authorities have been slow to fully appreciate the many nuances of international commerce associated with systematic and sizable trade deficits.

Table 8.4 is more significant than an indication of tax avoidance practices. It suggests a fundamental rethinking of government policies regarding cross-border trade. If foreign companies are, in fact, overstating their export figures to the United States, then the U.S. trade deficit is overstated while the U.S. investment balance is not just overstated but actually in deficit. Consequently, if much of U.S. imports constitute shipments to U.S. affiliates, traditional policies to discourage imports such as depreciation of the dollar will have only limited effect. Furthermore, to comply with various trade quotas, foreign companies could change practices by underbilling for shipments to U.S. affiliates while increasing the repatriating of funds as a return on their investment. The overall effect on the current account deficit would not change, but the countries could claim that they were complying with U.S. policy to reduce the trade balance.

TRADING PARTNERS

In the preceding discussion, economic analysis focused on trading volume. A full understanding of a country's influence on the global economic cycles requires an analysis of the array of trade relationships with trading partners. Two large industrial countries trading only with one another would report sizable exports and imports, but lacking a wider array of trade relationships diminishes the overall influence on the global economy. Accordingly, evaluating the cross-border commercial relationships requires an extensive three-step analysis of international trade data:

1. Calculate the dollar volume of trade business with partners.
2. Identify the relationship of cross-border trade to the domestic economy.
3. Determine the nature of the cross-border commercial relationship.

Evaluating the trading-partner relationship is commonly done by comparing the individual country's trade exports and imports with major trading partners together with the net trade balances. Table 8.5 presents figures for trading partners for six industrial nations both in dollar amounts and in share of total trade exports and imports. While these figures are only for 1991, trade relationships generally change slowly so that the identification of major trading partners can be considered representative for the preceding five-year period and probably for the succeeding five-year period to 1996.

Ideally, a country's cross-border commercial activity and influence on the global economy should be evaluated based on the entire spectrum of cross-border

Table 8.5
Principal Trading Partners of Selected Countries, 1991

United States	Export	%	Import	%
Total	417		491	
Canada	86	21%	93	19%
Japan	47	11%	92	19%
Mexico	33	8%	32	7%
Britain	22	5%	18	4%
Germany	21	5%	26	5%
Korea	15	4%	17	3%
France	15	4%	13	3%
Taiwan	13	3%	25	5%
China	6	1%	19	4%

Japan	Export	%	Import	%
Total	315		237	
United States	92	29%	54	23%
Germany	21	7%	11	5%
South Korea	20	6%	12	5%
Taiwan	18	6%	NA	
Hong Kong	16	5%	NA	
Singapore	12	4%	NA	
Australia	NA		12	5%
Indonesia	NA		13	5%
China	NA		14	6%

Germany	Export	%	Import	%
Total	403		390	
France	53	13%	48	12%
Italy	37	9%	36	9%
Netherlands	34	8%	38	10%
Britain	31	8%	26	7%
Belgium	29	7%	28	7%
United States	25	6%	26	7%
Austria	24	6%	16	4%
Switzerland	23	6%	15	4%
Japan	NA		24	6%

Britain	Export	%	Import	%
Total	185		210	
Germany	26	14%	33	16%
France	21	11%	20	10%
United States	20	11%	24	11%
Netherlands	15	8%	18	9%
Italy	11	6%	11	5%
Belgium	11	6%	10	5%
Ireland	9	5%	8	4%
Japan	4	2%	12	6%

Canada	Export	%	Import	%
Total	126		120	
United States	96	76%	75	60%
Japan	6	5%	9	7%
Britain	3	2%	4	3%
Germany	2	2%	2	2%

France	Export	%	Import	%
Total	217		233	
Germany	40	18%	36	15%
Italy	24	11%	24	10%
Belgium	19	9%	20	9%
Britain	19	9%	20	9%
Spain	15	7%	14	6%
United States	14	6%	13	6%
Netherlands	11	5%	12	5%
Switzerland	8	4%	9	4%

Sources: Moody's International Manual (New York: Moody's Investor Services, Inc., 1993);
Survery of Current Business, June 1992.
Note: Figures are in billions of dollars.

commercial activity previously discussed. Unfortunately, most readily available cross-border commercial data pertain only to merchandise trade, whereas some countries' relationships are also influenced by cross-border service and investment activity.

Table 8.5 summarizes trading-partner relationships developed by the selected countries in response to domestic economic conditions and their own unique economic systems. U.S. trade relationship data are particularly informative. In 1991, U.S. imports from Canada of $93 billion constituted only 19 percent of total U.S. imports, whereas the same dollar volume constituted 76 percent of Canada's total trade exports, making Canada's cross-border trade highly dependent on the U.S. market. Furthermore, Table 8.2 shows that Canada's 1992 trade exports represented 17 percent of its GDP, making trade with the United States a significant element to the Canadian domestic economy. It is little wonder that Canada's business cycle closely parallels U.S. business cycles and that the exchange rate with the U.S. dollar is a key Canadian economic indicator. Mexico's cross-border trade with the United States is also heavily dependent on the United States, and it pegs its currency to the U.S. dollar. Both countries, anxious to develop closer trading relationships with the United States, are strong advocates for NAFTA.

Japan's trading relationship has evolved in a different direction, reflecting trading patterns designed to capitalize on its domestic manufacturing capability. Though less dependent than Canada on international trade for domestic economic activity, Japan has concentrated 29 percent of its 1991 trade exports on the U.S. market, which enjoys the quality of its products but causes growing trade friction. Japan has sizable trade surpluses with industrial countries but sizable trade deficits with countries from which it imports primarily raw materials. Such an unusual balance of trade indicates either that all of the industrial countries produce inferior products unwanted by the Japanese consumer or that there is a deliberate policy of protecting domestic manufacturers in contravention of international trade agreements. That question cannot be resolved here, but trade partnership data such as those contained in Table 8.5 help in understanding various government policies affecting international economic trends.

Europe and the United States are major trading partners, with 1991 trade exports to the United States constituting 6 percent of German, 6 percent of French, and 11 percent of British exports. On the other side, comprising 5 percent of U.S. exports, Germany is vying with Britain as the leading U.S. trading partner in Europe. However, U.S. trade with Germany and France may be understated because the Netherlands and Belgium are major transhipment centers for products passing between the United States and Europe. Britain's declining trade relationship with the United States in contrast with its continuing large investments in the country explains some of the difficulty facing Britain as it proceeds to fully integrate into a European community which, as a whole, is less dependent on U.S. trade, as indicated by the trading partnership relationships of Britain, Germany, and France (see Table 8.5).

With the United States, Japan, and Germany constituting the three largest GDPs and the largest trading volume, the domination of international trade is clearly apparent. However, a review of the trading-partner data shows differences in their trade relationships with corresponding differences in cross-border transmission of economic conditions. U.S. trading partners tend to be widely dispersed around the globe, giving the United States significant influence on other countries while insulating itself from transmitting their economic conditions. Germany concentrates on its European neighbors, and Japan concentrates on the United States. Except for Canada, the United States is not heavily dependent on any one country, whereas Japan is dependent on the U.S. market while German exports are dependent on European markets.

INTERNATIONAL TRADE POLICY

With international trade being critical to many countries' economy, monetary and economic policies designed to manage the exchange rate or expand export financing may be insufficient to influence trade flows toward the desired objective, forcing countries to adopt more direct regulatory means. With the end of the Cold War, direct regulatory trade policy is again rising to center stage as countries sort out their international relationships previously built around security interests.

Types of Trade Policies

Individually or in conjunction with major trading partners, countries follow one of three broad regulatory trade strategies:

- Free trade
- Protection
- Managed trade

Free trade is the unrestricted cross-border trade of goods and services. A fundamental economic principle driving much of economic development is the division of labor allowing individuals and firms to specialize in specific process and skills, thereby becoming the most efficient and lowest-cost producer. Applied to international trade, this economic principle is in the form of comparative advantage whereby a country concentrates on producing those products it produces at the lowest cost using its surplus production to exchange for other products which it cannot produce at all or as cheaply as some other country. When firms are protected by a tariff wall, domestic wage rates and prices tend to be higher, contributing to domestic economic inefficiency. Accordingly, through free trade, maximum efficient use of national economic resources is achieved, benefiting individual countries both with lower-cost products and viable trading partners capable of purchasing more products.

In addition to free-flowing goods, full comparative advantage requires a free flow of capital and labor. During the Great Depression and World War II, countries created a complex control system regulating foreign ownership of financial assets and currency which inhibited free trade. Following World War II, considerable progress was made in removing these restrictions so that by 1990 cross-border flow of portfolio capital among the industrial countries was virtually unimpeded. Considerable progress has also been made in expanding foreign participation in domestic financial markets, although several countries still closely control such participation.

Free flow of labor has been a much more difficult goal. Differences in language, culture, religion, attitudes, and the like makes it highly expensive and socially disruptive to integrate immigrants into the domestic work force and general society. In addition, many people find it difficult to give up friends and lifestyles or disrupt their children's education and home life to relocate to more promising job opportunities. Accordingly, achieving comparative advantage in the face of an immobile work force unable to adjust to lower wage rates causes many companies to move production facilities to areas of lower-cost labor, thereby negating some of the benefits of free trade.

A principal advantage of free trade is that the central government can avoid responsibility for making politically painful choices of which domestic industries will be protected, thereby avoiding the constant lobbying and corruption efforts of industries seeking protection, which is demoralizing to democratic political institutions. When international competition or foreign policy requires elimination of protective regulation, the adjustment process can become a political millstone to the government, paralyzing its flexibility in international matters.

Opposite to free trade is *protectionism* whereby a country protects domestic industries less efficient than foreign producers and imports only those goods and services it is incapable of producing. Justification for protectionism rests primarily on national security and nation-building policies. Self-sufficiency in critical industries and avoiding industrial paralysis in the event of war are important security interests which can be compromised by free trade where a country becomes dependent on trading partners for lower-priced or strategic products. In the event of war, disruption, or trade dispute, replacing foreign suppliers places a high cost on the domestic economy as shortages occur; and precious capital and skilled labor must be quickly diverted to developing needed production capability. As an alternative to a full protectionist policy of self-sufficiency, some countries diversify foreign suppliers to avoid dependence on any one country.[1]

As part of a nation-building policy, discriminating against foreign producers while encouraging an internal free flow of goods has historically been an important means for developing strong national bonds. Such policy was successfully pursued by the United States following its independence from Britain; German states through the *Zollverein*,[2] a custom union, as a prelude to unification in the nineteenth century; and Europe in the late twentieth century in its quest for political unification. Fostering infant industries to develop new technology has been an important aspect of such a policy. Retaliatory tariffs or termination of most-favored-nation (MFN) privileges—allowing imports on favorable terms accorded other trading partners—have historically been a protectionist policy implemented to counter countries from practicing their own form of protectionism.

Countries following fixed exchange rate regimes may resort to protectionist policies as a means of adjusting cross-border trade flows. Countries such as Britain and the United States which have developed great financial centers become anxious to preserve the financial business by maintaining a fixed exchange rate regime. Where a country is undergoing major domestic economic changes or pegged the exchange rate at an unrealistic level, a fixed rate regime does not permit adjustment of exchange rates to correct for a trade deficit or surplus. Unwilling to adjust the exchange rate, a protectionist policy permits the country to maintain the fixed exchange rate regime while reducing imports.[3]

However, a protectionist policy may not achieve an overall improvement in the trade balance. Goods barred by a protectionist policy remain competitive in other countries. Hence, a protectionist country may experience greater export competition against the goods barred in its own country so that overall export growth declines along with the imports.

In reconciling the benefits of free trade with the survival elements of protectionism, many countries compromise and follow a *managed trade approach*. Under this approach, countries identify industries needing protection either for political or national security purposes, encourage free trade on behalf of those domestic industries with international competitive advantage, and negotiate bilateral concessions to remove protection of domestic industries with limited political influence. Despite the benefits of free trade to consumers, national governments are equally responsible for employment and are under constant political pressure to promote exports by opening cross-border markets while protecting domestic industries from cross-border competition. Furthermore, trading partners have different commitments to free trade and different definitions of national security interests so that a balance of trade is accomplished only by managing the trade by a government-administered process of tradeoffs with trading partners.

Post–World War II Global Trading System

Between World War I and World War II, most industrial countries practiced extensive protectionist policies in the form of high tariffs, import restrictions, and exchange rate depreciation, contributing to the decline in international trade which exacerbated weak domestic economies already suffering from depression. The overall economic dislocation greatly contributed to the political tensions that erupted into World War II.

Following World War II, the victorious Allied nations were determined not to repeat the mistakes of the interwar period and actively pursued global free trade policies ensuring equal treatment for all and inclusion of former enemies. Through U.S. leadership, considerable success was achieved toward a global free trade system. As a superpower, giant marketplace, and a large financial center, many governments supported the U.S. economic policy as a means of gaining access to its military and economic largesse. Furthermore, the adoption of the income tax system by industrial countries and its extension to the general population provided central governments with a revenue source that eliminated dependence on tariffs, making countries more willing to adopt free trade policies.

At the cornerstone of the post–World War II free trade system were three multilateral agreements establishing mechanisms for continuing cooperation and evolution in reducing impediments to free trade: the General Agreement on Trade and Tariffs (GATT), adopted in 1947; the Bretton Woods system, adopted in 1944; and the EEC, begun in 1951 as the European Coal and Steel Community.

GATT established an institutionalized system for periodic multilateral negotiations to reduce international trade restrictions. Beginning with twenty-three signatory nations, GATT grew to over 103 nations by the end of 1991. In pursuing this goal, GATT follows four basic principles: (1) nondiscrimination through application of the MFN principle to all signatories; (2) reduction of trade barriers; (3) reciprocal concessions as the basis of trading relations; and (4) establishing universal rules for cross-border commercial relationships. Recently, the GATT system has been renamed the World Trade Organization (WTO) and expanded to include cross-border commercial services and intellectual property.

In a radical departure from past practices, the EEC was established not only to promote free trade among its members but also to provide a broad institutional framework for political and economic consultation and negotiations to resolve the many questions raised by European economic interdependence. Although increasingly interdependent, European countries had followed independent protectionist and economic policies, adding to the insecurities prevalent from other sources of tension. An important parallel organization was the North Atlantic Treaty Organization (NATO), founded in 1949 to provide a military coalition that could remove the insecurity arising from interdependence.

Bretton Woods established an international monetary system that promoted free trade by providing a mechanism for exchange rate stability, free

convertability of currencies into other currencies, flexible international reserves, and lending facilities to assist in rebuilding war-torn economies. In
addition, elimination of capital controls was designed to encourage the free
flow of capital.

New Protectionism

Despite the substantial progress toward free trade, protectionism remains a
potent political and economic force. With the end of the Bretton Woods system of fixed exchange rates, countries can manipulate the exchange rate to
produce a trade barrier similar to a high tariff. More important, countries have
become sophisticated and subtle in furthering protectionism by a wide range
of nontariff barriers that add to the cost of foreign products competing in the
domestic marketplace.[4] These nontariff barriers include antidumping laws,
subsidies, government-imposed safety standards, government procurement
regulations, environmental regulation, labor standards, domestic content legislation, import quotas, credit guarantees, industrial cartels, free trade zones,
and tax incentives.

While the drive to reduce nontariff barriers is evident, the multinational
character of trade makes it difficult to achieve real success. When products
were manufactured and owned in one country and shipped to another, trade
relations were simpler to understand. Today, a manufacturing plant located in
one country and owned by a company headquartered in another country may
import raw materials or components from other countries and then ship its
products to another country for final assembly and distribution. As a result, a
complex web of economic alliances and production-sharing arrangements
between corporations and countries creates a political environment conducive
to expanded nontariff trade barriers.

This new emphasis on nontariff barriers also arises from a change in national economic objectives. Traditional protectionist policies had as their primary purpose the protection of threatened industries and substitution of
imported products with domestic production. Modern protectionist policy is
attuned to the economic objectives of free trade policy but achieves these
objectives by directly enhancing or guaranteeing a country's comparative
advantage in global trade. Hence, many protectionist restrictions are intended
to enhance technological high-end products where profits are high, and competitive advantages are achieved through quality rather than price while remaining obtrusive to avoid violations of GATT and other international
agreements.

There is also a corollary strategy accompanying protectionist trade strategy
called *mercantilism* where a country engages in protectionist policies to
stimulate exports, achieving a sizable trade surplus which is then invested
abroad to enhance national wealth. However, mercantilist policies cause other

countries to incur current account deficits and may trigger a strong protectionist reaction in defense.

The new protectionism and growing complexity in nontariff barriers is generating many different responses. Lax labor and environmental standards are
causing countries to impose tariffs to equalize the cost of different regulatory
systems. Section 301 of the U.S. Trade Act of 1974 was enacted in the United
States granting the President or the U.S. Trade Representative broad authority to take action against any foreign government practice that is "unjustifi-
able, unreasonable, or discriminatory and burdens or restricts United States
commerce." Unable to anticipate all possible nontariff barriers, trade negotia-
tors have begun negotiating market-sharing arrangements and import quotas
as a less complex means of regulating international trade so that in 1990, it
was estimated that 30 percent of U.S. imports were subject to some form of
quota restriction. The MFN principle is no longer unconditional but often
conditioned on additional concessions. Bilateral rather than multilateral bar-
gaining is expanding, making it easier to achieve agreement on complex issues but adding to the overall complexity of international trade regulation. By
1990, more than twenty regional trading arrangements had been established
to lower trading barriers among member countries while raising trading barriers against nonmembers.

Historical Experience

Despite the strong theoretical basis that free trade is the best trade policy
for economic growth, historical experience is mixed.[5] The United States grew
to great industrial prominence in the nineteenth and early twentieth centuries
under a high tariff wall; and Japan recovered from World War II, going on to
become the second-largest economic power utilizing strong protectionist policies. On the other hand, until the close of the Cold War, the Soviet Union,
Eastern Europe, and much of Latin America followed protectionist policies;
but their domestic economies declined relative to the Western industrial nations. Despite adopting a free trade policy, by the beginning of the twentieth
century, Britain was suffering a chronic trade deficit.

This historical experience indicates that successful trade policy does not
stand alone but must be incorporated into overall economic policy and that a
protectionist policy does not automatically result in poor economic performance. The United States and Japan were successful both because dynamic
domestic competition provided many of the advantages otherwise offered by
a free trade strategy and because their principal trading partner—Britain to
the United States and the United States to Japan—acquiesced to the protectionist policy for security purposes and to maintain a fixed exchange rate regime. In addition, in a competitive domestic market protectionist policies
bolstered overall domestic employment since employees of failed firms could
move to the successful domestic competitors. In contrast, protectionist policies

for domestic economies dominated by state-owned or -regulated industries or oligopolistic cartels, perpetuate entrenched business methods and inefficiencies resistant to innovative practices and products that could otherwise enhance economic growth.

If all trading partners follow the same free trade strategy, overall economic growth appears best achieved. The strategy breaks down when one or several trading partners follow protectionist or managed trade policies, creating a situation where countries following free trade are unable to export products to pay for imports from the protectionist country. This trade imbalance causes the sale of financial assets to pay for imports and thereby mortgage future capital flows. Contentious trade negotiations arise; and if trading partners cannot resolve the disparate trade relationship, the free trade countries either weaken—causing dislocation to the protectionist countries—or respond by banding together into free trade zones of like-minded countries and adopt protectionist policies against nonmembers.

NOTES

1. Economic analysis is often influenced by contemporary conditions, and it is helpful to review material from other periods to see the economic conditions considered in adopting economic policies. An excellent analysis of protectionist policy made during the height of its popularity is found in Richard T. Ely, *Outlines of Economics* (New York: Macmillan, 1926).

2. The role of the *Zollverein* to build German union and exclude Austria is described in A. J. P. Taylor, *Bismarck* (New York: Vintage Books, 1955).

3. J. M. Keynes favored free trade, but in the face of government determination to maintain the exchange rate, an expansionist domestic policy would not improve domestic employment unless increased spending was channeled solely to domestic business by means of a tariff wall. See J. M. Keynes, "Proposals for a Revenue Tariff," *The New Statesman and Nation*, London, March 7, 1931.

4. For a good in-depth discussion of contemporary international trading practices, see Robert G. Gilpin's article in Takashi Inoguchic and Daniel I. Okimoto, *The Political Economy of Japan*, Vol. 2 (Stanford: Stanford University Press, 1988).

5. Charles P. Kindleberger, *Economic Response* (Cambridge: Harvard University Press, 1978), in Chapter 3 discusses the rise of free trade in Western Europe (1820–1875) and found it difficult to isolate the consequences of free trade from the many other economic conditions then occurring.

CHAPTER 9

Cross-Border Investment Relationships

In the previous chapter, international investments were discussed in terms of the income and payments component of cross-border commercial activity. From another and more important perspective, international investment activity—better known as *capital flow*—is the cross-border deployment of financial assets constituting a separate and distinct activity transmitting economic conditions through their impact on changes in interest rates, exchange rates, and financing of trade flows.

When international communications were slow and hazardous, cross-border investment activity was limited to short-term liquid investments. International traders bought and sold goods in such a manner that the amount of claims and liabilities for payment equaled and canceled each other by short maturity dates on a country-by-country basis. Long-term cross-border investments were also undertaken but by a select and limited group of firms with a close network of reliable foreign agents to monitor local conditions.

Today, the situation has dramatically changed as a combination of advances has opened extensive opportunities in international investments. Removal of most currency and capital controls, together with deregulation of many financial markets, has enabled unimpeded acquisition of foreign financial assets. Improved global communications has greatly expanded knowledge of business and economic conditions throughout the world. Meanwhile, financial institutions have improved their expertise in managing cross-border investments while gaining confidence in national economic systems led by dependable governments and business institutions. In its 1993 annual report, BIS estimated that cross-border portfolio transactions had exceeded trade-related transactions.

These global advances have given confidence to expanded foreign participation in domestic financial markets, enabling countries with extensive domestic financial markets to finance greater trade flows—including larger trade deficits—by paying with financial assets rather than international reserves. Domestic financial markets also trade large volumes of government credit instruments with investment features particularly desirable to foreign investors, thereby expanding government abilities to finance large budget deficits through expanded cross-border investment activity.

While these advances allow investors to shift funds confidently between countries, greatly integrating individual national financial markets, local economic conditions remain the principal factor affecting financial markets. Cross-border investment activity is primarily participation in a country's domestic financial market. Accordingly, analyzing global investment activity requires an understanding of the following fundamental conditions:

- Structure of domestic financial markets
- Size of domestic financial markets
- Characteristics of cross-border investments

This interrelationship between domestic financial markets and international economic conditions is also important to the international matrix system. Not only do interest rates, share prices, and other domestic financial activities of the matrix countries have a significant impact on the global economy, but they are also an important source of key financial indicators integral to international economic trend analysis.

STRUCTURE OF DOMESTIC FINANCIAL MARKETS

Domestic financial markets of most countries mobilize financial resources for modern-day businesses and governments by organizing into three broad investment categories:

- Money market
- Portfolio
- Direct

An overview of the organized domestic financial markets of seven leading industrial nations consisting of short-term savings deposits, marketable stocks, and marketable bonds is found in Table 9.1 and illustrates the extensive capability of these nations to finance international trade.[1] Excluded are real

Table 9.1
Financial Markets of Selected Countries, 1990

Country	Demand Deposits	Savings Deposits	Stocks	Bonds	Country Total
		Billions of Dollars			
United States	$ 350	$ 5,243	$2,812	$ 4,406	$12,812
Japan	569	4,737	2,803	1,877	9,986
Germany	242	726	338	726	2,032
Britain	355	569	878	218	2,020
Canada	65	341	220	238	864
France	265	643	296	435	1,639
Netherlands	48	171	118	135	472
Other	NA	NA	971	2,333	3,304
Market Total	$1,894	$12,431	$8,444	$10,368	$33,137
		Market Share			
United States	18%	42%	33%	43%	39%
Japan	30%	38%	33%	18%	30%
Germany	13%	6%	4%	7%	6%
Britain	19%	5%	10%	2%	6%
Canada	3%	3%	3%	2%	3%
France	14%	5%	4%	4%	5%
Netherlands	3%	1%	1%	1%	1%
Other	NA	NA	12%	23%	10%
Total	100%	100%	100%	100%	100%
		Ratio to GDP			
United States	6%	97%	52%	82%	238%
Japan	19%	161%	95%	64%	339%
Germany	16%	49%	23%	49%	137%
Britain	36%	58%	90%	22%	206%
Canada	11%	60%	39%	42%	152%
France	22%	54%	25%	37%	138%
Netherlands	18%	65%	45%	51%	180%

Sources: Morgan Stanley Capital Markets; Solomon Brothers; World Bank.

estate mortgage, consumer installment credit, and several other major financial sectors important to the domestic economy but less significant to the international market. While all industrial countries maintain such financial market segments, custom, historical experience, regulation, and government policy have influenced their growth, size, and diversity. Using the ratio of domestic financial market segments to GDP, Table 9.1 describes the nature of the domestic financial markets and their influence on global capital flows. A further analysis of the size of financial markets in the global economy is provided in Appendix E, which lists the capitalization of equity and bond markets throughout most of the world, with the matrix countries having the dominant financial markets.

Money Market Investments

Considering the extensive news and literature covering portfolio investment activity, money markets remain the major repository of domestic savings (see Table 9.1); and their size in relation to other financial market segments is surprisingly large. In the United States and Japan, savings deposits alone consist of $5.2 and $4.7 trillion, respectively, and are larger than the entire liquid financial markets of the other countries in Table 9.1. Only Britain contains a financial segment, the stock market, that is larger than its savings deposits.

Money market investments are important because of their dual functions as a temporary repository of funds awaiting investment for other projects and as a principal component of the domestic money supply. In international economics, domestic money markets are also the backbone of the international currency markets supplying the principal medium of exchange for transacting international commerce. As discussed more fully in Chapter 10, international currency markets constitute the cross-border trade in domestic money market and deposit accounts; and growing international commerce cannot be accomplished without marshaling the large bank savings of the principal industrial nations. The market share and ratio to GDP analysis contained in Table 9.1 shows the dominating position of U.S. and Japanese savings deposits.

Table 9.2 presents the cross-border bank claims and liabilities component of short-term money markets, which also constitutes the principal component of the international currency market. At the end of 1992, the five matrix countries had in the aggregate foreign-owned bank claims of $2.2 trillion and liabilities of $2.4 trillion, constituting worldwide cross-border bank claims and liabilities of 42 percent and 45 percent, respectively.

The large size of these cross-border liabilities has enormous international economic impact indicated by comparing each country's ratio to GDP of cross-border bank liabilities in Table 9.2 with the savings deposit ratios in Table 4.1. For Britain, the ratio of liabilities to GDP in 1992 was 76 percent, which explains the unusually high ratio of bank deposits to GDP of 36 percent. For the United States, the large amount of foreign bank liabilities nevertheless is only 12 percent of its GDP because international commerce is less important to its giant economy.

Table 9.2
Cross-Border Claims and Liabilities, 1992

| | Billions of Dollars | | | Distribution | |
	Claims	Liabilities	Balance	Claims	Liabilities
World					
Industrial Countries	3,808	3,852	-44	72%	71%
Developing Countries	457	345	112	9%	6%
Offshore Banking Centers	934	1,105	-171	18%	20%
Other	96	161	-65	2%	3%
Total World	5,295	5,463	-168	100%	100%
Matrix Countries					
United States	537	663	-126	10%	12%
Japan	679	691	-12	13%	13%
Germany	252	184	68	5%	3%
Britain	728	804	-76	14%	15%
Canada	35	46	-11	1%	1%
Total Matrix Countries	2,231	2,388	-157	42%	44%
Selected Other Countries					
France	354	348	6	7%	6%
Belgium/Luxembourg	319	319	0	6%	6%
Switzerland	345	97	248	7%	2%
Netherlands	137	105	32	3%	2%
Selected Offshore Banking Centers					
Hong Kong	299	428	-129	6%	8%
Singapore	223	261	-38	4%	5%
Bahamas	135	122	13	3%	2%
Cayman Islands	212	237	-25	4%	4%

Source: International Financial Statistics (Washington, D.C.: International Monetary Fund, January 1994).

Portfolio Investments

Portfolio investments consist of marketable stocks and bonds where participants are passive and do not control the investment entity. Table 9.1 demonstrates the enormous size and breadth of the domestic stock and bond markets of several industrial countries which grew, in part, through recycling savings accumulated from substantial trade surpluses. In particular, with stock market capitalizations of $2.8, $2.8, and $0.9 trillion, respectively, the United States, Japan, and Britain represent about 60 percent of the global equity markets and attract much of international investment. Similar magnitudes are found in the bond and money markets. Major trading nations are supported by large domestic financial markets.

These strong domestic capital markets have allowed portfolio investments to play an important part in the overall expansion of international commerce. In an unrestricted international capital market, investors obtaining higher returns from cross-border stock and bond investments enable an integrated relationship between cross-border portfolio investments and trade. Growing demand for global investment creates growing demand for currencies, enabling trade exporters to expand trade by accepting payment in foreign currency and being reasonably assured that the currency can be easily sold. About 20 percent of European investments and 5 to 7 percent of Japanese and American investments now constitute cross-border investments, and the percentages are growing.

The large and diverse domestic financial markets described in Table 9.1 also attract investors located in countries with limited financial markets. The wide array of investment opportunities allow for portfolio diversification without the need of an unwieldy allocation of funds among several countries. Government supervision maintains market integrity, offering investors a fair return and reasonable expectations in achieving the return. Unrestricted convertability into other currencies and easy transfer of funds to new owners provides the liquidity and convenience so essential to modern-day commerce.

Organized financial markets also provide the ability to manage exchange rate volatility. Often, a fall in a currency value is offset by a rise in the domestic value of the investment. For example, a fall in domestic interest rates often causes a decline in the exchange rate matched by a rise in the value of domestic bonds offsetting the exchange rate loss. Another example is the London stock market where many of the listed companies earn 50 percent or more of their profits from foreign operations. A fall in the pound means these foreign profits will be translated into a higher figure when converted to the pound, often contributing to the rise in the London stock market when the pound exchange rate falls.

Direct Investments

Direct investments provide parent companies with controlled local business operations obliged to support and sell parent-company products. In turn, parent companies expand their domestic manufacturing operations and incur sizable capital commitments to produce parts and products for foreign affiliates. The strong relationship between cross-border trade and direct investment is demonstrated by comparing U.S. cross-border direct investments reported in Table 9.3 with the major U.S. trading partners listed in Table 8.5. Canada is the largest U.S.

Table 9.3
U.S. Cross-Border Direct Investment, 1991

	Billions of Dollars		Distribution	
	Overseas	In U.S.	Overseas	In U.S.
Industry				
Petroleum	56	40	12%	10%
Manufacturing	181	157	39%	38%
Wholesale Trade	48	64	10%	15%
Banking	21	22	5%	5%
Finance, Insurance, and Real Estate	118	79	26%	19%
Services and Other	37	52	8%	13%
Total All Industries	*461*	*414*	*100%*	*100%*
Geographic Distribution				
Europe	233	251	51%	61%
Canada	69	37	15%	9%
Latin America	76	18	16%	4%
Japan	25	93	5%	22%
Middle East and Africa	9	5	2%	1%
Other Asia	46	10	10%	2%
International Agencies	3	0	1%	0%
Total All Direct Investment	*461*	*414*	*100%*	*100%*
Selected Countries				
Japan	25	93	5%	22%
Germany	34	29	7%	7%
Britain	78	100	17%	24%
Canada	69	37	15%	9%
Netherlands	20	59	4%	14%
Switzerland	26	19	6%	5%
France	21	24	5%	6%
Brazil	15	1	3%	0%
Mexico	12	1	3%	0%
Bermuda	23	1	5%	0%
Hong Kong and Taiwan	9	3	2%	1%

Source: U.S. Department of Commerce, *Survey of Current Business,* June 1993, pp. 51 and 54.

trading partner, receiving 21 percent of 1991 U.S. exports, and is one of the largest locations for United States foreign investment, with 15 percent of the total. Japan is a major exporter to the United States, comprising 19 percent of total 1991 U.S. imports, and is the second-largest direct investor, constituting 22 percent of all foreign direct investment in the United States. With 24 percent, Britain is the largest foreign investor in the United States, sending 11 percent of its exports to this country and making the United States its third-largest trading partner in 1991.

This expanding relationship between cross-border direct investment and cross-border trade impedes implementation of traditional economic policies designed to improve a country's balance of trade. Parent companies must protect their foreign and domestic investments and parent company–affiliate trade flows by implementing policies resistant to exchange rate changes. One of the most common policies is hedging transactions, in which a company expecting to need or to receive in the future a foreign currency enters into a transaction to acquire or sell the currency, as the case may be, thus locking in the exchange rate price for the future transaction. Another policy is to disburse production facilities among several countries so as to be able to shift production to lower-cost facilities. As these policies suggest, unless exchange rate changes and competition are significant and sustained over an extended time period, the parent–affiliate trade flows are unlikely to be altered; and economic policies designed to improve trade balances are unlikely to be successful when unilaterally undertaken by a singe country.

An analysis of the industrial description of United States cross-border direct investments is also an example of the correlation of foreign direct investment to domestic economic characteristics. By 1991, U.S. direct overseas investment and foreign direct investment into the United States were roughly in the same proportion of industrial segments. Manufacturing is the largest segment—comprising 39 percent of U.S. overseas direct investment and 38 percent of foreign direct investment into the United States—closely followed by finance, insurance, and real estate at 26 percent and 19 percent, respectively.

Direct investment is a controversial cross-border investment activity. To capital-importing countries, direct investment is a means of obtaining new technology, management techniques, and equipment. On the other hand, there is the fear of foreign intrusion on local customs. To capital-exporting countries, foreign direct investment establishes a presence that allows the parent company to tailor products and service the local consumers. However, there is the concern of exporting high-paying domestic jobs.

SIZE AND STRUCTURE OF DOMESTIC
FINANCIAL MARKETS

The United States, Japan, and Britain operate the largest and most extensive financial markets which in 1990 (see Table 9.1) totaled $12.8, $10.0, and $2.0 trillion, respectively. Compared to other countries, the U.S. bond market is more developed as corporations and local governments directly cultivate the diverse sources of savings, bypassing the restrictive lending practices and high borrowing costs of U.S. banks and other financial intermediaries. In contrast, bank loans are a major capital source for Japan's public and private institutions as its population's large savings are funneled into $4.7-trillion savings deposits. British banks have opted to become internationally oriented by providing significant banking services, expertise, and support to world-wide trade and finance. A large portion of British savings supports an international currency market, indicated by an unusually high ratio of demand deposits to GDP of 36 percent. The London stock market is a large segment of its domestic financial market, reflecting a long history of extensive global operations by many publicly held companies.

The United States not only has the largest domestic financial market but offers the widest array of investment opportunities. Contributing to the size of the financial market are the substantial volume of U.S. government securities included in the $4.4-trillion bond market and the government-guaranteed deposits included in the $5.2-trillion savings accounts. With such protection against loss, it is no wonder that the U.S. financial market is a favorite destination of cross-border investment capital.

Compared to other countries, the U.S. and Japanese domestic financial markets are a much larger influence on their domestic economies as measured by the ratio to GDP of 238 percent and 339 percent, respectively. The capability of the U.S. financial market has also made it easier for the U.S. government to finance its budget deficits and importers to finance large trade deficits, thereby circumventing some of the disciplines of the marketplace described in international economic theory. Japan has restricted participation in its domestic financial market, but its great size and depth have caused pressures to build for expanded foreign participation.

Considering the economic importance of Germany and France to the European economy, the ratio of their financial markets to GDP of 137 percent and 138 percent, respectively, indicates the underdevelopment of their domestic financial markets. This situation may be a result of several historical factors. Both countries have a strong historical attraction to agriculture and a suspicion of finance and financial market manipulation, causing both countries to strongly support manufacturing and agriculture while closely regulating financial markets. In addition, the costs of two devastating world wars has wiped out much investment accumulation.

NATIONAL CHARACTERISTICS OF
KEY CROSS-BORDER INVESTMENTS

Characteristics of cross-border investment vary, reflecting a wide range in government policies, historical circumstances, and local attitudes, which is strikingly illustrated by the cross-border investment position of several major industrial nations for the period ending 1988 reported by the International Monetary Fund.[2] A summary of this rare and insightful report is found in Table 9.4 together with the ratio of cross-border-owned assets compared to the respective country's nominal 1988 GDP. An analysis of these data is discussed on a country-by-country basis in the following sections.

Table 9.4
International Investment Position of Selected Countries, 1988

Investment Items	United States	Japan	Germany	Britain	France	Switzer- land	Canada
				Billions of Dollars			
Assets							
Bank Claims	560	585	191	811	258	124	43
Official Assets	133	202	102	69	82	33	24
Securities	186	452	136	270	17	175	20
Direct Investment	334	111	70	192	51	47	59
Other Assets	53	119	191	68	2	57	42
Total Assets	1,266	1,469	690	1,410	410	436	188
Liabilites							
Bank Liabilities	596	767	130	926	250	102	72
Official Liabilities	369	58	127	48	11	1	83
Securities	438	275	71	107	58	76	78
Direct Investment	329	10	38	121	0	25	92
Other Liabilities	65	68	113	60	20	45	35
Total Liabilities	1,797	1,178	479	1,262	339	249	360
Net Worth	-531	291	211	148	71	187	-172
Nominal GDP	4,900	2,898	1,191	834	960	184	492
				Ratio to GDP			
Assets							
Bank Claims	11%	20%	16%	97%	27%	67%	9%
Official Assets	3%	7%	9%	8%	9%	18%	5%
Securities	4%	16%	11%	32%	2%	95%	4%
Direct Investment	7%	4%	6%	23%	5%	26%	12%
Other Assets	1%	4%	16%	8%	0%	31%	9%
Total Assets	26%	51%	58%	169%	43%	237%	38%
Liabilites							
Bank Liabilities	12%	26%	11%	111%	26%	55%	15%
Official Liabilities	8%	2%	11%	6%	1%	1%	17%
Securities	9%	9%	6%	13%	6%	41%	16%
Direct Investment	7%	0%	3%	15%	0%	14%	19%
Other Liabilities	1%	2%	9%	7%	2%	24%	7%
Total Liabilities	37%	41%	40%	151%	35%	135%	73%
Net Worth	-11%	10%	18%	18%	7%	102%	-35%

Source: International Monetary Fund, "Report on the Measurement of International Capital Flows" (Washington, D.C.: International Monetary Fund, September 1992), p. 97.

The United States

Compared to other countries, the hallmark of U.S. cross-border investment is the broad diversity, reflecting the important role its domestic financial markets perform in the global economy. Particularly noteworthy are the large cross-border direct investments. Table 9.3 provides further information on U.S. direct investment in 1991 showing that more than one-half of $461 billion in overseas direct investment and $414 billion in direct investment in the United States is with Europe.

In contrast to large direct investments, Americans have been reluctant overseas portfolio investors. However, since the IMF study of 1988, this situation is rapidly changing. The end of the Cold War in 1989 has eliminated major political and military concerns about cross-border investments. As Americans reevaluate the global marketplace, other governments and business are offering attractive investment opportunities that compare favorably to those found in the United States.

A comparison of official assets and liabilities reflects the key role played by the United States in the international monetary system. The United States and Germany have large official liabilities of $369 and $127 billion, respectively, arising from holdings accumulated by other countries as international reserve currencies. In many respects, the size of these official liabilities makes the United States the central banker for the world and Germany the central bank for Europe, raising issues regarding the burden and benefits of being a reserve currency (discussed in Chapter 10).

On the other hand, comparison of foreign official liabilities to private bank liabilities provides another insight into the international monetary system. U.S. official liabilities of $369 billion is well below the much larger foreign private bank liabilities of Japan and Britain of $767 and $926 billion, respectively. This comparison suggests that while dollars are still the preferred reserve currency, other currencies are being more widely used for daily commercial transactions. To be competitive, American businesses must become better versed in using multiple-currency strategies to enhance their international competitiveness.

The large amount of official assets held by Japan and Germany, $202 and $102 billion, respectively, follows their central bank purchases of foreign currency from their successful export industries. These purchases were necessary to forestall a rise in their exchange rates that would have occurred from foreign currency accumulated through the growing trade surpluses. These central banks also protect the price competitiveness of their export industries by purchasing foreign currencies to forestall an exchange rate appreciation.

Compared to other industrial countries, the large amount of U.S. cross-border investment represents a proportionately smaller share of U.S. economic activity, demonstrated by comparing the ratio of cross-border investments to GDP. On the other hand, the rising amount of U.S. negative net worth (see Table 9.4) gives the United States the dubious distinction of being the largest net debtor in the world. However, in terms of the domestic economy, the negative net worth in 1988 represents 11 percent of GDP, which is not so large as to be a major source of economic destabilization. Canada has a much more serious debtor problem with a negative net worth of 35 percent of GDP, which is burdening the Canadian domestic economy with continuing high interest rates.

Japan

Through many years of steady trade surpluses, Japan has recycled its surpluses into vast cross-border investments composed principally of portfolio rather than direct investments. Hence, Japan has become an international financial center of liquid funds similar to Switzerland and Luxembourg. Japan's balance-of-payments figures found in Appendix C further demonstrate its role as an international financial center. A large part of the overseas investments of Japanese banks is financed from cross-border short-term investments into the Japanese financial markets.

This role as an international financial center makes it more difficult for the Bank of Japan to conduct a monetary policy that can satisfy both domestic manufacturers that need low interest rates and declining exchange rates and the globally oriented financial industry increasingly dependent on obtaining foreign investors through high interest rates or appreciating currency. Consequently, Japan has limited its role and responsibility as a reserve currency or a stabilizing force in international commerce. It prefers concentrating on the commercial aspects of international banking and maintaining maximum flexibility in the conduct of domestic monetary policy.

Conspicuously, the limited foreign direct investments in Japan is in sharp contrast to the sizable foreign direct investments in the United States, Britain, and Switzerland, which is 7 percent, 15 percent, and 14 percent of their respective GDPs. Some commentators attribute this situation to a general policy of excluding foreign direct investment participation, while others point to the high cost of doing business in Japan because of high land prices, which are a prime factor in locating a manufacturing facility.[3]

Germany

Despite consistent trade surpluses, close proximity to its foreign markets, and the importance of international commerce to the domestic economy, Germany is also conspicuous by its low 6-percent ratio of foreign direct investment to GDP. Germany shares with Japan an apprehension of foreign participation in the domestic economy and consequently does not encourage foreign portfolio and direct investment. This situation probably arises from a combination of factors: lost overseas investments from war seizures, desire to minimize the risk of more seizures in the event of some future political dispute, and lingering antagonism from potential host countries because of the wartime deprivations delivered by German occupation forces.

The ratio of official liabilities to GDP shows Germany's role as a major reserve currency for the EMS. In addition, much international investment activity is conducted through Luxembourg to circumvent German financial regulation and share transaction taxes and noninterest-earning reserve requirements.

Subsequent to the IMF study of 1988, German cross-border investments are increasing, spurred on by the opportunities in Eastern Europe following the end of the Cold War. Furthermore, Germany has developed one of the largest bond markets to finance its unification process. Consequently, German long-term interest rates have a strong influence on world capital markets.

Britain

In contrast to the United States, Japan, and Germany, the dollar amounts and the GDP ratios for cross-border investment activity clearly illustrate Britain's role as a major international financial center and the importance of that activity to the domestic economy. Direct investment is a significant portion of its cross-border investment activity arising from the recycling of sizable and continuous trade surpluses earned when it was the great industrial power in the nineteenth century. More recently, the large direct investment flowing into Britain—15 percent of GDP—is a result of its strategic location and popularity for manufacturing, distributing, and servicing for the European market.

Particularly significant is the 97-percent ratio of cross-border bank claims to GDP. These figures provide a possible source for Britain's continuing sluggish economy; for its economic policies must cater to both domestic manufacturing needs, which requires low interest rates and a weak currency and the international financial industry which requires stable or appreciating currency. This figure is also another indication of the difficulty facing Britain in integrating its international financial industry with a European monetary and credit system that has more limited focus. Britain's balance of payments (see Appendix C) also shows its dependence on short-term capital to finance its current account deficits. It is difficult for a country to be a major financial center when incurring sizable current account deficits.

While Britain has been a major international financial center for several centuries, its international role has undergone some significant reorientation. Table 9.4 shows a small amount of official liabilities indicating not only its decline as a reserve currency but a declining role in regulating international finance. The image of the Bank of England as the epitome of the central bank with global responsibilities is no longer matched by the realities of the changes in the world economy.

France

France's limited international involvement is demonstrated by the low ratio of total domestic-owned foreign assets to GDP (43%), compared to 169 percent and 58 percent, respectively, for Britain and Germany. Despite a strong history of technological innovations, France has an equally strong desire to protect its domestic culture, contributing to a long history of controlling cross-border financial transactions. Thus, the $258 billion in bank claims—constituting more than one-half of all foreign investment—represents the financing activity supporting its cross-border trade in goods and services.

Switzerland

Switzerland's ratio of foreign investment to GDP is an astounding 237 percent, the highest of the countries shown in Table 9.4. With only a population of seven million, Switzerland has assiduously developed its international financial industry into a major global player by devoting substantial domestic assets to this enterprise. However, with $0.5 trillion in foreign-owned assets, the small size of the population limits its global financial strength despite the industry, astuteness, and ingenuity of its bankers.

A net worth equal to one year's GDP is a remarkable achievement testifying to the expertise in international investment, activity for which Swiss banks are famed. A source of this international financial strength is concentration on long-term cross-border portfolio investments, which contrasts with British international investment activity concentrated on currency trading and short-term money management. It is estimated that over 32 percent of Swiss banking assets are fiduciary accounts, which constitute investments owned by customers but managed by the banks.[4]

Despite the strong reputation as a dependable financial center and commitment to economic stability, Switzerland has eschewed any role as a reserve currency and has discouraged the use of its money market instruments for such a purpose through Federal and Cantonal stamp duties and turnover taxes that are high compared to the relatively low interest yields. Large foreign institutional holdings of Swiss currency would make its economy vulnerable to abrupt changes in international reserves and fluctuations in the exchange rate, reducing its ability to conduct monetary and exchange rate policy conducive to domestic needs.

Canada

Although not a major participant in international investment activity, Canada's cross-border investment position is instructive on a number of international investment issues facing many smaller nations. In relation to its GDP, foreign direct investment into Canada of 19 percent is the highest among the countries listed in Table 9.4. This high direct investment level is a combination of large capital projects necessary to develop the vast natural resources located in Canada and financing the large federal and provincial budget deficits. Canadian overseas investment of 12 percent of GDP is surprisingly large. The Canadian economy lacks diversification necessary for investment opportunities, and this outflow may be a consequence of its large immigrant population finding better investments overseas.

Canada's large amount of official liabilities appears to stem from foreign support of Canadian management of the exchange rate. The need for such support is indicated by Canada's large negative net worth caused by the sizable foreign investment in Canada and, more recently, foreign purchases of Canadian federal and provincial debt issued to finance large government budget deficits. As the balance-of-payments figures in Appendix B indicate, the interest payments on this debt are causing a large and recurring current account deficit with concurrent downward pressure on the Canadian exchange rate. Government monetary polices to support the Canadian dollar such as high interest rates would hurt the domestic economy.

THIRD-COUNTRY INVESTMENT INTERMEDIARIES

In pursuit of domestic agendas, industrial countries have developed a complex tax and regulatory framework which, in the rough and tumble of global competition, have been exploited by banking, finance, and holding companies catering to those seeking to circumvent—legally or illegally—loopholes in such regulatory and tax schemes. Several smaller countries have been particularly adroit at this activity and are commonly referred to as *offshore banking centers* or *tax havens.*

While considerable romanticism and mystery surround their activities and the volume of business is not inconsequential, their impact on global economics is not great; but they are adding to the complexities of understanding international commercial relationships and investment flows. For example, if a Japanese-owned financial subsidiary headquartered in the Bahamas establishes a branch in the United States, should the direct investment be considered an investment from the Bahamas or from Japan? Also, who is responsible for regulating the U.S. branch?

Offshore Banking Centers

Table 9.2 shows that 18 percent of cross-border claims and 20 percent of cross-border liabilities are with offshore banking centers comprised principally of Hong Kong, Singapore, the Bahamas, and the Cayman Islands. Their major attraction is the banking services provided without the regulatory restrictions that surround the commercial banking industry of the industrial countries.[5] Bank secrecy has been another important factor, although the

United States and other industrial countries have exerted sufficient pressure to be able to pierce the bank secrecy veil for legitimate criminal investigations. Most of the larger banks operating in these offshore centers are affiliates of major commercial banks of industrial countries.

As would be expected, a significant portion of the depositors in these banking centers reside in politically unstable areas such as the Middle East and Latin America. Offshore banking centers offer a safe investment haven without the political embarrassment of investing directly in Western financial markets. Another important advantage is avoiding freezing of assets which is a common U.S. practice when confronting a serious political or military contest with other countries.

Offshore banking centers deal primarily with money market investments because of several limitations on their ability to conduct portfolio and direct investment activities. Most industrial nations impose a withholding tax of 30 percent on the payment to nonresidents of dividend and interest income, which are reciprocally reduced or eliminated through an extensive network of bilateral tax treaties. Most offshore banking centers lack such a treaty network, preventing repatriation of dividend and interest income free of these withholding taxes. Portfolio and direct investment activity also requires a substantial infrastructure of highly trained professionals such as investment analysts, accountants, and lawyers; extensive telecommunications network; and frequent air traffic which only the major financial centers in the industrial countries can provide.

Offshore Investment Centers

In contrast to the offshore banking centers, several industrial countries have been successful in exploiting the regulatory framework surrounding portfolio and direct investments. Few Americans are aware that the United States offers a number of tax benefits to foreign investors which, when combined with the extensive network of income tax treaties, classifies the United States as a tax haven country. For example, interest income on bank deposits and capital gains from portfolio investments earned by foreign nonresidents are not subject to U.S. income tax.

Another country that has significantly exploited this regulatory framework is the Netherlands which has not only an extensive network of international tax treaties, including one with the United States, but also a domestic legal and tax system favorable to domiciled international holding companies. Through this favorable regulatory and tax framework, holding companies can shift funds between foreign affiliates with limited tax and other expenses. The success of the Netherlands as an offshore financial center is attested by Table 9.3. Despite its small size, it is the third-largest direct investor in the United States.

NOTES

1. For a more extensive analysis of domestic financial markets, see George F. Kaufman, *Banking Structures in Major Countries* (London: Kluwer Academic Publishers, 1992); Derek Honeygold, *International Financial Markets* (New York: Nichols Publishing Company, 1989); and Peter Newman, *The New Palgrave Dictionary of Money and Finance* (London: Macmillan, 1992).

2. The ability of financial markets to structure themselves to comply with religious, cultural, and other imperatives is illustrated in Zubar Iqbal and Abbas Mirakhor, *Islamic Banking* (Washington, D.C.: International Monetary Fund, 1987).

3. Mark Mason, *American Multinationals and Japan: The Political Economy of Japanese Capital Controls, 1899–1980* (Cambridge: Harvard University Press, 1992).

4. An extensive analysis of Swiss banking practices and organization is found in W. Blackman, *Swiss Banking in an International Context* (London: Macmillan, 1989).

5. An in-depth analysis of offshore banking centers is found in Yoon S. Park and Musa Essayyad, *International Banking and Financial Centers* (London: Kluwer Academic Publishers, 1989).

CHAPTER 10

International Monetary System

A vibrant and growing global economy requires an efficient and effective international monetary system. Despite disparate national policies, local customs, and a host of other obstacles, such a system has evolved; and its vitality has stimulated growth in international trade and investment. However, this system is uniquely different from most domestic monetary systems, and understanding its character and complexity provides an important context for evaluating the economic and financial indicators tracked by the international matrix system.

INTERNATIONAL MONETARY SYSTEM DESCRIBED

A universally accepted medium of exchange for conducting international commerce would seem a prerequisite for a successful international monetary system. In the context of national sovereignty, such a system would also require a mechanism for converting the international money into usable local currency, creating a dilemma for national governments committed to improving their respective domestic economies and therefore needing to control the domestic money supply. The international monetary system is characterized by the economic conditions created by this dilemma that periodically disrupts international commerce with attendant consequences to the business cycle.

International Monetary Development

A wide variety of instruments have been used as international mediums of exchange; but for hundreds of years, precious metals were the universally accepted medium of exchange extensively used for conducting both cross-border and domestic transactions. Gold and silver were widely used monetary forms in Europe, the Middle East, and Asia. By the nineteenth century, the international money system had evolved into a key currency system based on Britain's commitment to the gold standard; and countries pegged their currency exchange rates in terms of a fixed quantity of gold, settled their cross-border commercial balances through gold shipments, and based their domestic supply of money and credit according to a ratio of gold held by domestic monetary authorities.

As the Industrial Revolution progressed, the global trading network experienced rapid expansion, attributed by some to the international monetary use of gold but more accurately a result of improved transportation and transatlantic telegraphic communications in which gold became increasingly unsuitable. From 1815 to 1913, the proportion of gold and silver to the total international money supply is estimated to have fallen from 67 percent to 13 percent, whereas most of the monetary growth occurred in cross-border ownership of monetary instruments such as paper currency, bank deposits, trade bills, bankers' acceptances, and other money market investments.[1] Precious metals were too bulky and cumbersome to carry, too expensive to store and ship, and too slow to transport to act as an effective international medium of exchange. On the other hand, not only did bank deposits and other monetary instruments overcome these inconveniences, but they could earn interest income to the holders.

The final blow to the role of gold and silver as a universal money came with the depression of the 1930s and Britain's decline as a key currency country. A contributing factor to the depression was instability in domestic monetary policy brought on by unpredictable movements in gold and silver causing changes in the domestic money supply contrary to economic needs. As a consequence, many industrial countries abandoned the gold standard, floated exchange rates, and restricted domestic monetary use of precious metals. Use of gold and silver was limited to jewelry and conducting international business transactions, while domestic currency consisted of coin, paper currency, and bank checks.

As World War II was ending, officials from forty-five noncommunist countries met in 1944 at Bretton Woods, New Hampshire, to establish an international monetary system that would support expanded global trade to supply badly needed goods and services for war reconstruction, thereby promoting global political stability. Under the Bretton Woods system, the IMF was created as the administering agency of a set of rules and practices by which member nations agreed to carry out cross-border commercial transactions. At the heart of the system was the resurrection of a fixed exchange rate regime whereby member countries pegged their exchange rate in terms of both gold and the U.S. dollar, but only the dollar was convertible into gold at the fixed price of $35 an ounce. Member countries established a parity value with the U.S. dollar and agreed to maintain their bilateral exchange rate within ±1 percent of the parity value. Permission to change parity values required IMF approval. Under this system, both the dollar and gold became the principal exchange mediums for conducting international transactions, thereby creating by formal agreement a key currency system with the U.S. dollar as the key.

As envisioned by the creators of the Bretton Woods system, the United States emerged from World War II as the leading economic and military power which, combined with its strong domestic economy and political stability, gave great value to the dollar as an acceptable currency for international commerce. Expanded U.S. global trade increased the volume of dollars in international circulation, making it readily available for commercial transactions throughout much of the world. In technical parlance, the U.S. dollar became a *vehicle currency*, supplanting the British pound—which had held this position for over a century. By the 1960s, resurging German and Japanese economies were also contributing to expanding world trade, making their currencies valuable, plentiful, and desirable as vehicle currencies.

However, in the 1970s, the Bretton Woods system broke down. Dissimilar domestic economic policies, changes in cross-border commercial flows, economic revival of Japan and Germany, and financing of the Vietnam War made it impossible for countries to maintain fixed exchange rates at established parities. In 1971, the United States suspended the fixed exchange rate system of Bretton Woods in the hopes of reestablishing a different set of parities. However, the complexity and dynamism of global economic activity made it impossible. By 1973, the United States fully abandoned the Bretton Woods fixed exchange rate system in favor of floating exchange rates.[2]

Since then, the IMF and many central banks have been searching for a new system of fixed exchange rates. Meanwhile, the global financial markets have adjusted to the floating exchange rate regime, providing their own solutions by broadening the number of currencies used as vehicle currencies and smoothing out exchange rate fluctuations with an extensive forward currency market. Left intact and still a major aspect of the international monetary system is the IMF and its institutional arrangement by which central banks conduct business with one another, cooperate in managing exchange rate fluctuations, and regulate the cross-border payment process.

Composition of International Money

In today's international monetary system, monetary instruments have supplanted gold and silver as the principal exchange mediums for both domestic and cross-border commerce. Although loosely referred to as *currency*, these monetary instruments consist of government securities, short-term commercial paper, and bank deposits that comprise the money market segment of domestic financial markets. The daily cross-border and worldwide trade in these monetary instruments constitute the international currency market, permitting any one at any time to convert one currency into another for a wide variety of transactions.

This international monetary system differs markedly from the old gold-based system. Under the gold-based system, the supply of gold was dependent on mining production, which was a function of exploration, mining techniques, costs of production, and political stability of producing nations. In contrast, the supply of monetary instruments is a function of national monetary systems controlled by domestic authorities. Although the supply of monetary instruments can be unstable, leading to inflationary pressures and exchange rate volatility, it also provides flexibility and innovation to meet ever-changing economic and technological conditions not possible under the gold standard.

The international monetary system shares with domestic systems dependence on a dual source of money that is a source of instability: official reserves held by the national monetary authorities and bank deposits held by individuals and commercial enterprises. Official reserves consist of items defined by the IMF as acceptable to transact business between monetary authorities and therefore closely approaching a form of international money. The composition of official reserves is summarized in Table 10.1. In 1992, official reserves of all member countries of the IMF totaled $1,266 billion, comprising $64 billion in reserves with the IMF, $309 billion in gold holdings, and $893 billion in currencies of other countries.

Foreign exchange is the largest component of official reserves and has steadily grown to meet the needs of expanded global commercial activity. Foreign exchange reserves of all IMF member countries in 1988 comprised 59 percent of total official reserves, and by 1992 the proportionate share had grown to 71 percent. During this period, not only had gold fallen in value; more significant, the quantity of gold held as official reserves had little changed.

Denomination of official reserve currencies is concentrated with the major industrial countries, in particular, the United States, Germany, and Japan. The U.S. dollar remains the predominant reserve currency; but as is shown by Table 10.2, its proportionate share of all reserve currencies has fallen from 65 percent in 1985 to 56 percent in 1991. In contrast, the proportionate share of yen and the Deutsche mark reserve holdings have grown, constituting 10 percent and 17 percent, respectively, of all reserve currencies held in 1991. Since these two countries conduct extensive trading activity and contain large domestic financial markets, their currencies have become accepted as important vehicle currencies.

Table 10.1
Official Holdings of Reserve Assets, 1988, 1990, 1992

	Billions of Dollars			Percentage Distribution		
	1988	1990	1992	1988	1990	1992
Industrial Countries						
SDR and IMF Reserves	50	53	55	6%	6%	7%
Gold at Market Value	329	306	261	41%	34%	32%
Foreign Exchange	425	537	491	53%	60%	61%
Total Industrial Countries	*804*	*897*	*807*	*100%*	*100%*	*100%*
Developing Countries						
SDR and IMF Reserves	15	9	9	5%	2%	2%
Gold at Market Value	60	56	48	19%	15%	10%
Foreign Exchange	240	309	402	76%	83%	87%
Total Developing Countries	*316*	*374*	*459*	*100%*	*100%*	*100%*
Total All Countries						
SDR and IMF Reserves	65	63	64	6%	5%	5%
Gold at Market Value	389	362	309	35%	29%	24%
Foreign Exchange	665	846	893	59%	67%	71%
Total Official Reserves	*1,120*	*1,271*	*1,266*	*100%*	*100%*	*100%*
Gold Quantity (millions of ounces)						
Industrial Countries	801	796	785	84%	85%	84%
Developing Countries	147	145	145	16%	15%	16%
All Countries	*948*	*941*	*930*	*100%*	*100%*	*100%*

Source: International Monetary Fund, "1993 Annual Report," Washington, D.C.

In most cases, the foreign exchange component of international reserves constitutes monetary instruments of central governments or central banks and is the most liquid and least risky of available international investments. The rising supply of foreign currency reserves to meet the demand of expanded cross-border commerce has enabled governments to finance deficit spending by issuing monetary instruments. This process caused a worldwide increase in money supply that contributed to the global inflationary condition following abandonment of the gold standard in 1971.

Foreign exchange is also the principal component of the private-sector segment of the international monetary system. However, in contrast to the government-issued monetary instruments that comprise the foreign exchange component of official reserves, foreign exchange used in the private sector consists primarily of bank cross-border liabilities.[3] Table 9.2 shows the wide

Table 10.2
Share of National Currencies in Foreign Exchange Reserves, 1985–1991

	1985	1986	1987	1988	1989	1990	1991
Industrial Countries							
U.S. Dollar	65%	69%	71%	68%	60%	56%	52%
Japanese Yen	9%	8%	7%	7%	8%	10%	11%
Deutsche Mark	20%	17%	16%	17%	23%	22%	21%
Pound Sterling	2%	1%	1%	2%	1%	2%	2%
French Franc	0%	0%	0%	1%	1%	3%	5%
Swiss Franc	2%	2%	2%	2%	1%	1%	1%
Other or Unspecified	2%	3%	3%	3%	6%	6%	8%
Developing Countries							
U.S. Dollar	65%	63%	60%	58%	62%	61%	64%
Japanese Yen	7%	7%	9%	9%	7%	7%	8%
Deutsche Mark	10%	11%	11%	12%	11%	12%	11%
Pound Sterling	4%	5%	5%	6%	6%	6%	7%
French Franc	2%	2%	2%	2%	2%	2%	2%
Swiss Franc	3%	3%	3%	3%	2%	2%	2%
Other or Unspecified	9%	9%	10%	10%	10%	10%	6%
All Countries							
U.S. Dollar	65%	67%	68%	65%	60%	58%	56%
Japanese Yen	8%	8%	8%	8%	8%	9%	10%
Deutsche Mark	15%	15%	14%	16%	19%	19%	17%
Pound Sterling	3%	3%	2%	3%	3%	3%	4%
French Franc	1%	1%	1%	1%	1%	2%	4%
Swiss Franc	2%	2%	2%	2%	2%	1%	1%
Other or Unspecified	6%	4%	5%	5%	7%	8%	8%

Source: International Monetary Fund, "1993 Annual Report," Washington, D.C.

variety of national currencies used by the private sector. Nevertheless, the predominant currencies are bank deposits in the United States, Japan, and Britain representing 12 percent, 13 percent, and 15 percent, respectively, or a total of 40 percent of worldwide bank liabilities.

Although the international monetary system is based on multiple currencies, several attempts have been made for a universal currency. When the Bretton Woods fixed exchange rate system was in existence, a growing fear of insufficient gold supply to support global commercial activity combined with a desire to reduce dependence on the dollar triggered a search for an international money. In response, the IMF introduced the Special Drawing

Right (SDR) in 1970 to fill the need for a growing and flexible international money. However, the SDR was designed to act as a reserve currency for central banks and not as a commercially used monetary instrument.

A more recent monetary innovation introduced in 1979 is the ecu (acronym for European Currency Unit and also an ancient French coin), a medium of exchange for European commercial transactions and designed to circulate along with European national currencies. The ecu exchange rate is based on the weighted average of the EMS countries and has become an important element in the drive for European economic unification. Bonds and other credit instruments denominated in ecus have been issued for general public investment.

SDRs and ecus have had only limited success; and thus, despite these attempts at a single universal money, the goal remains elusive. The devastating 1930s depression expanded national government participation in economic activity, including a direct mandate to protect domestic employment. The disrupting influence of unregulated precious metal flows during the depression made control of the domestic money supply an essential element of government economic authority while creating a deep suspicion of a suprainternational currency. Today's global monetary system, composed of an extensive network of domestic financial markets, provides monetary instruments of flexibility and liquidity while remaining subject to national government supervision. Attempts to develop an international medium of exchange have, therefore, not received broad public or private support. While the current system has several weaknesses, there does not appear to be a better system that can provide the efficiency, flexibility, liquidity, government supervision, and wide support needed for a dynamic global economy. In addition, the current system avoids many contentious political issues best summarized as "who decides what face appears on the currency."[4]

Vehicle Currencies

In domestic economies, a nation's currency has a monopolistic position created by statutory authority that mandates its acceptance as legal tender for the payment of public and private debts. It is only compromised when the purchasing power is debased by runaway inflation. Internationally, there is no such monopoly, although by multilateral agreement such as Bretton Woods, member countries have agreed to the items that would be acceptable for transactions at the national government level. Instead, independent economic forces transform certain currencies into predominant international use. Using multiple currencies for the multiplicity of transactions exacts a cost in the currency-conversion process which can be substantially eliminated by the use of a single currency to settle all cross-border transactions. The choice of currency—the *vehicle currency*—depends on a number of factors, including availability, liquidity, transaction costs, and holding costs. These factors are, in turn, influenced by rates of inflation, exchange rate fluctuations, convertibility into other currencies, size of financial markets, wide and extensive cross-border commercial activity, and availability of supporting services.

Following World War II, the dominance of the U.S. economy in financing war recovery quickly made the U.S. dollar the predominant vehicle currency in the global economy. *Convertibility*—that is, the legal right of a foreigner to own a currency—is critical to the international monetary system; and until 1959, the U.S. dollar was the only major convertible currency. It became convenient for conducting international transactions requiring maintenance of large dollar holdings as working capital. This dominant role has continued because, compared to other currencies, the large volume and wide use lower transaction costs, administrative delay, and risks.

A country whose currency is used as a principal vehicle currency accrues several advantages. It becomes more convenient for residents to conduct international commerce, thereby reducing transaction costs. Domestic financial institutions gain business in currency and security exchange. Trading partners are willing to exchange goods and services to accrue vehicle currency balances to finance further trade. Political power and prestige are associated with vehicle currencies.

However, status as a vehicle currency presents major disadvantages. By definition, a vehicle currency is held in quantity by foreign entities, making it subject to greater exchange rate fluctuation and impeding central bank conduct of domestic monetary policy. To be effective for international commerce, a vehicle currency should retain a stable international value requiring a country to follow a fixed exchange rate regime. For this reason, leading industrial countries such as Germany and Japan have resisted the use of their currencies as vehicle currencies. In particular, they were concerned that increased demand for their currencies would appreciate the exchange rate to the disadvantage of export industries. With the establishment of the EMS in 1979 based on the Deutsche mark as the anchor currency, Germany acquiesced to the increased use of its currency for international transactions. By the early 1990s, the Deutsche mark was the second-largest vehicle currency after the U.S. dollar not only because of the expanded use in EMS but also because of its growing use in Eastern Europe.

Despite the U.S. dollar's diminishing share of international reserves and cross-border commercial transactions, it is the leading vehicle currency, playing a unique role in the international monetary system. The magnitude of the U.S. economy in the global economy; its openness to international commerce; its early dominance following World War II; and its continued global political, military, and economic leadership naturally places the U.S. dollar in great demand. Table 10.3 is an analysis of currency denominations of external financial obligations in 1989, showing the dominant use of the dollar. In foreign-issued Eurocurrency deposits, bank loans, and bonds, the U.S. dollar's

Table 10.3
Denomination of External Financial Obligations, 1989

Currency	Market Share (Percentage)		
	Eurocurrency Deposits	Bank Loans	Bond Issues
U.S. Dollar	59.7	77.0	51.9
JapaneseYen	5.5	5.3	8.3
Deutsche Mark	13.9	3.2	6.4
Pound Sterling	3.1	6.4	6.8
Canadian Dollar	0.0	0.0	4.0
French Franc	1.3	0.0	2.1
Swiss Franc	4.9	0.4	7.5
ecu	3.2	4.6	5.2
Other	8.4	3.1	7.8
Total	100.0	100.0	100.0

Source: Peter Newman, *The New Palgrave Dictionary of Money and Finance,* Vol. 1 (London: Macmillan, 1992), p. 697.

market share exceeds 50 percent in all categories. No other currency is so dominant, although after only ten years from its initial introduction, the ecu has become significant in relation to other European currencies.

The need for dollar working balances has also continued because prices of many internationally traded products are quoted and invoiced in dollars. Many internationally traded commodities such as oil are quoted on international exchanges in terms of dollars, and final settlement is in dollars. Many companies believe that quoting prices in dollars and accepting dollars as payment is a competitive advantage offsetting the risks and administrative costs of currency conversion. U.S. dollars are the principal currency used by central banks when intervening in the currency markets.

Although criticism of U.S. economic policy is expressed from time to time by the international community and there is a major transformation in the global economy—diminishing the role of the U.S. economy—the U.S. dollar remains the principal reserve currency, giving U.S. monetary policy great influence in global affairs. The U.S. government—in particular, the Federal Reserve—has played a leading role in maintaining the viability, stability, and integrity of the international monetary system, giving the U.S. dollar an added important function as a dependable store of value. In a floating exchange rate system, *dependable store of value* is a relative term meaning dependable in relation to other available forms of international money. Following abandonment of the Bretton Woods fixed exchange rate system in 1971, the U.S. dollar's exchange rate rose and subsequently fell. However, since the end of

1987, the Federal Reserve has worked to maintain a stable trade-weighted exchange rate.

Currency Market Overview

In response to the collapse of the Bretton Woods fixed exchange rate system, currency markets rapidly expanded their trading volume; and new financial centers arose to take advantage of the opportunities offered by floating exchange rates.[5] Since 1987, annual daily turnover in the international currency markets tripled, reaching $1 trillion a day by 1993. Spot transactions—that is, immediate delivery of the item—still remain the primary currency trading activity, which constituted 50 percent of all trades conducted in the London currency market during 1992. The next-largest currency trading activity is swap exchanges (47%), followed by forward contracts, futures, and options. The major currency markets are listed in Table 10.4, with the largest markets located in Britain, the United States, and Japan where *net daily* foreign exchange turnover in April 1992 averaged $300, $192, and $126 billion, respectively.

Table 10.4
Average Daily Net Foreign Exchange Turnover in Major Centers, April 1992

Country	Billions of Dollars	
United States	192	
Japan	126	
Germany	57	
Britain	300	
Canada	23	
Total Matrix Countries		698
Switzerland	68	
Singapore	68	
Hong Kong	61	
France	36	
Australia	30	
Denmark	28	
Sweden	21	
Total Other Countries		312
Total Daily Turnover		1,010

Source: Fact Sheet, Bank of England, February 1993.

Currency trading is conducted by a wide range of financial institutions, including commercial banks, security houses, nonfinancial corporations, central banks, mutual funds, pension funds, and insurance companies. The primary market makers are the thirty to fifty largest commercial banks along with a few large security houses. To manage the enormous currency trading volume, sophisticated electronic payment systems have been developed to settle daily currency balances in a manner similar to bank check clearing systems. The largest payment system is the Clearing House Interbank Payments System (CHIPS) owned by the New York Clearing House which, in turn, is owned by major New York banks. Settlement is made through a special account with the Federal Reserve Bank of New York. The next-largest payment system is the London-based Clearing House Association Payments System (CHAPS) with fourteen banks and the Bank of England as members.

Eurocurrency Market

A feature of the international monetary system that further distinguishes it from domestic monetary systems and adds complexity to international commerce is the Eurocurrency market. This term describes an international currency form first used in Europe but now an integral part of both the international monetary system and the broader global financial markets. Eurocurrency consists of cross-border claims and liabilities denominated in national currencies other than the country of the obligor and obligee. Between 80 and 90 percent of cross-border bank liabilities are estimated to be denominated in dollars; that is, the liabilities of banks, regardless of country of location, are payable to foreign holders in dollars. Thus, when a bank's dollar deposit liability comes due, the paying bank technically must purchase dollars in the currency market in order to make remittance to the customer. In practice, payment is made in the currency desired by the customer at the agreed dollar rate of exchange.

For example, a British bank may incur a Eurocurrency deposit liability to a French holder in the amount of £100.00 payable in dollars. If, at the time of payment, the exchange rate is £/$1.50, then technically the bank must pay the French holder $150.00. More likely, the French holder will want francs. If the dollar-to-franc exchange rate is Frfr/$0.20 then the French holder will receive Frfr 750. This transaction also creates a rate of exchange between the pound and franc of £/Frfr7.5 which may differ from the market exchange rate for direct pound-to-franc currency trades, creating opportunities for arbitrage currency traders.

The predominant use of dollar-denominated Eurocurrencies has important implications for the international monetary system and an example of the exchange rate management problem facing a country whose currency is used as a vehicle currency. Because U.S. cross-border bank liabilities are a proportionately smaller share of total cross-border bank liabilities denominated in dollars, bilateral dollar exchange rates may not correctly reflect U.S. cross-border commercial activity. Quoted bilateral dollar exchange rates are key economic indicators influencing other economic activity, and the distortions caused by the Eurocurrency market may contribute to inaccurate business and financial decisions. In addition, in the event of a crisis, the scramble to fulfill Eurocurrency commitments by buying or selling dollars could create harmful exchange rate volatility. Avoiding such volatility requires careful coordination among the central banks and places pressure on U.S. monetary authorities to pursue policies to stabilize the exchange rate at the expense of domestic economic needs. Because the U.S. government has been less willing to sacrifice domestic economic needs to maintain stable exchange rates, countries have been accelerating the use of other currencies to act as vehicle currencies.

INSTABILITY IN THE INTERNATIONAL MONETARY SYSTEM

Supplying sufficient quantities of money for stable economic growth while in the midst of diverging business cycles and economic policies is a difficult task. While the existing international monetary system has successfully fulfilled this task, the flexibility needed to provide necessary money supply has created several weaknesses that threaten continued economic development. Fortunately, many of these weaknesses are understood, and steps have been taken and continue to be taken to minimize or eliminate them. Nevertheless, these weaknesses remain and must be considered in economic trend analysis.

Overview

Cross-border currency trading volume of $1 trillion a day is often cited as evidence of the principal weakness that threatens to destabilize the international monetary system. However, the average daily trading volume solely in U.S. government securities in 1990 was $400 billion. Hence, a worldwide daily volume in currencies is large but not that much different from the daily volume of other large organized financial markets necessary to mobilize savings for investment. Historically, despite such volatile monetary situations, economies have functioned effectively.

The present multiple currency–based international monetary system resembles the rough-and-tumble banking and monetary system of the United States after 1837 when the demise of the Second Bank of the United States deprived the country of a functioning central bank. Often referred to as the period of *wildcat* banking, domestic money became a combination of government-minted coin and vault gold together with notes issued by numerous private banks located throughout the country. These bank notes were redeemable in coin or precious metals and circulated as money but at discount rates determined by the creditability and perceived financial strength of the issuing bank.

Coin and precious metals were in short supply, and a rapidly expanding economy created a growing demand for a medium of exchange. In response, banks rapidly expanded note issues augmented by a surge of new banks, often undercapitalized and imprudently managed, located in the new western territories where the mountain lions roamed—hence the term wildcat banks. The limited supply of coin and precious metals to meet note redemption and the absence of a central monetary authority to provide emergency liquidity caused many bank failures and a highly unstable monetary system. Nevertheless, the American economy grew and prospered.

Price volatility arising from expanded volume of currency trading is inherent in a floating or managed exchange rate system and is the accepted cost factored into the transaction pricing for market liquidity and flexibility in the face of diverging economic conditions and government policy. Nevertheless, exchange rate volatility is of great concern as an indicator of deeper underlying economic imbalances. Despite the liquidity and efficiency of the international monetary system, its present multicurrency composition is a source of worrisome instability because of four weaknesses not present in domestic monetary systems:

1. Growing speculative currency trading by financial institutions
2. Lack of an effective international monetary authority
3. Cost of exchange rate management
4. Foreign policy intrusion

Speculative Currency Trading

The growth of currencies as the mainstay of the international monetary system is similar to the growth of private bank notes that created the wildcat banking period. However, unlike wildcat banking, international monetary instability is not from lack of precious metals that bedeviled both the American and international monetary systems until the Depression, when abandonment of the gold standard prevented any redemption of currencies for gold. Increased currency trading combined with fluctuating exchange rates exposes financial institutions to collapse from speculative pressures.

Orderly changes in exchange rates is a normal part of the adjustment process as national economies reconcile their domestic economic situation to the global economic environment. The effect of exchange rate fluctuations on domestic and international commerce is discussed in Chapter 4. Financial institutions are expanding their currency trading activity beyond normal transaction needs, making speculative profits from such activity a separate profit center. Widely fluctuating and unpredictable exchange rates, combined with the growth in currency speculation, increases the exposure of many financial institutions to unusually heavy losses from unfortunate exchange positions, increasing the likelihood of the collapse of undercapitalized financial institutions with the possibility that panic will spread to other financial institutions and to the currency markets.

To a limited extent, the currency markets have responded to the volatility problem through a series of innovative techniques. Exchange rate fluctuations attract large sums of capital, providing currency markets tremendous liquidity and, therefore, the ability to engage in arbitrage operations to smooth out the fluctuations, providing a market-driven sense of orderliness. Derivative devices such as options, futures, and forward contracts have been widely used in commodity markets to help smooth price fluctuations and are achieving similar success in the currency markets. However, these techniques are not without risk, requiring participating companies to be adequately capitalized and managed.[6] The high leverage that has developed with these techniques means that the failure of one participating firm can have a devastating ripple effect.

Fortunately, this weakness has been recognized.[7] Monetary authorities of most industrial countries regulate the foreign exchange position of their domestic banks usually by placing a cap on the net currency position in relation to the bank's capital. There is also some regulatory oversight regarding disclosure of foreign holdings. Partially in response to this concern, central banks of the industrial nations adopted the Basle accords in 1989, which, among other things, required an increase in capital of commercial banks, thereby avoiding the undercapitalized banking system that characterized the wildcat period of U.S. monetary history.

However, there is a glaring weakness in this oversight. Industrial corporations, pension funds, and offshore mutual funds generally do not have specific regulatory oversight over their participation in the international currency market, making them vulnerable to overinvestment in currency trades to shore up lagging profits. Furthermore, the lack of management controls and experienced personnel has prevented companies from fully insulating themselves from inappropriate currency trading.

Lack of International Monetary Authority

A far more serious source of instability is lack of a central bank or monetary authority with the policy-making power or financial resources capable of operating an international monetary system. The supply and regulation of currencies is left to each country's monetary authority who are primarily concerned with domestic rather than global economic issues. International monetary policy occurs only when agreed upon by the principal monetary authorities and is effective only when supported by the central banks of the large industrial nations where sufficient resources can be used to carry out the policy.

Underlying much of current international economic thinking is that through floating exchange rates, each country is free to pursue its own domestic economic policy. However, in doing so, a country cannot ignore the transmission of economic conditions through the cross-border activity conducted by its trading partners. For example, in a floating exchange rate regime, a home country instituting an expansive monetary policy to increase demand would anticipate a fall in its exchange rate. Such a decline would cause an increase in its exports through lower prices and a decrease in its imports through higher prices. However, such an economic result assumes that trading partners will not initiate their own monetary policy in response. Competitive devaluations contributed to the chaotic economic conditions of the Great Depression.

Lack of a strong international monetary authority imposes a great burden on individual national monetary authorities attempting to stabilize international monetary conditions. If a central bank had sufficient international reserves, it could manage its currency exchange rate and at the same time conduct a monetary policy solely for domestic economic conditions. The growing volume in international currency, the growing number of financial institutions conducting currency trading as an investment opportunity, and the growing ability of the currency market to move swiftly and concentrate on a weak currency are making it impossible for many countries to maintain stable exchange rates without abandoning domestic economic policies.

Cost of Exchange Rate Management

Managing exchange rate fluctuations absorbs considerable effort, expense, and financial resources where combined costs are often disproportionately shared by countries, causing many monetary authorities to eschew any global economic responsibility. Managing exchange rate volatility through intervention in the currency markets exposes monetary authorities to risks of sizable trading losses as they attempt to restrain speculation and panic while more extensive exchange rate management requires domestic interest rate levels contrary to the needs of domestic economic conditions. In either situation, the cost is borne by only a few countries. Most monetary authorities have worked out procedures by which to share the cost and responsibility of exchange rate management. However, many economic conditions cannot be foreseen, resulting in continued disproportionate absorption of exchange rate management costs.

Foreign Policy Concerns

Nationalism remains a potent political force in international relations, creating continuous disputes and tensions. With the demise of the bipolar international structure and the return of multipolar international environment, economic issues and trade friction will dominate international relations. Use of currencies as the principal form of international exchange will become increasingly enmeshed in foreign policy issues because of the prestige and economic advantage associated with a national currency's status as a vehicle currency.

Currency issues have already been interjected into foreign policy issues. Although traded internationally, currencies are nevertheless claims on the respective domestic financial systems under the control of the respective national governments. One of the weapons to force resolution of international disputes is to freeze the assets of foreign claim holders. The U.S. dollar is the principal vehicle currency; and since 1945, the United States has frozen assets of nationals residing in a number of countries, including Cuba, Iran, and Iraq. As the principal reserve currency, declining U.S. dollar exchange rates have diminished its international currency reserve value for many countries, contributing to contentious responses to U.S. requests for support on other issues. While there is no reasonable substitute to the present international monetary system of multiple currencies, it is likely that countries will diversify their foreign currency holdings, which will probably result in further increases in currency trading volume and greater exchange rate volatility.

CAPITAL FLOWS

With the increasing use of national currencies for transacting international commerce, the capital flow process has become more complex than indicated by the term *capital flows*, making it one of the most misunderstood terms in international economic analysis. As often used, the term *capital flow* implies a flow of new money between the home economy and foreign sources. When gold and other precious metals were money for domestic and international purposes, a capital flow could indeed constitute a flow of money. Terms and concepts describing international commerce, such as capital flow, developed during this period are still used but do not accurately describe the true activity.

Capital Flows Explained

With no true international money, capital flow does not represent a cross-border flow of money in the classical sense (except in those rare instances where the domestic monetary system has collapsed, forcing residents to use foreign currency as a medium of exchange). A nation's money supply is solely controlled by its own domestic monetary authority. Under the existing international monetary system, capital flow represents a combination of two types of cross-border transactions: ownership change of existing financial assets and increase in financial assets to support cross-border commercial activity.

Each of these two types of capital flow transactions has different economic consequences. In the ownership change, residents of two countries exchange bank deposits in their respective domestic financial systems. Hence, through the currency market process, existing home-country bank deposits owned by home-country residents become owned by nonresidents with a similar transaction occurring in the other country. Under conventional balance-of-payments accounting the transaction is reported as a capital inflow and outflow. However, there is no immediate effect on a country's money supply. Such a capital flow could constitute an increase in the home-country money supply only if the cross-border acquisition of the home-country bank deposit was part of a home-country bank loan. In this situation, the home-country money supply statistics would record the loan as an increase in the monetary aggregates. Thus, the bank loan constitutes an expansion of the home-country money supply, not an inflow of foreign money.

On the other hand, this ownership change could have important international economic consequences not immediately registered in balance-of-payments reports. The ownership change is generally conducted through the international currency markets, affecting the bilateral exchange rate between the two countries. As discussed in Chapter 4, the exchange rate change could have a wide-ranging impact, affecting the competitive prices of internationally traded goods, value of financial assets, and attractiveness to foreign investors.

Another, but more subtle, economic consequence of ownership change is that cross-border holders may utilize home currency in a manner different from home-country residents. For example, cross-border holders tend to be investors, whereas home-country residents are both consumers and investors. Furthermore, will the cross-border investors place their newly acquired money in stocks, bonds, or real estate?

The other type of capital flow transaction is an increase in domestic financial assets to pay for commercial imports. This transaction type more closely resembles the classic capital flow definition but with some major differences. If a trading partner expands its domestic money supply to finance exports to the home country, then home-country credit has increased, although the money supply remains unchanged. Under this scenario, trading-partner exporters are selling their goods and services in exchange for financial instruments of the home economy. Although the home-country money supply has not increased, the trading-partner money supply has increased, counteracting the home-country monetary policy. With lost control over home-country monetary policy and expanded trading-partner export financing, home-country credit may grow faster than its money supply, creating domestic inflation and other imbalances that are similar to a home-country expansion of the money supply.

Under the classic gold standard capital flow, the international money supply remained static so that a capital flow theoretically caused one country to experience a decline in its money supply while another country experienced a rise. Consequently, the gold standard tended to be deflationary and was favored as a means of controlling inflation. Under present currency-based international monetary system, monetary authorities have greater independence in domestic monetary policy but less control over domestic credit because the rules and definition of eligible credit are determined by the trading partners

extending the credit. Consequently, this type of capital flow tends to be inflationary and has contributed to the inflationary tendencies of the post–World
War II global economy.

When the ownership change and financial asset capital flow activities are
netted together, they may appear inconsequential. However, if the capital
inflow constitutes acquisitions of short-term bank deposits while the outflow
is long-term investments, the domestic financial system becomes vulnerable
to economic shocks often experienced by banks that borrow short and lend
long. The U.S. financial system experienced such a dislocation in the early
1980s. Commercial banks had received significant offshore funds from
Middle East countries that had accumulated large dollar holdings in payment
of oil during the high prices of the late 1970s. The commercial banks then lent
the funds in long-term loans to developing countries. As the defaults in these
loans grew, the banks nevertheless needed to keep interest rates high to avoid
losing customer deposits. Accordingly, even after recovering from the 1982
recession, U.S. interest rates remained higher than necessary, allowing foreign countries to finance exports to the United States and causing dislocation
among a number of American industries.

Impact of Capital Flows

The previous description of modern-day capital flows has important implications to economic trend analysis. The increase in the financial assets type
of capital flow has an inflationary bias, causing monetary authorities to conduct their monetary policies with a principal concern of combating inflation,
whereas monetary authorities in the past were more concerned with deflationary pressures. However, traditional means of combating inflation through
tight monetary policy become less effective, not only because of the lack of
cooperation from trading partners but also because of the shift in burden.

Under traditional international economic analysis, a country attracted
cross-border capital by raising interest rates higher than prevailing world rates
and then using the acquired capital to pay for imported goods. Hence, the
primary cost and burden of attracting capital inflows fell on the home country, giving its monetary authorities more control over economic conditions.
International business of many developing countries are indeed conducted in
this manner, making interest rates and stable exchange rates a key factor in
attracting capital flows.

Today, nations have industries and regions dependent on export sales, making it imperative that they successfully sell products and services in the global marketplace. Consequently, the pressure to accept foreign currency in
payment becomes irresistible, making competitive interest rates a less significant factor for attracting capital while causing exchange rate changes to adjust for any trade imbalance. Here, the capital flow burden falls on the

exporting country to devise means for redeploying the foreign currency surpluses accumulated by the exporters. Historically, this burden was met by the rise of great financial centers that provided a global finance infrastructure and central banks that pursued monetary policies and exchange rate regimes in support of these financial centers, hence the rise of the great international financial centers of Amsterdam, London, New York, and Tokyo. In the 1980s, the United States financed its trade deficits through the ability and rapid expansion of the Tokyo financial market supported by Bank of Japan's easy monetary policy.

NOTES

1. Robert Triffin, *Our International Monetary System* (New York: Random House, 1968) discusses the historical development of international reserves.

2. An excellent discussion of post–World War II international monetary developments by two individuals that helped shaped government policy is found in Paul Volcker and Toyoo Gyohten, *Changing Fortunes* (New York: Times Books, 1992). As the global economy encompasses more industrial countries, making it difficult for any one country to exert decisive economic leadership, the comments of these two individuals underscore the difficulty in coordinating disparate economic systems.

3. Alessandro Leipold et al., *International Capital Markets* (Washington, D.C.: International Monetary Fund, 1991).

4. Frank T. Murphy, comments to the author, June 24, 1994.

5. A comprehensive analysis and description of the international currency market is Morris Goldstein et al., *International Capital Markets*, Part I (Washington, D.C.: International Monetary Fund, April 1993).

6. For central bank studies on derivatives, see *Recent Developments in International Interbank Relations* (Basle, Switzerland: Bank for International Settlements, October 1992), and *Derivatives: Report of an Internal Working Group* (London: Bank of England, April 1993).

7. For a summary of regulatory oversight performed by major industrial countries, see Goldstein et al., *International Capital Markets*, Part I.

CHAPTER 11

Central Banking

Virtually every major industrial country has as its principal monetary authority a central bank whose actions are intensely watched for the direction of monetary policy and the impact on economic trends. In the absence of a single international monetary authority, central bank actions not only affect the economic conditions of their respective countries but also have an enormous impact on the international monetary system and cross-border transmission of economic conditions. Accordingly, further elaboration on central banks and their influence on the domestic and global economy will enhance the use of the international matrix.

GENERAL FUNCTION

Central banking first began in 1668 with the establishment of the Swedish Ricksbank. However, it was the Bank of England, chartered in 1694 (and celebrating its three hundredth anniversary in 1994), that pioneered many of the monetary policy techniques used by modern central banks. Until acquired by the national government in 1946, the Bank of England was unusual in being a private bank devoted through historical tradition to the duties of central banking. In contrast, the United States operated without a central bank from the demise of the Second Bank of the United States in 1837 until 1913 when, by legislative action, Congress established the Federal Reserve System as a government agency to act as a central bank with a governing body semi-independent of government control. The Federal Reserve system has become a model emulated by other countries seeking to establish a semi-independent central bank. Table 11.1 lists the central banks of major countries, the date of their creation, and their principal governing bodies.

Through nearly 300 years of experience, developments in economic theories, and changes in national economic policy, the primary functions of central banks have evolved to their present orientation:

• Formulate and implement monetary policy.

• Regulate commercial banks and other depository institutions.

Table 11.1
Central Banks of Selected Countries

Country/Central Bank	Founded	Governing Body	Monetary Policy Committee
United States			
Federal Reserve	1913	Board of Governors	Open Market Committee
Japan			
Bank of Japan	1882	Policy Board	(Note 1)
Germany			
Deutsche Bundesbank	1957	Central Bank Board	Directorate
France			
Banque de France	1803		Monetary Policy Committee (Note 2)
Britain			
Bank of England	1694	Court of Directors	(Note 1)
Switzerland			
Swiss National Bank	1907	Bank Council	Management Board
China			
People's Bank of China	1948		(Note 1)
Canada			
Bank of Canada	1935	Board of Directors	(Note 1)
Mexico			
Banco de Mexico	1925		(Note 1)

Source: Schaefer Brothers.
Note1: Monetary policy directed by central government or finance ministry.
Note 2: Banque de France became independent effective 1994.

- Act as a lender of last resort in the event of a pending financial collapse of a financial or business institution.
- Supervise domestic bank activities in foreign countries.
- Act as fiscal agent for the national government.
- Hold the bank reserves of all or a majority of the commercial banks.
- Hold the nation's principal international reserves, including gold and foreign currency.
- Rediscount and loan against high-grade commercial paper and other collateral for member banks.
- Assist in check collection.
- Implement government-mandated credit policies.

Most industrial country central banks share several other similarities. They are owned or controlled by the central government, and there is generally a governing body or committee within the bank responsible for developing and implementing central bank policy. For central banks independent from their central governments, monetary policy is formulated and implemented by separate committees, although authority is still shared with a government finance ministry such as the Treasury departments in the United States and Britain and the Ministry of Finance in Japan. The degree of influence or control by the national government over monetary policy varies from country to country; but all central banks are aware that their authority is subject to public scrutiny and legislative oversight, making them sensitive to the same public pressures being exerted on the government.[1]

A distinguishing characteristic of most central banks is that they are granted a monopoly on the issuance and control of domestic monetary instruments constituting legal tender for discharging all public and private debts. They also hold the nation's domestic and international monetary reserves. These two functions make them uniquely capable of implementing monetary policy, acting as lenders of last resort, and providing assistance to commercial banks when encountering difficulties converting their deposit liabilities into domestic currency. Central banks normally restrict their business to commercial and other central banks, although several central banks—notably the Bank of France—continue to conduct some normal banking business.

Operationally, the central bank is responsible for coordinating, safeguarding, and influencing domestic financial markets to provide a steady flow of money and credit to the economic system consistent with growth, price stability, and full employment. In carrying out its responsibilities, the central bank attempts to anticipate economic problems and implement monetary policies guiding the credit markets in adjusting to changing economic conditions.

While all central bank functions impact the financial system, it is the formulation and implementation of monetary policy that has the greatest impact on the domestic economy and cross-border commercial activity. Monetary policy has the twin objectives of price stability and economic growth, but central banks tend to differ on the emphasis placed on either of these two objectives.[2] For example, the U.S. Federal Reserve Act mandates that the Federal Reserve "shall maintain long-run growth of the monetary and credit aggregates commensurate with the economy's long-run potential to increase production, so as to promote effectively the goals of maximum employment, stable prices, and moderate long-term interest rates." In practice, the Federal Reserve generally emphasizes price stability as the principal means of achieving these mandated objectives, since low interest rates and stable economic growth should lead to full employment. A few countries, notably Germany, mandate by law that price stability is the principal objective of monetary policy.

In implementing monetary policy, central banks utilize, almost exclusively, the following five methods:

1. Money supply operations
2. Official interest rates
3. Reserve requirements
4. Credit controls
5. Foreign-exchange operations

Money Supply Operations

Money supply operations constitute central bank management of the rate of growth in the domestic money supply. Generally, three types of operating methods are used: open-market operations, collateralized loans, and shifts in government deposits. All three operations are a means by which the central bank influences commercial bank reserves and interest rates and, therefore, the ability to make new loans and increase the domestic money supply. Use of these three operating methods is a function of historical custom and the nature of a country's domestic financial market.

In open-market operations, the central bank purchases and sells short-term securities debiting or crediting the accounts of commercial banks by the amount of security transactions, thereby changing their monetary base. With a large portfolio in marketable securities, a central bank engages in sufficient daily trading volume to affect security prices and their interest rate yields. The Federal Reserve uses this method by buying and selling government securities in a process originally developed to support the large government borrowings necessary in World War II. The Bundesbank and many other central banks also use this method but often include private securities such as bankers' acceptances.

In collateralized loans, the central bank influences the monetary base of commercial banks by its willingness to extend short-term loans collateralized by government and other securities which increase bank funds and the ability to increase commercial loans and the money supply. This method is heavily used by the Bundesbank, Bank of France, and other countries because the direct interaction with the commercial banks provides more direct influence over short-term interest rates than otherwise available under open-market operations.

Shifting central government funds into and out of deposit accounts at commercial banks is the least-used operating method. Tax collection and budget expenditures make central governments major customers of the commercial banking system. A transfer of deposits from commercial banks to the central bank has an impact on the monetary base similar to open-market operations, although it can be more immediate and direct. When the central bank wants to tighten monetary conditions, government deposits with commercial banks are withdrawn to the central bank. When an expansionary monetary policy is desired, the central bank deposits funds with the commercial banks. The Bank of Canada follows this method.

Central bank money supply operations may not always achieve the intended result. As previously discussed, if the banking system does not conform its lending activity to the monetary policy of the central bank, there may be a divergence between interest rates and growth in money supply, thereby nullifying the central bank's monetary policy. Nevertheless, with the ability to directly and immediately influence the supply of money and credit, money supply operations are one of the most powerful capabilities of the central bank implemented by day-to-day trading and other operations of the central bank's experienced staff.

One of the many policy debates is whether money supply operations should target interest rate levels or liquid asset levels and, therefore, the money supply. While the distinction is important for internal central bank management, both elements influence economic trends. For example, if the central bank engages in the purchase of securities, it tends to both reduce interest rates because of an increase in securities prices caused by the purchases, and increase the money supply because of the credit to commercial bank accounts that the central bank makes in payment. Conversely, if the central bank engages in the sale of securities, it tends to increase interest rates because of the decline in securities prices and to decrease the money supply because of the debit of commercial bank accounts as payment of the purchases.

Official Interest Rates

In addition to money supply operations, central banks influence interest rate levels by the official rates they charge commercial banks and other financial institutions when borrowing from central banks. These official interest rates are widely publicized, setting the base rate other financial institutions use to determine commercial loan rates. As described in Table 11.2, central bank lending methods vary but are generally divided into two principal methods. One method is the direct loan, which may be secured or unsecured by collateral.

Table 11.2
Official Interest Rates of Selected Central Banks

Central Bank	Official Rate	Description
Federal Reserve	Fed Funds rate	Interest rate for borrowing reserve funds charged by commercial banks
	Discount rate	Interest rate on short-term loans to commercial banks
Bank of Japan	Official Discount rate	Interest rate on short-term loans to financial institutions
Bundesbank	Lombard rate	Interest rate for collateralized short-term loans to financial institutions to bridge temporary reserve shortages (considered ceiling on short-term interest rates and above discount rate)
	Repurchase rate	Interest rate on securities repurchase agreements
	Discount rate	Interest rate for rediscounting eligible assets of financial institutions (considered floor on short-term interest rates and below Lombard rate)
Bank of England	Dealing rates	Interest rate on rediscounts of bills or loans to discount houses
Bank of France	Tender rate	Interest rate on repurchase agreements
	Rate on five- to ten-day repurchase agreements	Interest rate on five- to ten-day repurchase agreements for emergency funding
Bank of Canada	Bank rate	Interest rate on loans to financial institutions

Source: Dallas S. Betten et al., *The Conduct of Monetary Policy in the Major Industrial Countries,* Occasional Paper No. 70 (Washington, D.C.: International Monetary Fund, July 1990), p. 4.

The other method is central bank purchase at a discount of eligible paper such as short-term government securities with an obligation of the commercial bank to buy back the instruments.

The Federal Reserve uses the direct loan method. It prefers that commercial banks borrow from other sources, leaving the Federal Reserve as the lender of last resort. In this situation, the Federal Reserve's discount rate is official but is less significant because open-market operations are the principal means of influencing short-term interest rates. A more important interest rate is the Fed Funds rate charged for borrowings between commercial banks to satisfy reserve requirements mandated by the Federal Reserve and directly influenced by its open-market operations. The Bank of England, Bundesbank, the Bank of France, and many other central banks prefer discounting eligible paper using their quoted rates in the daily money market to directly influence short-term interest rates.

Thus, depending on the practice of the particular central bank, the official interest rates may or may not reflect a market rate of interest. For example, the Federal Reserve through the discount rate and the Fed Funds rate attempts to directly influence short-term interest rate levels, while the Bank of Canada pegs its Bank rate at twenty-five basis points above the average interest rate on ninety-one-day Canadian treasury bills. Most short-term interest rates will adjust in the same direction as a change in the official rate but will move to a market rate a few weeks later. Nevertheless, as an item of the commercial bank cost of funds, official interest rates influence short-term interest rates.

Official interest rates are generally used to signal changes in monetary policy that is both unambiguous and well publicized. When the official interest rate changes are in small increments over a long time period, it generally indicates a gradual change in central bank policy or simply an attempt to adjust to the market rate. However, if there are successive rate changes over a short period, it usually means that the central bank is implementing a changed monetary policy. A rise in the official interest rate indicates that the central bank is attempting to curtail credit. A decline in the official interest rate indicates that the central bank is attempting to increase credit.

Reserve Requirements

To protect bank liquidity, most industrial countries require that commercial banks maintain a minimum amount of reserve assets usually consisting of vault cash, deposits with the central bank, and eligible short-term marketable securities. From time to time, the central bank prescribes the minimum amount of required reserves usually stated as a percentage of bank deposits. An upward adjustment in the reserve requirement curtails commercial bank lendable funds while a reduction of the ratio increases their availability. Reserve requirements generally vary according to deposit type such as time and checking or demand deposits, with time deposits usually subject to a lower reserve ratio because of lesser daily withdrawals compared to demand deposits.

Changes in reserve requirements are the heavy hand of monetary policy because they can have an immediate and powerful influence on banks and their lending operations. Implementing monetary policy is like steering a speeding car over an icy road with money supply operations providing a flexibility that allows the central bank to study the economy's reaction and make minor adjustments while limiting the risk of "oversteering." Although intended as a means of protecting bank liquidity rather than an instrument of monetary policy, some central banks are further deemphasizing mandated reserve requirements in favor of reliance on prudent but flexible bank management practices to set reserve levels necessary for banking needs.[3] Canada has gone so far as to completely eliminate mandatory reserve ratios.

Nevertheless, central banks of the United States, Japan, and Germany still believe that mandatory reserve requirements in the form of deposits with the central bank are important for providing reserves essential to effective open-market operations and stable money markets. As commercial banks increase currency positions to meet expanding international needs, central banks are considering extending special reserve requirements to the foreign holdings of bank deposit accounts. However, many banks have resisted such action because the added cost of low-income earning reserves would place them at a disadvantage compared to banks operating in countries that maintain lower or no reserve requirements.

Although reserve requirements have become less important, should unbridled credit expansion threaten increased inflation, consideration may be given to their more active use. Decontrol of interest rates in the 1980s, combined with more independent and conflicting monetary policies among trading partners, has made it difficult for central banks to implement successful monetary policies that can contain inflation. The blunter power of the reserve requirement may become necessary.

Interest Rate and Credit Controls

Most central banks have some authority to directly regulate interest rates and credit which were widely used up to the late 1970s when the general movement toward deregulation began. Ceilings on interest paid by financial institutions were the most common form of credit controls which have been phased out by most countries. However, at the end of 1989, 49 percent of Japanese banks were still subject to some interest rate limitation. An important credit regulation administered for many years by the Federal Reserve and currently in force is the *margin account*—the amount of credit brokerage houses can provide for the purchase of marketable securities. In serious situations, national governments often adopt interest and credit controls usually delegating day-to-day implementation to the central bank.

Foreign-Exchange Operations

Foreign-exchange operations are the buying and selling of currency in the international currency markets to influence exchange rates. It is a central bank operation uniquely important to the international monetary system. These operations also include "swap" arrangements whereby cooperating central banks temporarily swap their respective currencies, while the foreign currency obtained in the swap may be sold or exchanged but then must be reacquired and returned to the other central bank.

The role of foreign-exchange operations varies depending on the monetary policy and type of exchange rate regime. Under a free-floating or managed float regime, the central bank engages in foreign-exchange operations to maintain an orderly market so that exchange rate changes will adjust gradually to market levels rather than by wide fluctuations characteristic of share markets. Under a fixed rate regime, in conjunction with other monetary methods, the central bank undertakes large foreign-exchange operations to maintain the fixed exchange rate even at the risk of sizable losses from exchange rate swings.

With daily foreign exchange volume exceeding $1 trillion, the ability of a central bank to maintain specified exchange rate levels solely by foreign-exchange operations without a high risk of loss is becoming increasingly difficult. Accordingly, counteracting exchange rate changes through direct central bank intervention in the currency markets requires considerable financial resources. For many industrial countries, intervention absorbs at least $1 billion, while U.S. intervention has often required more than $4 billion.

Because of the limited available resources, successful exchange rate management is a combination of foreign-exchange operations, interest rate levels, and other monetary policy tools.[4] Central banks have also developed an interventionist strategy to maximize the impact of such currency intervention.[5] Intervention appears best achieved if it is done unexpectedly and with much publicity, causing the markets to react in tandem with the intervention and without time for currency traders to assess the central bank's ability to carry out the interventionist policy. When coordinated with other central banks, intervention gains considerable credibility. However, with daily currency market volume exceeding $1 trillion, central bank intervention can maintain orderly currency markets but cannot compel markets to move in a direction contrary to the fundamental economic factors influencing exchange rates.

CENTRAL BANKING REACTION TO BUSINESS CYCLE

Notwithstanding the powerful tools at their disposal, central banks have a most difficult and awesome task in carrying out monetary policy. Most central banks are directed by a governing committee; and it is not unusual to find deep divisions over the role of monetary policy, interpretation of economic data, and differences in economic theory. In times of uncertainty when economic data are inconclusive and cannot show a definite trend line, these divisions sometimes prevent formation of the necessary consensus delaying implementation of central bank policy well beyond the point of time when it would be most effective in assisting the economy.

Implementing monetary policy is also made difficult by policy decisions and events outside central bank control. Domestic monetary policy is most effective if coordinated with domestic fiscal policy. However, fiscal policy is directed by national governments that are attempting to reconcile competing interest groups while pursuing issues beyond monetary policy such as national security and social policy. Contrary fiscal policies, combined with unanticipated cross-border economic conditions, may limit monetary policy options appropriate for domestic economic conditions.

Effective monetary policy must also be implemented at the early stage of changing economic trends when the situation is foggy and the data provide conflicting signals, making it difficult to conform actions from the banking and financial community. While the central bank can influence money supply and interest rates, it has limited influence on bank lending activity, availability of credit from nonbank institutions, and international currency markets. Differences in interpretation of economic data and transmission of cross-border economic disturbances may lead to divergent monetary directions.

Thus, despite all their power, central banks occasionally hesitate in responding to unfolding economic changes. This hesitation tends to follow a certain pattern. In the normal business cycle, there is a point where full capacity is reached and inflationary pressures build. To combat the inflation, the central bank adopts a tight monetary policy. As the policy takes hold, firms react by first reducing inventory and employment. As business activity slows, firms are reluctant to reduce prices; and therefore, inflation continues. However, even as production and employment are declining, the central bank often maintains a tight monetary policy until such time that it is confident that the credit markets are conforming to its policy and inflation is abating. Eventually the central bank realizes the economy is declining and that it has overreacted. It then reverses course and undertakes an easy monetary policy. Because the downturn has commenced, however, banks have become belatedly cautious, reducing their lending activity while increasing liquidity. Banks use the increased liquidity to purchase government securities rather than expand loans, thereby nullifying the central bank's attempts to refloat the economy by an easing of monetary policy.

Conversely, when the economy is in a recession, political pressure is placed on the central bank to reduce interest rates and increase money supply. This pressure usually stems from the unemployment numbers, which are lagging indicators of the economy. Hence, the central bank may respond by easing monetary policy at a time when, although unemployment is high, production is moving upward and consumer purchases are increasing. The additional monetary stimulus may have little effect on further production and, instead, only stimulate further price increases.

CENTRAL BANK INDEPENDENCE

Domestic Monetary Policy

A recurring economic and political issue is the division of monetary responsibility between the central bank and the central government or its finance ministry. Both institutions are responsible for economic policy and share the same overriding goal of full employment and a rising standard of living.

However, differences arise on the means of obtaining these objectives. Most central governments embrace the Keynesian economic theory regarding demand management by central government through tax and expenditure stimulus as the best means of achieving these goals. In contrast, most central banks believe that stable prices and low interest rates provide a conducive economic environment that allows the free-market system to achieve these goals.

Often, the two approaches lead to policy loggerheads, resulting in political tension between the institutions. Economically, such tension acts as a check and balance, preventing the policy of either institution from becoming destabilizing when policies are followed to extreme conclusions. By statute, some countries maintain the check and balance by insulating the central bank from government interference. Nevertheless, the central government has ultimate authority; and some central governments prefer exercising control by either directly formulating monetary policy delegating to the central bank the task of implementing the chosen policy or indirectly requiring the central bank to support central government bond market activities.

Thus, when studying central bank monetary policy, a judgment must be made about the central bank's ability and commitment to pursue price stability or its lack of independence requiring it to support central government directed monetary policy. After the Bank of England was acquired by the central government in 1946, it was made directly answerable to the Treasury, resulting in a monetary policy in support of government demand management fiscal policies. In contrast, the Federal Reserve and the U.S. Treasury reached an accord in 1950 relieving the Federal Reserve from responsibility for supporting the government bond market.

International Monetary Policy

While central banks of most industrial countries have considerable authority to develop and implement domestic monetary policy, central governments play a large role in international monetary policy where they can proscribe the central bank's ability to implement its monetary policy. Central governments often share with their central bank responsibility over foreign-exchange operations, including maintenance of a separate fund for foreign-exchange transactions. More significant, exchange rate regimes requiring the cooperation of trading partners are often established by multilateral agreement approved by the central government and binding upon the central bank. Any changes in such an exchange rate regime constitute a modification or abandonment of the multilateral agreement which only the central government can approve.

Consequently, in the absence of an international monetary authority, an exchange rate regime compatible with domestic economic policy usually requires that the central bank cooperate with the central government in obtaining support from the monetary authorities of major trading partners. These international economic activities propel some central banks into international diplomacy. Their shared devotion to domestic and international price stability as well as integrity of financial systems have achieved a high degree of cooperation and technical skills for joint activities, giving them a profound influence on certain aspects of international economic conditions. Such cooperation may be by means of informal discussion, commitment to a broadly defined international monetary system such as the gold standard, or by formal agreement as in the EMS and is usually in the form of coordinated changes in interest rates, exchange rate adjustments, and bank regulation.

However, a central bank can only be as cooperative internationally as permitted by the national government, the strength of the domestic financial market, and the nature of the domestic business cycle. When home-country and trading-partner business cycles are moving in parallel patterns, this cooperation is generally forthcoming. This is not the case when the countries are experiencing diverging business cycle phases in which case the central banks of the respective countries become preoccupied with their own domestic policy concerns.

OPERATING CHARACTERISTICS OF KEY CENTRAL BANKS

Central bankers of the major industrial countries share a strong commitment to price stability as their overriding objective not only to maintain the integrity of the credit markets but also in the belief that inflation retards economic growth. In other respects, different historical experiences, domestic economic conditions, legal requirements, and political environment have caused each central bank to develop unique characteristics and monetary policy techniques. The international monetary system is influenced by the characteristics of the central banks of the major industrial countries; and to the extent an international monetary policy requires agreement and coordination among these major central banks, such policy is shaped by their unique characteristics. Accordingly, a brief discussion of important characteristics of key central banks follows.[6]

The Federal Reserve

U.S. monetary policy is the principal responsibility of its central bank, the Federal Reserve, with economic growth and price stability as its twin objectives.[7] In carrying out monetary policy, the Federal Reserve uses a range of key economic indicators, including monetary aggregates, interest rates, and exchange rates. The key interest rate it monitors and attempts to influence is the Fed Funds rate, which is the interest rate banks charge when borrowing from one another to meet reserve requirements mandated by the Federal Reserve. While the Fed Funds rate fluctuates, it tends to lead other short-term money market interest rates.

The Federal Reserve has considerable autonomy from government direction and tends to emphasize price stability as its principal objective of monetary policy. However, the rate of unemployment is a publicly followed economic indicator, and its rising trend can exert powerful political pressure. Federal Reserve monetary policy has been hampered by central government fiscal policies focused on national security and social issues that have caused sizable government budget deficits.

Under the Bretton Woods system, fixed exchange rates were maintained in relation to the U.S. dollar, placing the burden of exchange rate management on America's major trading partners. This arrangement, combined with the lesser significance of international commerce, allowed the Federal Reserve to focus primarily on domestic economic conditions. With the switch to floating exchange rates in 1973, the Federal Reserve's international role has changed.

In the post-1973 managed exchange rate system, the dollar remains the principal international reserve currency; but maintaining a stable dollar exchange rate places an increasing burden on the U.S. economy. Managing the burden of a reserve currency without unduly harming the domestic economy requires that the Federal Reserve and other government agencies play a greater and more active leadership role in global monetary management. The two other principal global economic powers of Germany and Japan have been reluctant to play major roles in global monetary policy, preferring to concentrate on domestic concerns and their own key currency systems.

Foreign-exchange operations are a responsibility shared with the Treasury department, which is under the direction of the executive branch. The U.S. Treasury has direct foreign-exchange authority, and its own exchange stabilization fund can be used to intervene in the foreign currency markets independent of the Federal Reserve. In practice, since the dual authority could be destabilizing to currency markets, the Treasury and the Federal Reserve generally coordinate exchange rate policy with the Federal Reserve, the responsible agent for implementing the joint policy. Nevertheless, the choice of exchange rate regime is an executive branch policy decision.

Bank of Japan

Japan has fashioned a domestic financial system that concentrates savings in the banking system, thereby giving its central bank, the Bank of Japan, greater ability to carry out monetary policy compared to other central banks.[8] However, the Bank of Japan is required to support national objectives and consequently receives considerable direction from the central government through the Ministry of Finance.[9]

In contrast to the United States, the principal objective of Japanese monetary policy is noninflationary and sustained economic growth, making the industrial production index a more important economic indicator than the rate of unemployment. Under the Japanese economic system, unemployment is a primary responsibility of companies rather than government, which is fulfilled through the concept of lifetime employment where companies rather than government must utilize the unemployed. Relieved of unemployment responsibilities, the Japanese government concentrates its efforts on enhancing and protecting the industrial system. Although the recession of 1990–1993 strained this division of economic responsibility, it remains intact.

The government carries out its responsibility by managing much of its industrial system and circumventing undesirable market forces. Accordingly, in order to maintain control over domestic interest rates and exchange rates, Japan has resisted leadership in international monetary matters and a role as a vehicle currency. Furthermore, by limiting foreign participation in its domestic financial system, the Bank of Japan retains greater influence over the yen exchange rate which it has used to carry out a managed float regime favorable to its exporting industries.

However, manipulating economic conditions has limited both the government and industry from understanding market forces, in particular, the economic consequences of a protectionist trade policy. Thus, despite strong government involvement in domestic economic affairs, the recession of 1990–1993 has been particularly hard on the Japanese economy. A reconsideration of economic policy is under way, but the consensus nature of Japanese decision making indicates that monetary and economic policies tend to remain the same until they prove unworkable because of some major economic dislocation after which additional time is required to evaluate and develop new policy direction.

The Bundesbank

Experience with devastating inflation has provided strong political consensus for Germany's central bank, the Bundesbank, to be independent from the central government and pursue price stability as its principal objective.[10] Accordingly, changes in the consumer price index (CPI) and monetary aggregates are key economic indicators. Published Bundesbank targets for growth in monetary aggregates— in particular, M3—are taken seriously, although the central bank has had the same difficulty as other central banks in consistently achieving its targets.[11]

On the other hand, the German central government determines exchange rate policy and, by approving entry into the EMS, committed the Bundesbank to support a fixed exchange rate regime with the Deutsche mark as an anchor currency in the ERM exchange rate basket. Because of Germany's strong commitment to stable prices and large economy, the Deutsche mark became a reserve currency. Consequently, most European states pegged their currency exchange rates to the Deutsche mark. However, EMS placed the Bundesbank in an awkward position not generally understood by the originators. On the one hand, the Bundesbank is responsible for maintaining a stable exchange rate, while, on the other hand, it is required by law to maintain German domestic price stability.

This dilemma caused the currency crisis of 1992. Like Bretton Woods, the burden of managing the EMS key currency system fell upon Germany's trading partners. When the unification of East and West Germany created economic imbalances in Germany, including inflation, high interest, and current account deficits, the ERM fixed rate regime required its members to mirror German monetary conditions. The Bundesbank attempted a leadership role in ERM management by urging members to devalue their currency in recognition of Germany's high interest rates necessary to fight domestic inflation. The EMS members did not agree. Nevertheless, as required by law, the Bundesbank proceeded with a tight monetary policy; and under the ERM fixed rate regime, the member countries were forced to follow despite their domestic economies entering a recession. Eventually, deteriorating domestic economic conditions forced Britain and several other countries to abandon the ERM to pursue easy monetary policies. The ERM became a managed exchange rate regime with the Deutsche mark an anchor currency in recognition of Germany as a major trading partner.

Another factor creating difficulty for EMS is that Bundesbank monetary policy is an unusual combination. The EMS is a European key currency system based on the German economy and its European trading partners. However, Germany is not a major financial center, and its long-term interest rates tend to follow U.S. long-term interest rates. Furthermore, a historical suspicion of foreign ownership of domestic assets has restricted the growth of Germany's international financial sector. Accordingly, EMS remains influenced by the U.S. key currency system and U.S. economic conditions placing strains on the ERM exchange rate regime.

Bank of England

Despite a long and prestigious history as England's central bank and leader of the international financial system during the nineteenth century, following the Bank of England's nationalization in 1946, its role in monetary policy has substantially diminished. There are no statutory objectives for monetary policy, thereby allowing such objectives to be formulated by Parliamentary leadership—usually the Chancellor of the Exchequer and the Treasury—with the Bank of England responsible for carrying out the directives. Economic growth tends to be the principal objective of monetary policy. It is unclear which economic indicators are important, and they tend to change according to the policy of the sitting Chancellor of the Exchequer. Reflecting the political desire to sustain economic growth, money supply growth has been chaotic, contributing to high and stubborn inflation.

The crux of the Bank of England's problem is its lack of independence from government policy, inhibiting it from taking a leadership role in formulating British economic policy. While no central bank is totally immune from political pressure or government influence, the other central banks are a step removed, giving them the ability to provide more objective economic advice, develop long-range policies, and maintain consistent monetary goals rather than abrupt policy changes. Although primarily a political decision, the economic consequences of joining the ERM and maintaining a fixed exchange rate does not appear to have been well thought through; and presumably, the Bank of England was a key advisor. Collapse of the Bank of Credit and Commerce, International (BCCI) appears attributable in part to Bank of England lax regulatory review. In recognition of these problems, steps were taken in 1994 to grant the Bank greater independence in monetary policy.

Bank of Canada

Like many other central banks, Canada's central bank, the Bank of Canada, has the twin monetary policy objectives of economic growth and price stability with general emphasis on the latter. However, economic dependence on cross-border commerce with the United States limits the central bank's ability to pursue independent monetary policies so that domestic monetary policy tends to mirror U.S. monetary policy. Canada operated a floating exchange rate regime well before collapse of the Bretton Woods system. Nevertheless, the bilateral exchange rate with the U.S. dollar remains a key economic indicator. Federal and provincial government budget deficits averaging –3 percent of GDP is creating a large current account deficit and making it difficult to implement domestic monetary policies without a sharp reaction in the Canadian exchange rate.

NOTES

1. A noticeable exception to state ownership is Hong Kong, where, as a thriving British colony, it developed a distinct and separate monetary system by having its leading commercial banks—principally the Hong Kong and Shanghai Banking Corporation (HKSB)—assume many central bank duties. Accordingly, Hong Kong currency consists primarily of HKSB notes; and the bank regulates its note issue in accordance with directives of the monetary committee, works with the colonial administration in bank regulation, and provides primary market support in pegging the Hong Kong dollar to the U.S. dollar.

The Hong Kong monetary system is undergoing rapid change as the colony prepares for reversion to China scheduled in 1997. Under the current transition, China's official currency, the yuan, is being introduced into Hong Kong's monetary system to circulate alongside the Hong Kong dollar. As the yuan circulation increases, China's central bank, the People's Bank of China, will expand monetary influence in Hong Kong. It remains unclear whether Hong Kong will peg one or both currencies to the U.S. dollar during and after the transition period. The process of integrating Hong Kong's financial and monetary system into China's system will be a strong indicator of the character of China's approach to the global economy.

2. Survey of monetary policy objectives of seven industrial countries is discussed in International Monetary Fund, "World Economic Outlook" (Washington, D.C.: International Monetary Fund, May 1993), p. 24.

3. An analysis of reserve requirements and the approach of various central banks, see Joshua N. Feinman, "Reserve Requirements: History, Current Practice, and Potential Reform," *Federal Reserve Bulletin*, Washington, D.C., June 1993, pp. 569–589.

4. For an overview of Federal Reserve exchange rate management, see B. Dianne Pauls, "U.S. Exchange Rate Policy: Bretton Woods to Present," *Federal Reserve Bulletin*, Washington, D.C., November 1990, pp. 891–908.

5. A detailed account of central bank intervention in the ERM crisis of 1992 is discussed in Morris Goldstein et al., *International Capital Markets*, Part I (Washington, D.C.: International Monetary Fund, 1993).

6. Additional operating characteristics for these and other central banks can be found in Peter Newman, *The New Palgrave Dictionary of Money and Finance* (London: Macmillan, 1992), and Glenn G. Munn, *Encyclopedia of Banking and Finance* (Pasadena, Calif.: Salem Press, 1991).

7. There are many books on the Federal Reserve, and one of the most popular overviews is William Greider, *Secrets of the Temple* (New York: Simon & Schuster, 1987). A more technical discussion of Federal Reserve monetary policy is found in William C. Melton, *Inside the Fed* (Homewood, Ill.: Dow Jones–Irwin, 1985), and Thibaut de Saint Phalle, *The Federal Reserve* (New York: Praeger Publishers, 1985).

8. An analysis of Japanese monetary policy is found in Ramon Moreno and Sun Bae Kim, "Money, Interest Rates and Economic Activity: Stylized Facts for Japan," *Economic Review* 3 (1993), Federal Reserve Bank of San Francisco, pp. 12–24.

9. Andreas R. Prindl, *Japanese Finance* (New York: John Wiley & Sons, 1981).

10. For a general overview and history of the Bundesbank, see David Marsh, *The Bundesbank* (London: Heinemann, 1992).

11. An overview of Bundesbank monetary policy was provided by the President of the Bundesbank, Hans Tietmeyer, in "Changing Capital Markets: Implications for Monetary Policy—An Overview," *Economic Review* 4 (1993), Federal Reserve Bank of Kansas City, pp. 5–11.

PART III

THE INTERNATIONAL
MATRIX SYSTEM

CHAPTER 12

International Matrix Indicators: Definitions and Benchmarks

With a general model of business cycles, cross-border transmission of economic conditions, and the existing global economic system, attention can now be turned to the international matrix system designed not only to follow economic trends but also to indicate impending changes. This system accumulates current key economic and financial indicators that have consistently demonstrated an ability to forecast current economic trends and arranges these indicators in a format (shown in Table 12.1) by which several analytical techniques can be applied.

While these indicators can be studied through trend line analysis, quantitative benchmarks indicating changes in trends are more important. Through historical analysis of key indicators for the matrix countries during the period 1978 to 1991, many indicators demonstrated quantitative benchmarks at certain phases of the business cycle, which are included in the discussion that follows. Through relationship analysis, additional quantitative benchmarks have also been developed (discussed in Chapter 13). Current reports of these indicators can be evaluated in light of these benchmarks providing a more informative context by which to better understand current economic and financial indicators.

This chapter describes each of the key indicators used in the matrix system and their significance with special attention to the benchmark data that signal

Table 12.1
International Matrix Format

	Jan	Feb	Mar	Apr	May	Jun	Jul	Aug	Sep	Oct	Nov	Dec
Industrial Production												
Unemployment Rate												
Consumer Price Index												
Wage Index												
Producer Price Index												
Weighted Currency												
Currency to Dollar												
% from December												
% from December												
Narrow M												
Broad M												
Real Broad M												
Money Market Yield												
Government-Bond Yield												
Yield Spread												
Real Money Market Yield												
Real Govt.-Bond Yield												
Bank Prime Rate												
Spread - Money Market												
Spread - Govt. Bond												
Balance of Trade												
Current Account												
Balance of Trade % GDP												
Current Account % GDP												
Share Index												
% from December												
WTI Oil per barrel												

Source: Schaefer Brothers.

impending changes in economic conditions. In the next chapter, these indicators are discussed in their relation to one another providing further benchmarks and insight into economic trends. The remaining chapters discuss incorporation of the data into the matrix system and the various analytical techniques to discern economic trends.

THE INTERNATIONAL MATRIX INDICATORS

Keeping with the purpose of this book to utilize timely data that are easily and inexpensively available, the international matrix system primarily utilizes the key economic and financial indicators reported each week in *The Econo-mist*. In this section are found more than twenty-eight key indicators for more than fifteen industrial countries that represent in the aggregate more than 90 percent of industrial country output and more than 70 percent of world output. Most of these indicators are derived from indexes prepared by govern-ments, international organizations such as the IMF and the OECD, and financial firms, which *The Economist* accumulates and publishes in a conve-nient format at the back of each week's edition.

The international matrix system uses sixteen of these indicators for the five matrix countries that in the aggregate comprise more than 50 percent of world output. One additional indicator, the price of West Texas Intermediate (WTI) Crude Oil, is available in most daily financial papers. The matrix system can be expanded to include data from the other industrial countries and the more limited economic and financial data on thirty developing countries, including China, India, Mexico, and Brazil, which *The Economist* began publishing in 1994.

For several important indexes such as industrial production and consumer prices, *The Economist* conveniently reports both the year-to-year rate of change rather than the actual index and the rate of change from the prior quar-ter to the current quarter. The international matrix system uses the reported year-to-year rates of change in the indexes because of their wider use in eco-nomic reports, analysis, and historical studies. A more helpful figure for iden-tifying impending changes in economic trends would have been a month-to-month rate of change in such indexes; but keeping to a principal goal of this book, the international matrix system uses the published data.

Through historical analysis of *The Economist* indicators during the period of 1978 to 1991, the following seventeen indicators have been particularly useful in understanding international economic trends:

- Year-to-year change in industrial production index
- Unemployment rate
- Year-to-year change in the consumer price index
- Year-to-year change in wage index
- Year-to-year change in the producer price index
- Trade-weighted exchange rate index
- Exchange rate to the U.S. dollar
- Year-to-year change in narrow M
- Year-to-year change in broad M
- Yield on three-month money market investments
- Yield on government bonds
- Bank prime rate
- Annual balance of trade
- Annual current account balance

- Foreign reserves
- Share index
- Price of West Texas Intermediate Oil

In contrast to *The Economist* format, the international matrix groups these key economic and financial indicators on a country-by-country format as shown in Table 12.1. Under this format, economic trend analysis begins with understanding the economic condition and business cycle of each country. Furthermore, many of the indicators included in the international matrix system were developed by each country to reflect their own needs and consequently are not uniformly comparable. They become more meaningful in the context of other indicators for the same country.

YEAR-TO-YEAR CHANGE IN INDUSTRIAL PRODUCTION INDEX

The year-to-year rate of change in each country's industrial production index is a good indicator of the country's economic conditions as of the most current month reported. Industrial production indexes measure the change in output of a nation's industrial sector comprising primarily factories, mines, electric utilities, and gas utilities representing 40 to 50 percent of total economic output for most industrial countries. Generally, there is a close correlation between changes in a nation's industrial production index and changes in the GDP with the advantage that industrial production indexes are reported monthly and are, therefore, more current than the quarterly GDP data. These indexes measure the rate of change in industrial output and not the level of output so that following a severe recession, a steady rise in the rate of change of the industrial production index may not be matched by other indicators until such time as more industrial capacity comes into active use.

Industrial production indexes are prepared by each government's statistical organizations based on monthly surveys but generally do not include the other major economic activities of services and construction which are also an important component of overall economic activity. An exception is the industrial production index for Germany, which does include construction activity. While services traditionally consist of low-paying jobs such as retail clerks, it also includes consulting and computer software services which are critical to high-technology industries and are becoming one of the fastest growing segments of business activity contributing a larger share of economic output. Construction is a small but critical component of GDP because sustained economic growth cannot be achieved without adequate and modern plant facilities.

Table 12.2 summarizes historical rates of changes in the industrial production indexes for each of the matrix countries during the period 1978 to 1991.

Table 12.2
Industrial Production Index Analysis, 1978–1991

Benchmark: 2.5 percent average growth.

| Country | Parameters | | |
	Largest Growth	Largest Decline	Average Growth
United States	15%	-10%	2.1%
Japan	12%	-8%	5.2%
Germany	5%	-5%	2.2%
Britain	4%	-11%	0.4%
Canada	17%	-13%	1.5%

Source: "Economic and Financial Indicators," *The Economist,* 1978–1992 issues.

This table demonstrates the accuracy of the industrial production index to reflect structural economic conditions in the matrix countries as well as the phase of the business cycle. During this period, Japan's average industrial production growth of 5.2 percent was the best of the matrix countries. Germany and the United States were next, reporting similar average rates of industrial production growth of about 2.2 percent. However, the fluctuations in the rates of change between high and low were greater in the United States (15% and –10%) than in Germany (5% and –5%), reflecting the severity of the 1982 recession in the United States. Britain and Canada have experienced significant below-average growth in their industrial production indexes of 0.4 percent and 1.5 percent, respectively.

Historical analysis indicates that an annual rate of change in the industrial production index for each matrix country of 2.5 percent or better is a good benchmark indicator of economic growth when sustained for more than three months. A strongly growing economy is indicated by a sustained year-to-year change in the industrial index of 4 percent, although a country recovering from a significant economic downturn may generate a faster growth rate. Countries have substantially enhanced their standard of living by maintaining an industrial production growth rate of 4 percent or more over a sustained period. As indicated by Table 12.2, only Japan has achieved this growth rate among the matrix countries. If the annual rate of change is less than 2.5 percent, economic growth is sluggish or declining.

Industrial production benchmark figures are also significant because some countries, notably Japan, view the index as the most important indicator upon which to base economic and monetary policies. Significant variations from the benchmark level may signal changes in economic and monetary policy. Other countries, such as the United States, are more sensitive to unemployment figures and base their economic and monetary policies accordingly.

A declining industrial production index raises concern about the severity in economic decline, and the Great Depression provides several benchmarks by which to measure such severity. Table 12.3 shows the worst annual decline in industrial production indexes reported during the depression period for several countries. Though calculated from indexes used at the time, the rates of change remain a helpful guide in evaluating current economic data. In 1932, the United States suffered the worst annual decline in its industrial production index of −22 percent, while Japan, less dependent on manufacturing, was less severely affected suffering its worst annual decline in its industrial production index in 1931 when it reached −3 percent.[1] Japanese industrial production appears to have suffered more in the 1990–1991 recession where year-to-year declines in the Japanese industrial production index were reaching −5 percent.

UNEMPLOYMENT RATE

The unemployment rate is another important government-prepared indicator of current economic conditions and is also useful in indicating changes in economic and monetary policy. Because of the depression, industrial nations have given governments broad authority to implement high employment economic policies. The United States is particularly sensitive to this responsibility where monthly unemployment figures receive the widest public attention. Unemployment rates usually lag other key economic indicators, but through trend analysis the slope of the trend line can be a useful indicator.

Table 12.3
Depression Period Decline in Industrial Production

Country	Largest Annual Decline	Year
United States	-22%	1932
Japan	-3%	1931
Germany	-18%	1931
Britain	-6%	1931
Canada	-15%	1932
France	-15%	1931
Italy	-8%	1931

Source: Ronald Dore and Radha Sinha, *Japan and World Depression* (New York: Macmillan, 1985).

International economic trend analysis is complicated by the wide disparity in unemployment rates, reflecting the different views of government responsibility toward employment. Europe and the United States view unemployment as a government responsibility, although U.S. benefits are less generous contributing to lower unemployment rates. In times of economic distress, companies more readily shed themselves of unnecessary employees transferring the financial burden of unemployment to the government. Japan, on the other hand, has a concept of life employment so that in times of economic downturns companies, not the government, bear the primary responsibility for utilizing unnecessary employees such as loaning them to other companies. These underused individuals are not included in Japanese figures, contributing to an underreporting of unemployment conditions. During the 1990–1993 recession, it was estimated that the rate of underused Japanese employment was 4 percent. If this number were added to the 2.5 percent reported unemployment rate, a more realistic unemployment rate would be 6.5 percent.

These varying views on unemployment are reflected in differences in unemployment definitions, measurement procedures, programs, and social norms. For example, U.S. unemployment data are derived from monthly statistical surveys, integrating the reports of federal and state agencies administering unemployment programs together with interviews of individuals no longer receiving benefits. In contrast, Britain, with a more comprehensive government unemployment program, maintains a centralized system of claims and registration of unemployed, providing more accurate data. To overcome these differences, some experts suggest that a better indicator of economic conditions is the rate of change in employment. However, internationally comparable employment data are not readily available on a timely basis.

Because of the wide differences in unemployment concepts reflected in different rates, developing a single benchmark figure was not possible. Table 12.4 reports the highest rate of unemployment for each of the five matrix countries and the lowest rate of unemployment during the period of 1978 to 1991. Except for Japan, unemployment levels in the matrix countries exceeding 10 percent were during periods of economic recession, while levels of 5 percent followed periods of sustained economic growth. For Japan, unemployment levels had lesser modulation, reaching 3 percent during severe economic downturns and moving to 1.9 percent following periods of sustained economic growth.

As with the previous discussion regarding the Great Depression, unemployment rates from this period are helpful benchmarks in evaluating the severity of an economic downturn. Table 12.5 reports the highest rate of unemployment during the depression, which exceeded 22 percent for the United States, Germany, and Britain. During this period, Japan also experienced severe and prolonged declines in industrial production index but, reflecting the smaller manufacturing sector, kept the unemployment level at 7 percent.

Table 12.4
Rate of Unemployment Analysis, 1978–1991

Benchmark: Varies by country.

| Country | Parameters | | |
	Highest Rate	Lowest Rate	Average Rate
United States	10.8%	4.9%	6.9%
Japan	3.0%	1.9%	2.4%
Germany	9.6%	3.5%	7.2%
Britain	13.2%	5.2%	9.3%
Canada	12.8%	7.1%	9.1%

Source: "Economic and Financial Indicators," *The Economist,* 1978–1992 issues.

Table 12.5
Depression Period Unemployment Rate

Country	Highest Unemployment	Year
United States	25%	1933
Japan	7%	1932
Germany	30%	1932
Britain	22%	1932

Source: Ronald Dore and Radha Sinha, *Japan and World Depression* (New York: Macmillan, 1985).

YEAR-TO-YEAR CHANGE IN CONSUMER PRICE INDEX

Consumer price indexes, commonly referred to as CPI indexes, are the most widely followed indicator of inflationary conditions so that changes in these indexes indicate economic imbalances that will generate responses by the government and financial markets. While the price deflator used to adjust nominal GDP to real GDP is considered a more accurate measure of inflation, CPI indexes are more widely publicized and have more immediate impact on financial markets.

Based on monthly surveys, CPI indexes measure the average price paid by consumers for a basket of goods and services that usually include food, clothing, shelter, fuel, medicines, transportation, doctor's fees, dentist fees, and related local sales taxes. The government-prepared indexes reported in *The*

Economist are generally the most internationally comparable of government-prepared indexes. However, there are differences such as in Britain where the commonly used CPI index—called the retail price index—includes changes in mortgage interest rates. These indexes generally do not consider price changes in financial assets such as stocks and real estate investments, which can also indicate inflationary pressures, as they absorb excess liquidity that otherwise would be spent on goods and services.

Maintaining stable prices is an important condition for steady economic growth, and changes in the CPI index indicate the magnitude of imbalance occurring in an economy. Fear of inflation generates inefficient resource allocation, resulting in enormous unbalanced economic activity. Consumers accelerate purchases of goods and services to beat price increases. Employees demand higher wages without relation to productivity. Investors switch assets from income-earning assets to investments that can appreciate faster than inflation. Businesses accelerate price increases because of lack of consumer resistance. Financial institutions increase interest rates and engage in speculative ventures.

A principal reason for ongoing inflationary pressures is the growing impact of government taxes and regulation on consumer prices, which in Germany are called *administered prices*, composed of the following broad categories:

• License fees and motor vehicle taxes
• Excise and sales taxes
• Regulated prices such as rent control, environmental regulation, and health care services
• Prices influenced by international agreements such as voluntary import quotas and agricultural price supports

Administered prices cover about 40 percent of the items included in the basket of goods and services used in the German CPI index and are an indication of growing government contribution to inflationary pressures occurring in many other countries.

Table 12.6 summarizes historical rates of changes in the CPI indexes for each of the matrix countries during the period of 1978 to 1991, reflecting the traumatic inflationary experience of 1978 to 1983 where the CPI annual rate of change for many countries exceeded 10 percent. While zero price inflation would be ideal, the dynamic and ever-changing global economy combined with expanded government-administered prices indicates that such a policy would be detrimental to long-term growth and stable employment. As a benchmark, a year-to-year rate of change in the CPI of 3 percent or less is conducive to long-term economic growth, although some countries such as New Zealand prefer an annual rate of change in CPI of no more than 2 percent. Compared to other industrial countries, Japan and Germany have been much more disciplined in controlling inflation as indicated by the average annual change in CPI during the 1978–1991 period within the 3-percent

Table 12.6
Consumer Price Index Analysis, 1978–1991

Benchmark: 3.0 percent average growth.

Country	Parameters		
	Largest Growth	Smallest Growth	Average Growth
United States	14%	1%	6.0%
Japan	8%	-1%	2.8%
Germany	7%	-1%	3.0%
Britain	22%	3%	8.0%
Canada	13%	1%	6.7%

Source: "Economic and Financial Indicators," *The Economist,* 1978–1992 issues.

benchmark rate. During the same period, Britain experienced an average rate of change in its CPI of 8 percent, contributing to the poor performance in industrial production.

YEAR-TO-YEAR CHANGE IN WAGE INDEX

For most manufacturers, labor is the single largest component averaging in excess of 50 percent of manufacturing costs making changes in a wage index, an indicator of inflationary pressures. However, wage indexes tend to lag trends indicated by changes in the CPI indexes for the matrix countries. Nevertheless, in formulating monetary policy, the Bundesbank closely follows the German wage index because of the strong trade union movement which incorporates wage index data in industry-wide labor contract negotiations. In the United States, the trade union movement is weaker, and less attention is given to the wage index except when there is an unusual spurt in inflation. Table 12.7 summarizes the year-to-year rates of change in the government wage indexes reported by *The Economist* for the matrix countries during the period 1978 to 1991, indicating the close parallel to the rates of change in the CPI indexes.

There are several other reasons limiting the use of wage indexes as key economic indicators. Each country compiles data from different groups such as (1) all industrial labor or (2) only manufacturing labor. Generally excluded from such data are the retail and service sectors. Compensation policies vary widely; and wage rates generally do not include other forms of pay mandated by local custom, laws, and government programs such as fringe benefits, holiday policies, or payroll taxes which in some areas may exceed 35 percent of cash wages. Wage rates generally measure gross pay with no reduction for the wide variety of withholding taxes among the countries.[2] Some of these dif-

Table 12.7
Wage Cost Index Analysis, 1978–1991

Benchmark: 3.0 percent average growth.

| | Parameters | | |
Country	Largest Growth	Smallest Growth	Average Growth
United States	10%	1%	5.0%
Japan	9%	0%	4.8%
Germany	7%	2%	4.5%
Britain	22%	6%	10.5%
Canada	13%	2%	6.7%

Source: "Economic and Financial Indicators," *The Economist,* 1978–1992 issues.

ferences are reflected in the performance of the wage index as in the case of Japan, where year-to-year changes in the wage index fluctuate more than the other matrix countries, reflecting Japanese compensation policies of low fixed monthly payments periodically augmented by substantial bonuses based on profitability and productivity. These compensation policy differences make international comparability of employment compensation particularly difficult.

Some economists also calculate changes in real wages by subtracting from the rate of change in the wage index the change in the CPI for the comparable period. For example, the year-to-year change in the German wage index in March 1991 was 6.3 percent; and the year-to-year change in its CPI index for the same period was 2.5 percent, resulting in a theoretical real wage increase of 3.8 percent. While in theory, this resulting change in real wages could be an important indicator, an analysis of the historical matrix indicates a wide divergence in reliability. This lack of reliability seems to stem from wide national differences in fringe benefits, taxation, and compensation practices (discussed previously) which affect overall employee take-home pay and their true purchasing ability. Accordingly, changes in the real wage index are not used in this international matrix system.

YEAR-TO-YEAR CHANGE IN PRODUCER PRICE INDEX

Producer prices are the prices charged at the point products enter into the distribution stream and before the additional costs of transportation and distribution. Like CPI indexes, producer price indexes (PPI) are prepared by government agencies based on monthly surveys. Wholesale prices are similar to producer prices but are usually determined at a level closer to the end user and may include some carrying and holding costs.

PPI indexes were begun in the nineteenth century, and their popularity continues providing extensive historical data on price level changes. By measuring prices at an earlier stage in the economic chain, some view PPI indexes as a more reliable indicator of inflationary trends unaffected by less sensitive consumer behavior. In international matters, many domestic manufactured products include significant imported raw materials and components so that some view changes in the PPI as better measures of international price competition and pressures. International price changes may be reflected by similar changes in the PPI. With Britain dependent on a high portion of imports, the Bank of England considers its PPI index an important indicator of inflationary pressures.

In practice, the CPI has been a better measure of inflationary pressures than the PPI. Employment and government-administered prices are significant cost factors at the retail and distribution level, while manufacturing is subject to other costs not reflected in producer prices. In addition, most manufacturing is based on standing orders or contractual commitments where prices are fixed, thereby preventing rising commodity and cross-border component prices from immediate influence. PPI tends to follow rather than lead the inflationary trend while lagging other changes in economic conditions. Nevertheless, the British PPI index has been a helpful indicator because 50 percent of the items included in the index are imports. However, the index covers only manufactured products. The U.S. PPI index excludes imported goods, making it a less reliable price indicator.

Table 12.8 provides the range of changes in the PPI indexes for the matrix countries during the period of 1978 to 1991. Except for Japan, the year-to-year rates of change in the PPI indexes for the matrix countries fluctuated between 7 and –3 percent, which is less than the CPI indexes. A general benchmark

Table 12.8
Producer Price Index Analysis, 1978–1991

Benchmark: 2.0 percent average increase.

Country	Largest Increase	Smallest Increase	Average Growth
		Parameters	
United States	6%	-2%	2.1%
Japan	4%	-11%	-1.4%
Germany	3%	-5%	1.1%
Britain	7%	3%	5.1%
Canada	5%	-3%	1.9%

Source: "Economic and Financial Indicators," *The Economist,* 1978–1992 issues.

indicating stable prices was a year-to-year change in the PPI of no more than 2 percent. During the Great Depression, wholesale price indexes based primarily on commodities were the principal means of measuring international price changes. Table 12.9 shows that the decline in wholesale price indexes of the matrix countries from August 1929 to September 1930 exceeded –10 percent. This figure is a helpful historical benchmark. As indicated in Table 12.8, Japan's largest decline in its PPI of –11 percent occurred in 1986 following a rapid rise in its trade-weighted exchange rate that contributed to a decline in industrial production. A year later, the unemployment rate rose to 3 percent, the highest level during the 1978–1991 period.

TRADE-WEIGHTED EXCHANGE RATE INDEX

The trade-weighted exchange rate indexes for the matrix and other countries reported in *The Economist* are those used by the Bank of England, which are based on a common methodology for the weights, making these indexes comparable for all the matrix countries and highly useful for current and historical comparison purposes. Unlike other indexes, *The Economist* reports the index numbers themselves, making it useful for other analytical techniques. As discussed more fully in Chapter 13, the rate of change in a country's trade-weighted exchange rate is an important indicator of the cross-border transmission of economic conditions because of the type of exchange rate regime indicated and the monetary policy followed to support the regime.

BILATERAL DOLLAR EXCHANGE RATE

Changes in the U.S. dollar bilateral exchange rates tend to parallel changes in the trade-weighted exchange rate for that country. Hence, following the daily dollar exchange rate provides a more current understanding of exchange rate activity, which is then more fully reflected in the Bank of England's

Table 12.9
Depression Period Decline in Wholesale Prices, August 1929 to September 1930

Country	Rate of Change
United States	-12%
Japan	-22%
Germany	-12%
Britain	-14%
Canada	-16%

Source: Charles P. Kindleberger, *Historical Economics* (Berkeley: University of California Press, 1990), pp. 302–303.

trade-weighted indexes published weekly in *The Economist*. Following the
U.S. dollar bilateral exchange rates is also important because many countries
peg or manage their exchange rates directly with the dollar; and, as the principal international vehicle currency, currency markets respond to its trend,
thereby affecting both the bilateral and trade-weighted exchange rates of
many other countries.

In some cases it may also be beneficial to follow a country's bilateral exchange rate with each of its cross-border partners. As previously discussed,
many countries peg or manage their exchange rates in relation to the exchange
rate of a major trading partner or in relation to a basket of currencies anchored
by a major trading partner such as the Deutsche mark in the case of the ERM.
In addition, the Bank of England's trade-weighted index is based on manufacturing trade and does not consider other important commercial relationships such as investments.

YEAR-TO-YEAR CHANGE IN NARROW M

Modern economic analysis has been dominated by Keynesian economic
theory, which emphasizes government fiscal policies to influence consumption, investment and interest rates. In the early 1970s, a major revolution in
economic thinking occurred emphasizing the role of money supply and free-
market activity as being the principal influence on economic activity. The
revolution was spearheaded by Milton Friedman, who co-authored with Anna
Schwartz *A Monetary History of the United States, 1867–1960*, which in ex-
haustive detail demonstrated the relationship of money supply changes to U.S.
economic growth and prices. A similar study on British monetary history
demonstrated the same relationship.

Based on these and other scholarly works, economists began serious study
of the impact of monetary conditions. However, just as monetary theory became widely understood, high interest rates caused depositors to switch funds
out of commercial bank deposits and into other higher-yielding investments,
triggering a dislocation in the monetary system of many countries, chaos in
monetary statistics, and difficulty in implementing effective monetary policies. In response, central banks undertook a more systematic approach to
money supply data by developing a system of monetary aggregates, M1, M2,
M3, and so on, that classify different types of financial assets used as money.
While attempts were made at uniform definitions for each monetary aggregate, local custom, historical experience, and commercial needs resulted in
wide variations in definitions and influence on the domestic economy. Definitions of various monetary aggregates reported by central banks of several
matrix countries are located in Appendix D.

Several of these monetary aggregates have proven useful in indicating current and future economic conditions. As required by law, or as a matter of
policy, central banks prepare growth rate projections or targets for monetary

aggregates which are publicly announced as a guide for monetary conditions. Comparing actual rates of change in monetary aggregates to projected growth rates is an important indication of monetary policy.

In publishing money supply data, *The Economist* provides international comparability by dividing the data into two broad categories—*narrow M* and *broad M*—and then reporting the year-to-year rate of change in a country's monetary aggregate that closest resembles these two categories. Narrow M consists of financial assets held for immediate transactions and normally resembles monetary aggregate M1, consisting of currency in circulation and commercial bank deposits.

M1 is the traditional definition of money supply used in the early analysis of monetary theory, and the definition among the countries is more uniform. However, there are differences such as the Federal Reserve's inclusion in its M1 of traveler's checks and Germany's inclusion in its M1 of interest earning bank deposits that can be withdrawn on up to one month's notice. For Britain's narrow M, *The Economist* reports the year-to-year change in the more widely followed M0, 85 percent consisting of currency in circulation plus bank deposits with the Bank of England, and is similar to the monetary base. Until deregulation of the financial markets, M1 was the principal monetary aggregate followed by most central banks; but the relationship broke down in the 1980s, causing central banks to develop other monetary aggregates with a better relationship to economic activity.

Although monetary aggregates have experienced diminished use for guiding central bank monetary policy, an analysis of historical data indicates their continued significance as an economic indicator. Table 12.10 provides experience in the rate of change in narrow M for each of the matrix countries.

Table 12.10
Narrow M Analysis, 1988–1993

Benchmark: 6.5 percent average growth.

Country	Parameters		
	Largest Growth	Smallest Growth	Average Growth
United States	14%	-1%	6.5%
Japan	14%	1%	5.7%
*Germany**	12%	2%	8.3%
Britain	21%	1%	6.7%
Canada	19%	-4%	5.2%

Source: "Economic and Financial Indicators," *The Economist,* 1988–1994 issues.
*Narrow M figures not reported from December 1991 to June 1992.

Changes in narrow M reflect central bank attempts to expand or contract the money supply. A 6.5-percent increase in narrow M indicated stable economic growth; but if the rate of change declines, industrial production would begin declining in about twelve months. Conversely, if current economic conditions are weak, a rising rate of change in narrow M would indicate expanding industrial production.

YEAR-TO-YEAR CHANGE IN BROAD M

Broad M consists primarily of the year-to-year rates of change in monetary aggregates having a greater influence on a country's economic activity and, therefore, closely followed by its central bank in conducting monetary policy. Generally these aggregates consist of M1 items plus interest-earning demand-and-time deposits held at depository institutions. However, the particular aggregate varies from country to country, reflecting variations in the financial system so that a general benchmark level could not be developed. For example, Japan's broad M consists of its year-to-year rate of change in monetary aggregate M2 + CDs, while Britain's broad M is the year-to-year rate of change in monetary aggregate M4. For the United States, *The Economist* reported the year-to-year changes in the M3 monetary aggregate but in 1994 switched to the M2 monetary aggregate, which is more widely followed by U.S. economists. A definition of these monetary aggregates is found in Appendix D.

Studying the rate of change in broad M must be made in relation to existing economic activity. If the economy is operating at full capacity, continued increases in broad M will translate into increases in the price level with no discernable impact on economic output. In a persistent inflationary environment, money supply tends to increase to accommodate the inflationary expectations of people and not economic output. A more meaningful analysis of broad M is to adjust the year-to-year rate of change by an inflation factor to arrive at a rate of growth in the real money supply. The international matrix system makes a rough adjustment to approximate the real growth in broad M by using the CPI index (discussed in the next chapter).

YIELD ON THREE-MONTH MONEY
MARKET INVESTMENTS

Short-term interest rates are an indicator of the liquidity level of a country's overall financial market. When money is abundant, short-term interest rates decline. As the economy grows, investor confidence returns and investment opportunities expand, causing short-term interest rates to rise as long-term capital markets compete for funds. As shown in Figure 12.1, interest rate levels and trends among the matrix countries vary widely in response to different liquidity levels, economic conditions, and central bank monetary policy.

Figure 12.1
Three-Month Money Market Yields for Selected Countries, 1978–1991

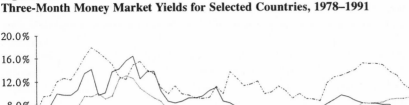

Source: "Economic and Financial Indicators," *The Economist,* 1978–1992 issues.

Accordingly, short-term interest rates are an important economic indicator for each country but have little impact on international financial markets or global economic conditions until such time as their interest rate level rises above the respective country's long-term interest rate.

A key indicator of short-term interest rates is the yield on three-month money market investments which comprise principally certificates of deposit and other three-month interest earning bank deposits available in most industrial countries. Three-month money market yields provide an internationally comparable short-term interest rate that is only slightly above three-month government bills. A preferred indicator of short-term interest rates would have been the yield on three-month treasury bills because in the United States, Britain, and several other countries, these yields are considered more important for monetary policy, are more widely followed by financial markets, and are the base by which many institutions price their offerings of short-term investments, including money market accounts. However, not every country has an active treasury bill market. Japan, in particular, does not actively trade its short-term government paper. The use of interest rates in economic trend analysis is discussed in Chapter 13.

YIELD ON GOVERNMENT BONDS

Government general-obligation bonds are considered the most marketable and least risky of long-term investments and are usually backed by the full faith and credit of the central government, which has the power to tax to pay for the obligations. Accordingly, yields on marketable government bonds set a minimum level for long-term interest rate levels and are the best indicator of long-term interest rate trends. All other long-term investments—shares, real estate, corporate bonds, and collectibles—must offer the potential for higher returns to compensate for the greater risks and lack of marketability.

While not all industrial countries have active markets in short-term government obligations, they borrow extensively in the capital markets, creating active government-bond markets. Government obligations, often referred to as treasury obligations, are classified into three broad categories according to maturity:

- Bills
- Notes
- Bonds

Treasury bills are obligations of one year or less and are normally issued without a coupon interest payment. Accordingly, treasury bills are sold at a price discounted below the face redemption amount, reflecting the interest rate that will be paid at maturity. Treasury notes are generally obligations of maturity of greater than one year but less than ten years with interest generally paid semi-annually or quarterly. Bonds are obligations of ten years or more in which interest is paid semi-annually or quarterly. The government-bond interest rates reported by *The Economist* are generally derived from indexes for bond maturities of ten to fifteen years or, where such indexes do not exist, a widely traded bond maturing in ten to fifteen years.

With the reduction in capital controls, government-bond interest rates of the matrix countries tend to move in similar directions as their domestic capital markets become more integrated causing interest rates to be internationally competitive. Nevertheless, participants in domestic financial markets are predominately local residents; so while interest rates may move in the same direction, nominal interest rate levels still vary as shown in Figure 12.2, reflecting local economic conditions as well as international conditions of exchange rate risk, inflation differentials, withholding taxes, and transaction costs.

BANK PRIME RATE

The *prime rate* is generally defined as the interest rate most large banks charge their better customers for short-to-medium-term loans. However, the precise definition of the prime interest rate varies from country to country. In the United States, the *Wall Street Journal* defines prime as the interest rate charged by 75 percent of the thirty largest U.S. commercial banks. In Britain, clearing banks use a *base rate* interest which is widely reported, but *The Economist* understands that the best customers are charged 1 percent over the base rate, making this adjusted interest rate the bank prime rate used as the

Figure 12.2
Government-Bond Yields for Selected Countries, 1978–1991

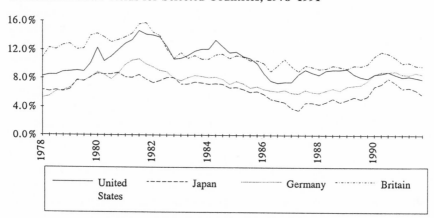

Source: "Economic and Financial Indicators," *The Economist,* 1978–1992 issues.

key indicator. For Germany, the prime rate reported by *The Economist* is the overdraft rate for prime corporate customers. In practice, the interest rate actually charged customers for bank loans is a variation on the prime rate after considering many factors such as transaction costs and risk, with the published prime rate acting as a reference for subsequent negotiations.

For economic trend analysis, it is not the interest rate but the level of bank lending activity which is important in economic activity. Banks must review their lending activity, deposit activity, and cost of funds to arrive at the published prime rate. Central banks carefully monitor bank prime rates to determine the effectiveness of monetary policy. Lowering of bank prime rates is not an indication of a greater willingness to lend but a reaction to market forces as banks become more cautious because of declining activity and attempt to retain their better customers by offering lower interest rates. When analyzed in relationship to other interest rates (as discussed in the next chapter), the prime rate becomes an important indicator of bank liquidity and willingness to lend, signifying future economic trends.

ANNUAL BALANCE OF TRADE

As an important measure of cross-border trade, most governments report monthly balance-of-trade figures; but annual balance-of-trade figures are more widely used and discussed in economic reports. Appendix B contains balance-of-trade figures for the matrix and other countries during the period 1988 to 1992. *The Economist* provides both monthly and annualized balance-of-trade figures derived from cumulating the preceding twelve-month-period balances. For easy comparability, these figures are reported in U.S. dollars for all the countries. However, because of inflation, trade balance figures reported at current prices provide limited analytical use. A more important indicator of international commerce is the ratio of the annualized trade balance figures to nominal GDP as more fully discussed in the next chapter.

ANNUAL CURRENT ACCOUNT BALANCE

As discussed in Chapter 8, a more important measurement of cross-border commerce is the aggregation of trade, services, and investment balances into an overall commercial balance. Most countries do not regularly report such a figure but instead report the current account balance, which approximates the commercial balance net of official transfers such as foreign aid and cross-border military expenditures. Appendix B contains current account figures for the matrix and other countries during the period of 1988 to 1992. As with the trade balance figures, *The Economist* reports an annualized current account balance in U.S. dollars for all the countries based on the preceding twelve-month period. Because of inflation, the ratio of the annualized current account balance to nominal GDP is a more important economic indicator than the actual dollar balance and is discussed in the next chapter.

Unfortunately, despite the increasing importance of the current account balance, the United States, Canada, and many other countries report such figures only quarterly so that balance-of-trade figures remain a more timely means of following cross-border commercial activity. On the other hand, Japan reports monthly figures for both trade and current account balances. With the increased importance of global economic matters, all major trading industrial nations should develop monthly current account figures. In the fast-paced global economy, such data will permit more timely evaluation of international competitiveness and international economic trends contributing to development of better international economic policies.

FOREIGN RESERVES

Foreign reserve balances are an indicator of a country's management of its exchange rate and cross-border investment activity. A country with low foreign reserves and a deteriorating domestic economy is likely to experience an exchange rate depreciation and difficulty in paying obligations denominated in foreign currency triggering a default on such obligations. Countries in this deteriorating situation may respond by raising domestic interest rates and implementing stringent exchange controls. On the other hand, rising foreign reserves and rising exchange rates indicate that the domestic interest rates are too high; and the country can accept a lowering of interest rates and still maintain stable exchange rates. Foreign reserves also indicate ability to support a stable exchange rate by intervening in the foreign exchange market without resorting to other monetary policies such as changes in interest rates.

The foreign reserve figures reported by *The Economist* are in current U.S. dollars for easy comparability and are derived from monthly IMF reports of official reserves consisting primarily of foreign currencies, SDRs, and accounts with the IMF, which are the primary instruments used in currency market intervention. Gold holdings, which constitute as much as 32 percent of industrial countries' total 1992 international reserves, are not included because they are rarely used for currency intervention purposes. The balance-of-payment figures in Appendix B show the yearly changes in reserves for selected countries during the period of 1988 to 1992.

SHARE INDEX

The Economist reports principal share price indexes used by major stock exchanges throughout the world.[3] For the matrix country stock markets, the principal indexes reported are as follows:

New York   Dow Jones Industrial Averages (DJIA)

Tokyo   Nikkei 225 Average (Nikkei)

Frankfurt   Deutscher Aktienindex (DAX)

London   The Financial Times/Stock Exchange 100 (FTSE 100)

Toronto   Toronto Stock Exchange 300 Composite Index (TSE 300)

These indexes were developed by financial news publications to provide a more systematic approach to following stock market activity. The oldest and best-known index is the DJIA, which follows the New York Stock Exchange (NYSE) and traces its roots to 1888. Although called an average, the many changes throughout the years required that it be prepared using index methodology. It comprises thirty large capitalization industrial companies representing 25 percent of the value of stocks traded on the NYSE, which is the principal U.S. stock exchange. While often criticized for the inclusion of only large capitalized companies, the DJIA is the best internationally known share index whose movements influence most other stock exchanges and whose long history allows for substantial historical analysis.

The other indexes are of more recent development reflecting the dramatic changes occurring in the international capital markets. The Nikkei is not a true index but rather an average of the 225 shares of principal companies traded in the Tokyo stock exchange and is not weighted by share market capitalization. Nikkei is a Japanese abbreviation for *Nihon Keizai Shimbum*, Japan's main financial daily newspaper and developer of the average. Germany's DAX was introduced July 1, 1988, comprising thirty of the most heavily traded stocks listed on the Frankfurt Stock Exchange, which represent 75 percent of the total turnover in German equity markets. The FTSE 100 was begun in 1984 to provide a more effective index system that could also be the basis for option and index trading on the London Stock Exchange following the merger of many regional exchanges in 1973. Shares included in the index represent 70 percent of the London equity market. Canada's TSE 300 Composite Index represents Canada's five stock exchanges with the largest located in Toronto. In addition to share indexes for stock exchanges in other countries, *The Economist* also reports the Morgan Stanley Capital International Index of major world stock markets, which in 1993 included stock markets for twenty-three countries.

Some economists believe that stock market indexes remain an important leading economic indicator based on the theory that the public changes its consumption level in accordance with changes in net worth caused by changes in the stock market values. For that reason, leading composite indexes of economic indicators for many countries include a stock market index. In 1987, that contention was weakened when the October stock market crash was not followed by a cataclysmic decline in the global economy as had occurred following the market crash of October 1929.

Although share market values have some impact on consumers' confidence levels, financial systems have changed considerably since 1929, making their use as a leading economic indicator less significant compared to other indicators. Direct individual ownership of publicly traded stock is declining as individuals switch to mutual funds and pension plans, causing these institutions to be the dominant force in many stock markets. At the end of 1992, it was estimated that 46 percent of the market value of shares traded in established U.S. stock exchanges were owned by institutional investors. While institutional investors are active daily traders, they are also committed to keeping funds in the market because their customers are individuals saving primarily for future retirement. Changes in consumption levels are unlikely to cause individuals to withdraw existing savings already committed for long-term investment. Accordingly, it is more probable that the economy influences the stock market than vice versa.

Nevertheless, the stock market is a large segment of the financial market of most industrial countries. If properly understood, stock markets' reaction to events can be a helpful clue to economic trends. In the post–World War II period, movements in stock market prices of industrial countries appear to have been influenced primarily by two items: (1) changes in interest rates and (2) changes in expectations of future profit growth, both of which are a function of the business cycle. These relationships are discussed more fully in the next chapter. Furthermore, with industrial country consumers becoming increasingly affluent but also concerned about retirement, stock exchange indexes also provide some indication of excess liquidity indicating future inflationary pressures (discussed in the next chapter).

PRICE OF WEST TEXAS INTERMEDIATE OIL

Energy has always been a critical factor to industrial-based economies; and they have been blessed with abundant, inexpensive, and readily available diverse energy resources ranging from hydroelectric, coal, and nuclear energy, to domestic oil. Oil is of particular significance because it is one of the cheapest and versatile energy sources. The transportation system of trains, planes, and automobiles relies almost exclusively on oil; and there are few readily available substitutes. In the first half of the twentieth century, U.S. oil demand was supplied principally from domestic sources, while European demand was supplied by Russia and a European-controlled Middle East, contributing to a stable source of energy supply and prices. Today, the United States, Europe, and Japan import over one-half of their oil from foreign sources located in regions with political tensions. Because of prior experiences with oil boycotts and disruptions, industrial countries are very sensitive to this dependence on foreign oil.

In the event of disruption of the oil supply or unreasonably high prices, the full cost falls on the transportation system and the goods and people that use it. A rapid increase or decrease in the price of oil does not allow time to redirect the transportation system to adjust to the new price, causing a major economic dislocation. Hence, oil prices and oil supply are critical factors to industrial country economies and significant changes in oil prices have a major impact on consumer behavior.

In monitoring oil prices, there are a variety of crude oil prices and international markets. *The Economist* reports the Brent per barrel crude oil price, which is derived from trade in North Sea oil and a major oil source for the European economies. Before the North Sea oil discoveries in the early 1980s, Europe imported most of its oil from the Middle East; and the principal market was in Rotterdam, whose prices were key indicators.

In the United States, the principal indicator of oil prices is the price per barrel of WTI Crude Oil. The international matrix system utilizes the WTI oil price because of greater historical data. Since 1978, the monthly price of WTI oil has gone from a low of $11.83 in the third quarter of 1978 to a high of almost $40 in October of 1990. It is generally believed that the price of WTI oil will probably remain at between $20 and $25 per barrel, which is a price level that is not disruptive to most countries. At this price range, sufficient domestic and foreign oil can be profitably produced and refined to meet international demand, while exploration for new fields can be economically undertaken. If the price of WTI oil begins rising above $25 per barrel at a rate faster than the annualized rate of change in the CPI and if the rise is rapid, the cost impact on the transportation system and winter heating can cause a serious economic dislocation. Conversely, a fall in the price of WTI oil below $15 per barrel, adjusted for subsequent inflation, can adversely affect the domestic oil industries in the United States and Britain. Under existing technology and oil-recovery methods, most marginal wells cost at least $15 to produce one barrel of oil. Newer wells cost closer to $18 per barrel. When oil prices approach these price levels, oil exploration and development ceases in Britain and the United States, thereby crippling their domestic oil industries and increasing dependence on volatile foreign oil.

NOTES

1. An excellent comparison of economic conditions in Japan and other countries during the Great Depression is found in Ronald Dore and Radha Sinha, *Japan and World Depression* (New York: Macmillan, 1985).

2. See the extensive comparison of employee taxes and take-home pay in thirteen industrial countries including the matrix countries, *The Economist*, March 13, 1993, pp. 83–84.

3. For a discussion of share indexes and other financial indicators, see Howard M. Berlin, *The Handbook of Financial Markets, Indexes, Averages, and Indicators* (Homewood, Ill.: Dow Jones–Irwin, 1990).

CHAPTER 13

International Matrix Indicators: Relationships

An economic indicator measures activity in a particular economic sector, and Chapter 12 provided a concise explanation of the economic sectors being measured by the seventeen key economic and financial indicators of the international matrix system. Yet each sector interacts with others; influences others; and is, in turn, influenced by the other sectors so that studying changes in individual indicators solely by trend line analysis is an incomplete economic analysis. A more timely and complete method is studying the relationships among these key indicators, which is the subject of this chapter.

RELATIONSHIP ANALYSIS

A *relationship* is defined as a connection of economic meaning between one indicator and another. More specifically, the relationship must be one that will identify current economic conditions or indicate future economic trends. For the international matrix, examining the relationship between indicators within each country provides further understanding of current economic conditions and indicated economic trends. Historical relationship analysis of the key economic and financial indicators for the matrix countries during 1978 to 1991 provides additional benchmarks to understand phases of the business cycle.

Current Snapshots of the Economy

The unemployment rate and year-to-year rate of change in the industrial production index for each matrix country provides a snapshot of its current business cycle for the month reported. The significance of these indicators is discussed in Chapter 12. In relationship analysis, these two indicators represent different segments of the economy which, under normal conditions, should be telling the same economic story, thereby complementing one another.

If the year-to-year rate of change in the industrial production index is 2.5 percent or greater and shows a rising trend from preceding months, then the unemployment rate for the country should be falling. Three consecutive months of rising or falling industrial production index indicates a trend line that the unemployment rate should be complementing. If the unemployment rate is not proceeding in the complementary trend, it is an indication of a growing imbalance in the country's economy. For example, if the year-to-year rate of change in the industrial production index is systematically exceeding 2.5 percent but the rate of unemployment is not declining, it is an indication that the economy is growing—however, weakly—and could reverse direction.

This snapshot of a country's economic activity will also be studied by its industry and government, which will respond with appropriate modifications in economic behavior or changes in economic policy. The most influential response will come from the country's central government which, following the depression, is entrusted with authority to utilize its vast resources for creating conditions conducive to full employment. Each country has a benchmark unemployment rate and rate of change in CPI that historically triggers a response from the country's central government. In the case of the rate of unemployment, the threshold figure is 7.5 percent for European countries and Canada, 6.5 percent for the United States, and 2.5 percent for Japan. When unemployment reaches the benchmark level in a particular country, the initial reaction will come from the central bank which will usually be a monetary policy shift reducing interest rates—in particular, the official rate—and increasing the rate of growth in broad M money supply. Depending on the magnitude of the unemployment rate increase, pump-priming by the central government may also follow such as reduction in taxes and increased government spending.

In the case of the CPI, the benchmark figure triggering government response is more uniform among the matrix countries occurring when the year-to-year rate of change in the CPI rises above 3.5 percent. In this situation, expect the central bank to tighten credit by increasing the official interest rate and curtailing the rate of growth in broad M. If inflation persists for more than nine months, there should be a move toward reducing government spending.

In formulating responses to domestic economic conditions, countries are often restrained by formal or informal commitments to maintain stable exchange rates which prevent them from adopting monetary or fiscal policies that may cause instability or a change in the exchange rate. Evaluating the nature of the exchange rate regime and the degree of commitment is discussed below. Governments must also manage a number of economic and noneconomic issues which often make them slow to recognize changes in the economic environment and even slower to develop a consensus for the appropriate response.

Rate of Change in Trade-Weighted Exchange Rate Index

Exchange rates fluctuate daily, but significant changes in a country's trade-weighted exchange rate index over a period of time are one of the principal indicators of the economic relationship between trading partners. These significant changes are indicated by calculating the change in the Bank of England's trade-weighted exchange rate index from the beginning of the year to the current period and comparing these changes to several benchmarks indicating economic conditions. For example, at the end of December 1988, Japan's trade-weighted index was 152.2 and by June 1989 had fallen to 141.8. The rate of change during this six-month period was, therefore, –6.8 percent.

As a benchmark, under stable economic conditions or under a fixed exchange rate regime, the trade-weighted exchange rate should not change more than ±2.5 percent within a six-month period as countries manage their exchange rates to maintain stable cross-border economic conditions or act in accordance with a fixed exchange rate regime by maintaining exchange rates within the agreed narrow band.

This benchmark is also helpful where a country is part of a formal fixed exchange rate regime such as the ERM. In such a situation, the multinational agreement establishing the fixed rate regime normally specifies the exchange rate level. This level is the permitted band width around which the exchange rate must be maintained before member countries are required to intervene in the currency market to avoid further fluctuation. The agreement may also specify the mechanisms for intervention or realignment of the exchange rates. Such an exchange rate level is normally based on a currency basket that includes many of the trading partners whose exchange rates are already included in the Bank of England's trade-weighted index. Consequently, changes in the Bank of England's trade-weighted index indicates a country's adherence to the formal fixed rate regime. For example, from 1979 to 1992, the ERM band width was ±1.5 percent; but because of lags in implementing intervention to maintain the band width, the trade-weighted exchange rate of many member countries showed greater fluctuations, in some cases reaching ±3.5 percent.

Maintaining the trade-weighted exchange rate within the ±2.5-percent band width during unstable economic conditions may require a monetary policy contrary to domestic economic needs. An analysis of real broad M and interest rate yield spreads discussed later in this chapter will indicate whether a country is following a monetary policy to maintain the fixed exchange rate regime or to deal with domestic economic conditions. For example, a country experiencing a declining industrial production index and rising rate of unemployment may nevertheless be compelled to impose a tight monetary policy of high interest rates to maintain exchange rate stability under a fixed exchange rate regime. In such a situation, Britain was compelled in 1992 to abandon membership in the ERM. Its rate of unemployment was rising above 10 percent, and year-to-year changes in the industrial production index were declining. The tight monetary policy to maintain the exchange rate, indicated by three-month money market yields exceeding government-bond yields, was incompatible with Britain's worsening domestic recession.

Conversely, a country experiencing strong economic growth but committed to a fixed rate regime may be prevented from raising interest rates to combat inflationary pressures. If unemployment rates, year-to-year rates of change in industrial production, and year-to-year changes in the CPI exceed benchmark figures, indicating growing economic imbalances, a country may be compelled to realign the exchange rate or abandon the fixed exchange rate regime altogether.

Trade-weighted exchange rate fluctuations beyond ±2.5 percent indicate growing economic imbalances caused by economic conditions such as inadequate domestic monetary policy. When the rate of change reaches 10 percent or more within a nine-month period, it is an indication that domestic economic conditions are becoming significantly disrupted. For an economy dependent on cross-border commerce, such a rapid rate of change in a short period does not provide sufficient time for the economy to adjust, thus resulting in severe domestic economic dislocation.

A rapid rise in the exchange rate of 10 percent or more often indicates a rapid increase in domestic interest rates, a tight monetary policy, and eventual slowdown in domestic industrial production. Export industries will also be hurt by the exchange rate rise; and if these industries are more important than the import sector, a fall in the industrial production index may occur in the next three to six months. Furthermore, a fall in the PPI may also occur if imports of raw materials are important to domestic industry. On the other hand, an exchange rate decline of 10 percent or more indicates falling interest rates which may spur domestic industrial production to replace higher-priced imports. In the meantime, the trade balance may not reflect the benefits of declining imports because the higher import prices offset the lower import volume. However, the lower exchange rate may cause a rise in the PPI reflecting the higher cost of imported raw materials and components that could disrupt economic activity of countries highly dependent on foreign imports of goods and capital.

Table 13.1 provides a summary of annual changes in the trade-weighted indexes and dollar bilateral exchange rates for the matrix countries from 1988 to 1992. Exchange rates experienced considerable fluctuations, reflecting different

Table 13.1
Changes in Matrix-Country Exchange Rates, 1988–1992

Annual Change in Bank of England's Trade Weighted Exchange Indexes

	1988	1989	1990	1991	1992	5-Year Average
United States	1.1%	2.1%	-9.6%	-0.8%	9.5%	0.5%
Japan	5.3%	-15.0%	-0.2%	9.1%	7.9%	1.4%
Germany	-0.7%	5.1%	1.3%	-0.3%	3.9%	1.9%
Britain	6.3%	-11.3%	-0.9%	6.4%	-11.3%	-2.2%
Canada	6.5%	4.3%	-3.2%	0.1%	-7.0%	0.1%

Annual Change in U.S. Dollar Bilateral Exchange Rates

	1988	1989	1990	1991	1992	5-Year Average
Japan	-0.8%	15.9%	-6.8%	-7.4%	-0.8%	0.0%
Germany	12.9%	-7.1%	-12.9%	2.0%	7.2%	0.4%
Britain	3.6%	8.8%	-16.1%	3.8%	20.4%	4.1%
Canada	-7.7%	-3.3%	0.0%	0.0%	10.3%	-0.1%

Annual Change in Mark/Pound Exchange Rate

	1988	1989	1990	1991	1992	5-Year Average
Britain	9.1%	-14.6%	4.0%	-2.1%	-10.7%	-2.9%

Source: "Economic and Financial Indicators," *The Economist,* 1988–1992 issues.

economic conditions in each country and oil supply dislocation threatened by Iraq's invasion of Kuwait in July 1990. Germany's trade-weighted exchange rate showed the most stability reflecting monetary policies pursued to maintain the EMS. In contrast, Britain's trade-weighted exchange rate was the most volatile, reflecting domestic economic conditions incompatible with its principal trading partners.

Rate of Change in Bilateral Dollar Exchange Rate

Many countries conduct much of their cross-border commerce in U.S. dollars, peg or manage the exchange rate with the U.S. dollar, or have the United States as a principal trading partner so that monitoring the bilateral exchange rate with the U.S. dollar is an important indicator. Calculating the bilateral rate of change from the beginning of the year to the current period measures the extent of fluctuation. For example, at the end of December 1988, the dollar-to-yen bilateral exchange rate was 126 and by June 1989 had risen to 141, resulting in a six-month rise in the dollar's value to the yen of 11.9 percent.

Change in the dollar's bilateral exchange rate can be compared to several benchmarks. About thirty countries peg their exchange rate to the U.S. dollar, so their bilateral exchange rates are the basis of a fixed exchange rate regime and should not fluctuate more than ±2.5 percent. On the other hand, many countries only include the dollar as part of an overall currency basket composed of principal trading-partner currencies. In managing their exchange rate, fluctuations in the U.S. dollar can be offset by opposite fluctuations in other currencies. Under this system, overall exchange rate stability is maintained if the bilateral exchange rate with the dollar is within ±5.0 percent.

A change in the bilateral exchange rate beyond these parameters within a nine-month period indicates growing economic instability that may trigger a reaction from the monetary authorities to arrest the change before it becomes more disruptive. A change in the bilateral exchange rate of more than 10 percent within nine months is an indication of a serious disruption in economic conditions, which is particularly disruptive if the rate of change is paralleled by the rate of change in the trade-weighted exchange index.

Some countries have a stronger commercial relationship with a trading partner other than the United States or may be a member of a fixed rate regime, such as the EMS, where exchange rates are pegged to a basket of currencies that usually includes a major anchor currency such as the Deutsche mark. Monitoring the bilateral exchange rate with the principal partner or anchor currency may thus be more important to help understand exchange rate fluctuations. This can be accomplished using the same benchmark calculation discussed for understanding changes in the dollar bilateral exchange rate. Table 13.1 shows the annual rate of change in the pound-to-mark bilateral exchange rate which more closely correlates with Britain's change in its trade-weighted exchange rate than the pound-to-dollar bilateral exchange rate.

Real Money Supply

In previous chapters, the relation between money supply changes and economic growth was discussed. However, evaluating money supply changes using traditional trend line analysis of monetary aggregates has become less meaningful because of the global inflationary environment that began in the 1970s. Industrial country economies have become adept at absorbing inflationary price increases with no appreciable impact on real economic output. Accordingly, money supply changes may only be a response to inflationary pressures rather than more fundamental economic conditions.

Adjusting the money supply growth rate by an inflationary factor results in a more meaningful money supply figure for economic analysis. Commonly

referred to as the *real* rate of money supply growth, this adjusted figure reflects the amount of money available to support increased output and is a
more useful figure for historical comparison. It is the rate of change in real
money growth that is the key influence on economic output.

From time to time, economists calculate real money growth rates but such
information for the matrix and other countries is not readily available on a
timely basis. Using the matrix data, a calculation can be made approximating
a real growth rate in broad M. This calculation is made by taking the year-to-
year change in broad M for a given month and subtracting the year-to-year
rate of change in CPI for the same month. The resulting figure, referred to
here as real broad M, is a rough but very helpful indication of real monetary
growth or decline for the year. For example, in the fourth quarter ending December 1992, the year-to-year rate of change in nominal broad M for the
United States was 0.1 percent and for the same month, the year-to-year rate
of change in the CPI was 3.0 percent. Accordingly, the year-to-year rate of
change in real broad M for the period ending December 1992 is the difference, –2.9 percent, indicating a tight money supply.

A review of the rate of change in real broad M during the 1985–1991 period indicates a relationship to changes in both the industrial production index and short-term interest rates. A rising or falling trend in the year-to-year
rate of change in real broad M for at least three consecutive months will normally accompany or be followed by a comparable rising or falling industrial
production index three months following the first month of the changing trend
in real broad M.

Table 13.2 shows the highest and lowest rates of change in matrix country
real broad M. The wide variations make it difficult to develop a general
benchmark. However, improvement in the industrial production index will be

Table 13.2
Real Broad M Analysis, 1988–1993

Benchmark: Varies by country.

| Country | Parameters | | |
	Largest Growth	Smallest Growth	Average Growth
United States	5%	-3%	-0.8%
Japan	12%	-2%	4.2%
Germany	6%	0%	3.1%
Britain	17%	1%	6.4%
Canada	8%	0%	4.3%

Source: "Economic and Financial Indicators," *The Economist,* 1988–1994 issues.

even more likely if a matrix country's year-to-year rate of change in real broad M is greater than 1 percent for each of the three consecutive months. Note the substantial increase in real broad M for all matrix countries except for the United States. Trading-partner monetary expansion to finance exports to the United States offset the tight monetary policy of the Federal Reserve.

The magnitude of change in real broad M is another important economic indicator. One of the more significant conclusions arrived at in Friedman and Schwartz's *A Monetary History of the United States, 1867–1960* was the decline in the money supply that occurred as the economy slid into the Great Depression. In fact, the rates of change in the money supply then are still helpful benchmarks in understanding the impact of a current rate of change in real broad M. Table 13.3 shows the extensive decline in the U.S. money supply during the depression, with each year constituting a different phases of the business cycle. In the 1929–1930 period, the U.S. economy was sliding toward a recession consistent with the model of a normal business cycle. The United States was in the midst of the recessionary economic downturn during the 1930–1931 period. The dramatic decline in the money supply reached a climax during the 1931–1932 period, when it fell –17 percent, clearly showing the fall into the depths of the depression.

In projecting future economic conditions resulting from changes in real broad M, it is equally important to consider the relationship with current economic conditions that may negate the effect of changes represented by this indicator. The experience of the high inflationary period of the late 1970s indicates that a decline in real broad M takes longer to work its way through the economy before ultimately causing a decline in the industrial production index. It appears that once the general public is convinced that there is a significant and continuing inflation, creative financing techniques expand credit to replace a decline in real broad M. During a weak economy, however, expansion of real broad M will not necessarily translate into increases in production if the credit markets are not equally prepared to expand credit.

Thus, to be effective, change in a country's real broad M must also be supported by conforming changes in a country's credit markets and vice versa. Since data on lending activity are often not timely, interest rate relationship

Table 13.3
Depression Period Decline in U.S. Money Supply

Period	Rate of Change
1929-1930	-2%
1930-1931	-7%
1931-1932	-17%
1932-1933	-12%

Source: Federal Reserve Bulletin, Washington, D.C., 1929–1934 issues.

analysis (discussed in the following section) indicates the degree of conformity (or lack thereof) of the credit markets to changes in real broad M. A weak economy struggling to grow requires both an expanding money supply and credit manifested by low short-term interest rates, indicating surplus bank liquidity levels capable of supporting credit expansion. On the other hand, combating a harmful inflationary spiral requires both a contracting money supply and high short-term interest rates. High short-term interest may simply indicate the price banks are charging for loans; but if such condition is in conjunction with a contracting money supply, it confirms that bank liquidity levels are no longer sufficient to support further credit expansion that is fueling inflationary pressures. If there is a divergence between changes in real broad M and lending activity, changes in industrial output are not likely to digress from the existing trend.

Yield Spread: Money Market Yield Less Government-Bond Yield

It is generally held that rising interest rates increase costs to businesses and consumers, causing a curtailment in economic activity, while declining interest rates reduce costs, thereby causing an increase in economic activity. Yet twentieth-century economic experience shows long periods of low interest rates that failed to invigorate the economies of many countries and long periods of high interest rates that did not deter many countries' economic growth and stability.

Changes in interest rate levels do not have the expected economic impact because of the interrelationship with other economic conditions. If interest rates are high but profits are even higher, borrowers will continue to pay high interest and will continue profitably. In inflationary periods, increasing borrowing costs will not stop inflation if (1) businesses continue increasing prices to cover increasing costs; (2) banks continue lending money even though interest rates are higher; and (3) workers obtain cost-of-living adjustments, providing higher compensation to cover higher interest costs.

Conversely, lower interest rates will not necessarily spur an economy. Lower interest rates will not cause economic expansion if consumers choose to pay off debts previously contracted at higher interest rates rather than purchase goods. In a deteriorating economy, normally prudent investment projects often cannot demonstrate a reasonable ability to generate sufficient income to cover even the lower interest rate obligations, while declining interest income may reduce funds available for lending. This condition causes financial institutions to curtail lending in favor of investing in lower-earning but less risky government bonds. Furthermore, while interest is a cost to a borrower, it is income to a lender; and lower interest rates feed back into the economy, reducing consumer purchasing power and thus negating the benefit of lower interest rates.

Therefore, it is not interest rate levels that are the primary influence on the economy but rather the growth (or lack thereof) in both money supply and bank lending. Yield spreads between interest rates from different sectors of the credit markets are good indicators of the supply and demand for credit, changes in the money supply, and financial institution lending activity. The spread between the money market yield and the government-bond yield indicates the liquidity level for short-term funds. If the yield spread is positive (i.e., the money market yield is higher than the yield rate on government bonds), liquidity is contracting as demand for short-term funds is growing faster than the supply. If the yield spread is negative (i.e., the money market yield is below the yield rate on government bonds), liquidity levels are expanding as supply of short-term funds is satisfying or growing faster than the demand.

Many financial publications maintain a chart plotting interest rate yields which usually include a graph of the spread between short-term and bond interest rates. A more helpful approach for historical benchmark analysis is to calculate the spread, which is a simple process. For example, in December 1992, the yield on Canadian three-month money market investments was 7.0 percent; and the yield on Canadian government bonds was 8.6 percent. The difference of −1.6 percent is the yield spread. In the international matrix, a negative yield spread indicates that the three-month money market yield is below the bond yield, while a positive yield spread indicates that the three-month money market yield is above the bond yield.

An analysis of the spread between three-month money market and government-bond yields for the matrix countries from 1978 to 1991 provides some important benchmarks for economic trend analysis, which are summarized in Table 13.4. In a healthy and growing economy, the yield spread for a matrix country other than Japan should be −2 to −2.5 percent and accompanied by sustained growth in real broad M. Japan has maintained significantly lower

Table 13.4
Benchmark Yield Spreads

Country	Indicated Monetary Conditions				
	Money Market Less Government Bond			Prime Less Money Market	Prime Less Bond
	Tight	Easy	Normal	Normal	Normal
United States	1.0%	-3.0%	-2.0%	2.0%	1.0%
Japan	1.0%	-2.0%	-1.0%	0.8%	1.0%
Germany	1.0%	-3.0%	-2.0%	2.0%	1.0%
Britain	1.0%	-3.0%	-2.0%	1.0%	1.0%
Canada	1.0%	-3.0%	-2.0%	1.0%	1.0%

Source: Schaefer Brothers.

interest rate levels, so the yield spread for its growing economy should be –1 percent. When a matrix-country central bank is stimulating a deteriorating economy by expanding the money supply, the yield spread will usually expand to between –3 and –3.5 percent. For Japan's lower interest rate levels, the yield spread should be –2 percent. When the yield spread for any matrix country approaches 1 percent, the respective central bank is usually trying to combat inflationary pressures and should be significantly curtailing the money supply growth.

This analysis of yield spreads should also be made in conjunction with the rate of change in a country's real broad M. For a country's monetary policy to be effective, the change in real money supply requires a conforming response by commercial lenders, indicated by the yield spread and rate of change in broad M. If both conditions complement one another, the central bank's monetary policy will more likely bear fruit. For example, a negative yield spread should be in conjunction with growth in real broad M, while a positive yield spread should be in conjunction with a decline in real broad M. If the yield spread and rate of change in real broad M do not complement one another, the central bank is not likely to achieve its intended policy goal.

Yield Spread: Prime Rate Less Money Market Yield

With commercial banks performing a critical role in the nation's money supply and credit, measuring their response to economic conditions and central bank monetary policy is an important relationship analysis. Banks earn their money by lending at a higher rate of interest than the rate they pay to savers. Among the matrix countries, the yield spread between the bank prime rate and the yield on three-month money market investments varies from 0.8 to 2 percent because of different domestic financial markets. In the case of Japan, a tightly controlled banking and money market system distorts the interest rate relationship. Table 13.4 summarizes for each of the matrix countries the spread between the prime rates and three-month money market yields under normal liquidity levels based on interest rate data for 1989 to 1992.

Comparing the yield spread between a country's bank prime rate and its three-month money market yield is an indicator of banking system liquidity levels. A deviation from these benchmark figures indicates changes in liquidity levels and pending changes in lending activity. If the spread between the prime rate and money market yield narrows from the benchmark level (e.g., falls below 2 percent in the United States or Germany; 1 percent in Japan, Britain, or Canada), as usually occurs in a growing economy, liquidity levels are tightening; and banks will be under pressure to increase their prime lending rate. If the spread begins to widen (e.g., grows above 2 percent in the United States or Germany; 1 percent in Japan, Britain, or Canada), as usually occurs in a weakening economy when liquidity levels are rising, the banks are in a position to lower the prime lending rate. However, pressure on the banks to lower interest rates is limited because, in a weak economy, customers are unable to liquidate inventories and accounts receivable. Consequently, banks tend to continue lending at high interest rates beyond the peak in business activity, curtailing lending only after the economy is already moving downward.

The spread between the bank prime rate and the three-month money market yield also indicates the potential for money supply expansion through new bank lending activity. If a central bank is attempting to spur a weak economy by reducing interest rates and expanding the money supply—typically indicated by a decline in the money market yield faster than a decline in the government-bond rate—the banks should respond by reducing the prime rate to encourage new lending. However, if after central bank monetary easing the spread between the prime rate and the money market yield rate remains above the benchmark level, it is an indication that bank lending is still restrictive and that the banks are not conforming to central bank monetary policy. A central bank policy to expand money supply will not bear fruit until the banks move in line.

On the other hand, if the central bank implements a tight monetary policy by increasing interest rates and restricting the growth in the money supply— as evidenced by an increase in the money market yield above the yield on government bonds—the banks should be increasing the prime rate to conform. However, if the spread between the prime rate and the money market yield remains at the benchmark level or smaller, it is an indication that the banks are not conforming to central bank policy. Such a narrowing yield spread indicates that there is a strong demand for capital, that banks are liquid, and that lending is continuing as if the economy were still expanding.

Yield Spread: Prime Rate Less Government-Bond Rate

In providing funds to both the public and private sectors, commercial banks face two fundamental choices: (1) invest in public-sector government bonds where the interest rate is low but the risk is minimal, or (2) invest in the private-sector commercial and personal loans where the interest rates are higher but the risks and cost of loan administration are also higher. Exercising their investment judgment, banks switch loans and investments between the public and private sector depending on their economic outlook.

Expanded bank lending to the private sector is the key for economic growth. An important indicator of bank economic outlook and willingness to lend is the spread between the bank prime rate and government-bond yield. When banks are positive about the economy and believe the lending risks are manageable, they will aggressively seek loan customers in the private sector who, if equally positive about the economy, will pay an interest rate greater than the government-bond yield. In a growing economy, customers should have no difficulty paying an interest rate several points greater than the government-bond yield. Hence, a bank prime rate in excess of the government-bond interest rate indicates that the banks are continuing to lend to the private sector.

On the other hand, when the economy is declining and the risk of loan default is rising, a higher interest rate offered by private-sector firms is insufficient to attract bank lenders. In a downturn, banks become cautious, piling up excess funds in short-term government obligations. The prime rate often declines below the yield on government bonds, not because the banks want to expand loans but because the banks are vigorously competing for the dwindling number of good customers. A narrow yield spread between the prime rate and the yield on government bonds often indicates a slowdown in bank lending to the private sector. A negative yield spread between the prime rate and the yield on government bonds, where the bank prime rate is significantly below the government-bond rate, indicates that the banks are liquid but cautious in their lending practices. Such a negative yield spread may also indicate extensive government budget deficits whose financing requirements are crowding out the private sector.

In analyzing the yield spread between the bank prime rate and the yield on government bonds for each of the matrix countries between 1978 and 1991, several benchmark patterns emerge. A small positive or negative yield spread between the prime rate and the yield on government bonds indicates normal bank lending activity. When the prime rate exceeds the yield on government bonds by 1 percent or more, bank lending may be too aggressive and may be contributing to a speculative investment environment. When the prime rate falls below the bond rate so that the yield spread is −1 percent or lesser, bank caution has caused a serious decline in credit availability, which may impede an economic recovery.

A major problem of industrial economies is lack of coordination in bank lending activity with business cycle phases. At major cyclical turning points, banks in most countries do not timely adjust their lending activity to changes in the business cycle. Usually the spread between the prime rate and the government-bond rate is only slightly positive just when the growth in real broad M is being curtailed. As the money supply tightens, interest rates respond quickly so that the money market yields rise above the government-bond yields. However, several months will elapse before a decline in the growth in real broad M impacts industrial production. Meanwhile, despite the tight money supply that should warn of a slowdown in the economy, the banks continue lending at the profitable higher interest rates.

Then, as the unemployment rate rises and the economy weakens, the central bank steps in, reversing its tight monetary policy by reducing short-term interest rates and expanding the money supply. Banks are very profitable because of the high interest rates on loans as manifested by a strongly positive yield spread between the prime rate and the yield on government bonds. This high spread makes them reluctant to reduce the prime interest rate in anticipation of a slowing economy. Eventually, the weak economy causes the money market yield to fall below the yield on government bonds so that the spread turns negative. The central bank aggressively expands the money supply to avoid acceleration of the downturn, but the bank prime rate tends to remain higher than the yield on government bonds. Banks keep their interest rates high to earn income necessary to offset rising losses from bad loans caused by the deteriorating economy. Although the demand for credit may be falling because of the weak economy, banks may curtail lending activity (but not interest rates) even faster in light of deteriorating loan collateral. At the bottom of the economic downturn, the central bank attempts to stimulate the moribund economy by additional reductions in short-term interest rates and faster expansion of the money supply. However, commercial banks are reluctant to conform. Cautious about future prospects, banks maintain high liquidity levels, as evidenced by a prime rate well below the yield on government bonds. Furthermore, commercial banks may be unable to expand the deposit portion of the money supply by new loans because of borrowers' unwillingness to increase debts. In fact, paydown of debts may contribute to a reduction in the money supply.

Real Three-Month Money Market Yield

Although short-term money markets are less sensitive to inflationary conditions, the real money market yield is an important indicator of monetary conditions. This real money market yield is calculated by subtracting the current year-to-year change in the CPI from the current nominal three-month money market yield. For example, if in December 1992 the Canadian three-month money market yield is 7.0 percent and the year-to-year change in Canadian CPI is 2.1 percent, the real three-month money market yield is 4.9 percent.

Based on the interest rate experience during the depression summarized in Table 13.5, under most economic conditions the nominal three-month money market yield should always be higher than the year-to-year rate of change in

Table 13.5
Depression Period Interest Rates, 1932–1937 Averages

	United States	Japan	Germany	Britain	Canada
Short-term	0.4	2.6	3.6	0.9	1.4
Government Bond	3.1	4.3	6.1	3.2	3.9
Yield Spread	-2.7	-1.7	-2.5	-2.4	-2.5

Source: Sidney Homer, *A History of Interest Rates,* 2nd ed. (New Brunswick: Rutgers University Press, 1977).

the CPI but generally not greater than 1 percent. However, a country experiencing chronic current account deficits will need to increase the real three-month money market yield to 2 percent; and if the real money market yield exceeds 2 percent, it is an indication of a tight monetary policy and perhaps a monetary policy that is overrestrictive. Such a high real three-month money market yield may also indicate a policy to maintain an exchange rate level that is higher than warranted by economic conditions. On the other hand, if the real three-month money market yield is less than 0.5 percent or even a negative figure, it is an indication of an excessively easy monetary policy that could fuel future inflation or cause a declining exchange rate. In the aforementioned example, the high Canadian real money market yield indicates an unusually tight monetary policy apparently undertaken to arrest a decline in Canada's trade-weighted exchange rate, which had fallen 7 percent, and its bilateral U.S. dollar exchange rate, which had fallen 10 percent.

Real Yield on Government Bonds

While central and commercial banks have a unique influence on short-term interest rates, long-term rates are another matter. Long-term capital markets are large and competitive, preventing any one institution from influencing prices through market intervention. Long-term interest rates are thus influenced by general credit conditions of supply, demand, and risk. However, inflation expectations are particularly important because most obligations are not subsequently adjusted for inflation. At the time bonds are issued, lenders must include in their interest rate a factor for anticipated future inflation.

A calculation isolating the inflation element in long-term interest rates is useful in evaluating trends from both a current and historical prospective. As with the calculation of growth in real broad M, the interest rate adjusted for inflation is called the *real interest rate*. However, unlike calculating for real broad M, which uses the existing inflation rate as measured by the actual year-to-year rate of change in the CPI, the inflation element in long-term interest rates is the expectation of the future rate of inflation. This expected inflation rate is an imprecise number in constant fluctuation. Nevertheless, a rough estimate of the real long-term interest rate on government bonds can be calculated by subtracting from the government-bond yield the expected rate of change in the CPI. The difference constitutes the real rate of return anticipated by bond investors. For example, if in December 1992, Canadian government bonds are yielding 9.3 percent and the expected annual rate of change in the CPI is 5 percent, the difference of 4.3 percent would constitute the real interest rate.

Attempting to determine the expected rate of inflation is a subjective analysis, and reasonable people will arrive at different conclusions. Most bond investors develop their expectations about future inflation rates from experience in the preceding year or two. Accordingly, bond investors' perceptions of the necessary interest rate on bonds usually lag the current inflationary trend. In a period of slowly rising inflation, bond investors are caught unaware of the rising inflationary trend and may not seek a sufficiently high rate of interest as compensation. When inflation is declining, bond interest rates often remain high as investors fear the trend in lower inflation is only temporary.

Economists have devoted considerable research to determining the minimum level of real interest (assuming very little risk) an investor would require. Some of the better analyses base their conclusions on a study of interest rates during the Great Depression. Table 13.5 summarizes average short- and long-term interest rates during the depths of the depression (1932–1937). The United States, Britain, and Canada suffered the worst, as is reflected by the very low nominal rates where short-term interest were about 1 percent while government-bond yields were closer to 3 percent. On the other hand, during this period, Japanese and German rearmament created domestic inflationary pressures.

This 3-percent nominal government-bond interest rate experienced by the United States during the depression is considered by many to be the minimum expected real interest rate for long-term investment capital. Investors in today's government bonds should, therefore, earn a real interest rate in excess of 3 percent to compensate both for rate of inflation and other risk factors. Referring to the example in the preceding paragraph, if the minimum real rate of interest is considered 3 percent and the current real rate is 4.2 percent, then it appears that the financial markets are demanding a 1.2-percent premium in addition to the expected rate of inflation.

Real government-bond yields above or below the 3-percent benchmark reflect other economic conditions. Matrix-country real government-bond yields for 1978 to 1991 often averaged closer to 4 percent. This higher real interest rate coincided with a country's current account deficit to avoid exchange rate depreciation. In instances where real government-bond yields exceeded 4 percent, the exchange rate often appreciated indicating a domestic interest rate policy higher than necessary for stable economic conditions. On the other hand, countries incurring a current account surplus experienced real government-bond yields below 3 percent as foreign investors flooded domestic-bond markets anticipating earning additional income from rising exchange rates and rising bond prices.

Real interest rates are also important in evaluating the economic consequences of a fixed rate regime. Where the real government-bond yield exceeds 4 percent and a country is incurring chronic current account deficits, the higher real government-bond yield may be necessary to maintain the exchange rate level pursuant to the fixed rate regime. However, such a policy places an interest rate burden on the entire domestic economy. Monetary authorities must decide whether to maintain the exchange rate level or reduce interest rates and accept the consequences of an exchange rate depreciation. Conversely, when a country is incurring current account surpluses, a real bond yield below 3 percent indicates that the exchange rate is too low and should eventually appreciate.

An analysis of the historical data from 1978 to 1991 indicates a relationship between real interest rate and current account levels necessary to maintain stable exchange rates. A country with a current account deficit near –2 percent of GDP maintained stable exchange rates with a real government-bond yield above 4 percent. A current account deficit closer to –3 percent of GDP required a real government-bond yield above 5 percent. A current account surplus exceeding 2 percent of GDP enabled real government-bond yields to fall below 3 percent.

In comparing interest rate movements for the matrix countries, real government-bond yields tend to move in close parallel directions, as shown in Figure 13.1. This close correlation indicates that capital markets are becoming more interrelated, that inflation rates are used as a proxy to reflect anticipated changes in exchange rates, and that exchange rate movements are integrated with interest rates in influencing cross-border investments. Nominal three-month money market yields are more volatile than government-bond yields, reflecting their significance in monetary policy rather than in investment decisions.

Ratio of Trade Balance to Nominal GDP

Calculating the ratio of a country's annualized balance of trade to current or year-end forecasted nominal GDP provides a highly useful indicator for analyzing economic conditions. It is particularly useful for comparison against historical benchmark data. Table 13.6 provides a range of ratios for both the trade and current account balances of the matrix countries during the period 1983 to 1991.

Figure 13.1
Real Government-Bond Yields for Selected Countries, 1978–1991

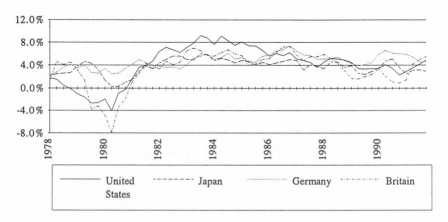

Source: "Economic and Financial Indicators," *The Economist,* 1978–1992 issues.

Table 13.6
Ratio of Current Account and Trade Balances to GDP, 1983–1991

Country	Trade Balance			Current Account		
	Best	Worst	Average	Best	Worst	Average
United States	-1.1%	-4.0%	-2.5%	0.4%	-3.5%	-2.1%
Japan	4.6%	-2.0%	3.2%	4.3%	0.8%	2.5%
Germany	6.5%	0.8%	3.9%	4.7%	-1.4%	2.0%
Britain	0.6%	-5.0%	-1.9%	1.3%	-4.2%	-1.0%
Canada	4.8%	0.5%	2.3%	0.9%	-4.3%	-1.6%

Source: "Economic and Financial Indicators," *The Economist,* 1983–1992 issues.

Under normal economic conditions, a country should maintain a consistent ratio of its annualized trade balance to nominal GDP of no more than ±0.5 percent. Such ratio indicates that its trade exports and imports are about balanced and that financial assets are not being sold cross border to pay for higher imports. On the other hand, a country with sizable foreign-owned debt must generate a higher trade balance surplus to earn sufficient foreign exchange to pay down the debt. Canada's average ratio of trade balance to nominal GDP during the 1983–1991 period was 2.3 percent, indicating a strong domestic economy comparable to the economic strength reflected by similar ratios of 3.2 percent for Japan and 3.9 percent for Germany during the same period. However, Canada must make substantial payments on foreign-owned debt obligations so that after a sizable trade surplus, its average ratio of current account balance to nominal GDP was –1.6 percent. If a country's trade balance constitutes a major component of cross-border commerce, this trade balance ratio approximates the ratio of the current account balance to nominal GDP, indicating economic conditions more fully discussed in the following section.

Ratio of Current Account to Nominal GDP

For industrial countries with complex cross-border commercial activities, the ratio of a country's annualized current account balance to actual or forecasted year-end nominal GDP is more important than the trade balance ratio discussed previously. Many countries experience trade balance surpluses but high foreign-owned debt payments, creating a current account deficit. Canada is a prime example; and the United States, as the world's largest debtor nation, may soon be in a similar situation.

Based upon this current account ratio, a historical analysis provides some significant benchmarks. During the peak of Britain's industrial might from 1870 to 1910, its current account surplus is estimated to have averaged 4 to 5 percent of its nominal GDP. This sustained surplus was invested in overseas securities, providing a future stream of investment income that offset subsequent reversal in Britain's balance of trade. Table 13.6 summarizes the ratio of current account to GDP for the matrix countries during the period 1983 to 1991. During this period, Japan maintained an annual current account surplus averaging 2.5 percent of GDP, which was invested overseas. The resulting stream of investment income enabled it to become a major financial center. During the same period, Germany's ratio of annualized current account balance to nominal GDP has averaged 2 percent. In contrast, the current account ratio to GDP for the United States and Britain has averaged –2.1 percent and –1.0 percent, respectively.

As a benchmark, a current account balance (surplus or deficit) of 1 percent or more of nominal GDP creates currency supply-and-demand pressures, triggering a change in a country's exchange rate. In the case of a fixed rate regime, a change in government-bond interest rates—in particular, real government-bond yields—relieves the pressure on the exchange rate. For example, a current account deficit of –2 percent of GDP may cause real government-bond yields to climb to 4.5 percent; and if the year-to-year rate of change in CPI remains stable, nominal bond yields will likewise rise. On the other hand, if the year-to-year rate of change in CPI declines, nominal-bond yields may not decline to maintain a stable exchange rate. Countries experiencing a current account surplus exceeding 2 percent of GDP often experience declining domestic interest rates that encourage investment of the surplus into higher-yielding cross-border investments.

Foreign Reserves and Trade Balance/Current Account

In the absence of government intervention in the currency markets, foreign reserves should reflect adjustments in the current account balance. Rising foreign reserves should accompany a rising current account surplus as exporters sell foreign currency to monetary authorities in exchange for domestic currency. Declining foreign reserves should accompany a deteriorating current account as the monetary authorities sell foreign currency to domestic companies to enable them to pay for imports and foreign debts.

However, with the expansion of cross-border commercial activity and the role of currency in the international monetary system, changes in foreign reserves reflect other economic activities, namely,

• Monetary policy
• Exchange rate stability
• Central bank support for export trade
• Ability to maintain import purchases

The monetary policy reflected by changes in foreign reserves depends upon the country's exchange rate regime. In a fixed or stable exchange rate regime, an unusual rise in foreign reserves often indicates tight monetary policy attracting cross-border purchases of domestic currency. An unusual decline in reserves indicates a monetary policy that is easier than warranted by domestic economic conditions. In particular, a current account deficit accompanied by rising foreign reserves indicates an overly tight monetary policy, while a current account surplus and falling reserves indicates a domestic monetary policy that is too loose. On the other hand, where there are large current account deficits or surpluses that are not matched by changes in foreign reserves, it is an indication of significant cross-border portfolio investment activity: A rising current account surplus allows domestic residents to invest abroad, while a current account deficit encourages use of financial assets rather than reserves as payment for imports.

Exchange rate policy will also be reflected by changes in foreign currency reserves. In a free-floating exchange rate regime, changes in currency supply and demand caused by current account balances should be reflected through exchange rate changes rather than changes in the reserves. Hence, a current account surplus should trigger an appreciation in the exchange rate, while a deficit should trigger an exchange rate depreciation with no change in the foreign reserves. A managed exchange rate regime will normally be indicated by a combination of foreign reserve and exchange rate changes. Intervention in the currency markets to maintain stable exchange rates or a fixed rate regime is often indicated by changes in the foreign reserve balances.

An important analysis is whether a country has sufficient foreign currency reserves to manage the exchange rate without resorting to other monetary policies which will more directly impact the entire domestic economy. An important comparison is the ratio of a country's foreign reserves to its cross-border bank liabilities reported by the IMF. For industrial countries with extensive domestic financial markets, this ratio should be no greater than 10 to 1. If the ratio is greater, as is the case of Britain, downward pressure on the exchange rate cannot be countered by currency intervention; and the monetary authorities will need to maintain stability through implementation of other monetary policies. A smaller ratio indicates that the monetary authorities have sufficient foreign reserves to withstand speculative pressures.

Unfortunately, the debt information is not published regularly by *The Economist*. Table 13.7 provides some debt figures and reserve ratios, indicating which of the matrix countries have strong foreign reserve positions and which do not. Germany and Canada have developed strong positions with reserve-to-bank liability ratios of 49.5 percent and 30.4 percent, respectively. At 4.7 percent, Britain's reserve position is weak, indicating that to maintain a fixed exchange rate regime it must rely on domestic monetary policy. The United States and Japan have similar reserve-to-bank liability ratios of 9.1 percent and 10.4 percent, respectively.

Changes in foreign reserve balances may indicate central bank activity in support of cross-border commerce. Adjusting cross-border commercial rela-

Table 13.7
Adequacy of Foreign Reserve Balances, 1992

Country	Billions of Dollars			Reserves as % of Liabilities
	Currency Reserves	Current Account	Bank Liabilities	
United States	60	-66	663	9.1%
Japan	72	118	691	10.4%
Germany	91	-25	184	49.5%
Britain	38	-21	804	4.7%
Canada	14	-24	46	30.4%

Source: International Financial Statistics (Washington, D.C.: International Monetary Fund, January 1994).

tionships is normally accomplished through the currency and financial markets. However, if exporters accumulate sizable foreign currency balances in payment for goods and services, they will be unable to sustain export growth unless there is a market for foreign currency. Countries with sustained current account surpluses develop a financial market sector specializing in foreign investments which absorb the accumulated foreign currency. However, a sizable trade surplus accompanied by a sizable growth in the foreign reserves indicates that the private market for foreign currency is saturated and that the central bank is purchasing the foreign currency in support of further export trade.

Foreign reserves are particularly critical to a country dependent on essential imports, such as food and oil, that is experiencing chronic current account deficits. In such a situation, imports must be paid by financial assets of the domestic economy and, if such assets do not exist, then by foreign reserves. Dividing foreign reserves by one-twelfth of annual commercial imports indicates the number of months a country could continue to purchase imports, assuming termination of all exports. Although such situation is generally unlikely except in an extreme emergency, this calculation has been helpful in evaluating economic conditions of developing countries.

For many industrial countries, the foreign reserve-to-import ratio is not an effective measure. As previously discussed, extensive domestic financial markets allow the continued purchase of imports because foreign suppliers will be able to dispose of any currency received as payment.

Share Indexes and Interest Rates

With tremendous growth in public and private debt, domestic interest rate levels have become more competitive relative to equity investments; and investors have become nimble in switching between the two investment types for maximum earnings. Since 1978, changes in interest rates have been more significant to share prices, while changes in corporate profits have become less of a factor. The stock market of industrial countries is composed mostly of established companies that have experienced several business cycles, survived, and prospered. Accordingly, even in a significant economic downturn, the market assumes that, upon economic recovery, most companies will share in the prosperity and return to profitability.

Consequently, share index movements tend to occur in conjunction with major or anticipated moves in interest rates. Higher interest rates cause a share index decline, indicating that investment funds are being pulled from equity into credit markets; and there is concern of rising business costs. Lower interest rates improve share indexes as share investments provide attractive yields, and there is anticipation of improving corporate profits.

The stock market anticipates that if the economy is rising, interest rates will also rise. If the economic growth means that profits will rise faster than interest rates, the market will continue rising. When interest rates accelerate faster than the rise in profits, which often occurs at the top of the business cycle, the share index begins to falter. Conversely, at the bottom of the recession, interest rates are low and the share index often anticipates a recovery causing share prices to rise. If the share index is reacting to a factor other than current or anticipated interest rates, it is an indication of public reaction to an event, which may constitute only a temporary adjustment to the longer-term trend in share prices.

While both short- and long-term interest rates impact share prices, the principal relationship is yield on government bonds. Most investors, including institutions that trade daily, are long-term investors comparing the available returns between stocks and bonds. Though attractive, money market yields are short-term investments and, over the long run, generally cannot offer returns comparable to long-term investments. However, rapid changes in money market yields over a short time period of several months indicate a major change in monetary policy that will become reflected in government-bond yields and will influence investment decisions.

A rapid change in share indexes may reflect changes in monetary policy, indicating future inflationary pressures. Table 13.8 shows the largest advances and declines for the principal share indexes of each of the matrix countries. Industrial countries have accumulated substantial liquid funds that can be spent either on goods and services or on financial assets. When spent on goods and services, it triggers the traditional inflationary impact reflected in rising CPI indexes. When spent on financial assets, it triggers speculative rises in financial asset prices reflected in rapidly rising share indexes. Normally, share indexes should not rise more than 20 percent per annum. When they rise above 30 percent, it is an indication of growing monetary surplus, triggering speculative activity. Eventually, interest rates will rise, depressing stock prices and causing investors to shift money into money market and bond invest-

Table 13.8
Share Index Analysis, 1978–1991

Benchmark: Over 30 percent indicates speculation.

	Parameters		
Share Index	Largest Growth	Largest Decline	Average Growth
U.S. - Dow Jones	31%	-16%	12%
Japan - Nikkei 225	44%	-41%	14%
Germany - DAX	76%	-37%	8%
Britain - FTSE 100	41%	-15%	11%
Canada - TSE 300	38%	-25%	11%

Source: "Economic and Financial Indicators," *The Economist,* 1978–1992 issues.

ments, adding to increased domestic spending and rising prices of goods and services. The period 1978 to 1991 indicated that inflationary pressures increased twelve to eighteen months following a year-to-year rise in a country's share index above 30 percent.

As a major international trader in goods and services with the largest financial market, the U.S. stock market has a substantial international influence. Under the key currency system, many countries manage their exchange rate in relation to the U.S. dollar, thereby maintaining similar monetary policies and interest rate trends. Hence, when the U.S. stock market reacts to U.S. domestic interest rate developments, as indicated by movements in the DJIA, other stock markets tend to follow, as shown in Figure 13.2. With heavy British investments in the United States, the London stock exchange is highly sensitive to U.S. economic conditions; and changes in the FTSE 100 often indicate future changes in the DJIA. A notable exception to the close relation to the DJIA has been the Tokyo market. As reflected by the Nikkei 225, it experienced several years of speculation, followed by a severe correction. An independent monetary policy put the Japanese business cycle in a direction different from the United States, even though the country is its principal trading partner.

The cross-border relationships between capital markets are becoming more pronounced, which may cause changes in several relationships. Presently, the DJIA reflects primarily economic and political conditions in the United States because the companies included in the index earn most of their revenue from U.S. sources and are headquartered in the United States. An increasing number of foreign-domiciled companies are being listed on the NYSE, while U.S. companies are expanding their global business. By the end of 1993, more than 9 percent of the listed companies were foreign domiciled; and a concerted

Figure 13.2
Selected Share Indexes, 1988–1993

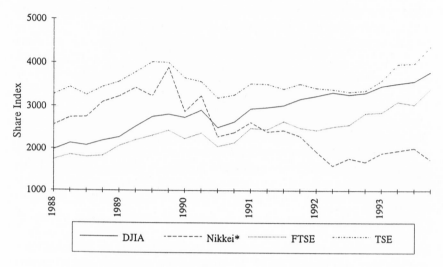

Source: "Economic and Financial Indicators," *The Economist,* 1988–1994 issues.
*Nikkei shown at one-tenth of index.

effort is being made to increase the number. Hence, global economic and political factors are going to have a greater influence on the DJIA.

Bear in mind that stock market investors represent a narrow slice of the population and are attempting to beat the market by anticipating economic changes. There is a tendency to overreact at the first sign of economic change. In their hurry to avoid losses or maximize profits, market participants do not always make a reasoned analysis of economic data or other events and may incorrectly judge economic trends. Consequently, share indexes of stock market prices remain faulty leading indicators.

CHAPTER 14

Other Economic
Indicators

Limiting economic indicators to readily available data allows for an understanding of international trends using a minimum amount of executive and investor time and resources. When accumulated in the international matrix system, the seventeen key economic and financial indicators discussed in this book keep executives and investors abreast of complex international economic conditions and future trends. Other indicators are also available.[1] Several of these other indicators are included in *The Economist* section of key indicators but tend to duplicate those used in the matrix system. Indicators not reported by *The Economist* are generally those tailored to individual countries but could become key indicators if compiled on a uniform basis by more countries.

A brief discussion of selected other popular economic and financial indicators may provide further insight into international economic trend analysis. If available on a timely basis, these indicators can also be included in the matrix system.

OFFICIAL INTEREST RATES

Official interest rates discussed in Chapter 11 are an important indication of the central bank perception of current economic conditions and monetary policy. While under stable economic conditions, each central bank will adjust its official interest rate to reflect financial market conditions. Successive changes in official interest rates over a one- to six-month period indicate change in monetary policy. Each central bank uses different official interest rates with different policy purposes, making it difficult to provide a simple uniform reporting system for the international matrix. *The Economist* does not include many official interest rates in its section of key economic and financial indicators, although the influence of some official interest rates such as the Fed Funds rate is reflected in overnight money market rates found in that section. While these overnight rates may be useful indicators, major changes in central bank official interest rates are normally reported more timely in the daily financial press such as the *Wall Street Journal* or the *Financial Times*.

Whether official interest rate changes significantly influences a country's economy is dependent on two conditions which can be subsequently followed in the international matrix: (1) the degree the official interest rate change influences the money market as indicated by a change in the yield spread between the three-month money market yield and the government-bond yield, and (2) the degree the official interest rate change is supported by conforming money supply operations indicated by a subsequent change in the year-to-year rate of change in a country's narrow M and real broad M.

Banks and other financial institutions may not necessarily conform to central bank monetary policy. This situation occasionally occurs when, in implementing its policy, a central bank has misread the supply-and-demand forces affecting short-term funds. For example, to spur the economy, a central bank may attempt lowering short-term interest rates by lowering its official interest rate. If banks are concerned about the economy, they may prefer maintaining a high prime rate, limiting their loan portfolio, and investing in high-yielding and safer government bonds. The divergence in interest rates indicated by the yield spreads between the prime rate and (1) the three-month money market yield and (2) the government-bond yield indicates commercial bank loan growth. This activity may nullify the intended effect of the change in the official interest rate.

OTHER INTEREST RATES

In its economic and financial indicators section, *The Economist* also reports interest rates on commercial bank three-month deposits, corporate bonds, Eurocurrency three-month deposits, Eurocurrency bonds, and LIBOR (London Interbank Offering Rate) three-month and six-month loans. These additional interest rates parallel the three-month money market yields and government-bond yields used in the international matrix system; therefore, including them in the international matrix would be a duplicative effort. Commercial bank three-month deposit interest rates could be an important economic indicator; but a review of interest rate data from 1978 to 1991 indicates that these rates are regulated, particularly in Japan, and do not reflect market interest rates as well as the three-month money market yields.

While following these additional interest rates is unlikely to provide further insight into economic trend analysis, they are important for some investment analysis and decision making. Comparing corporate bond and Eurocurrency yields with the respective three-month money market and government-bond yields in each country may provide risk assessment information on financial markets and economic conditions. LIBOR is an increasingly popular interest rate for basing loan interest rates, particularly variable interest rate loans. LIBOR interest rates tend to parallel U.S. money market yields.

INTEREST RATE DIFFERENTIALS

According to interest parity theory, interest rates among the industrial countries should be at the same level. If they are not, international capital flows will move to the country offering the highest interest rate, causing all interest rates to move toward a similar equilibrium level. Under a fixed rate regime where countries commit themselves to a common monetary policy, interest rate parity has great validity. However, under the floating exchange rate regime of the current international monetary system, there are major factors preventing equilibrium interest rate levels.

Different business cycles, domestic economic conditions, economic policies, exchange rate changes, and political changes are only some of the factors contributing to different nominal interest rate levels. In fact, no more than 25 percent of a country's investors engage in cross-border investment activities, limiting the influence of global capital flows and cross-border interest rate levels. Furthermore, countries experiencing high interest rates usually have unstable economic conditions, making investments in their financial markets more risky and discouraging cross-border capital flows. These unstable economic conditions are better understood through the key indicators of the international matrix system. Accordingly, while nominal interest rate differentials are an important factor for cross-border investors looking for the highest yield, they do not provide significant additional insight into economic trends.

RETAIL SALES

International economic thinking is heavily influenced by the demand management concepts of Keynesian economics in which consumption is a key factor for economic growth. In most industrial countries, consumption constitutes two-thirds of GDP so that monitoring consumer activity and attitudes is considered important in understanding a country's economic trends. As an indicator of consumer spending, *The Economist* provides year-to-year rates of change in monthly retail sales for industrial countries, including the matrix countries. It appears that year-to-year increases of 3 percent are reasonable for a normal economy.

However, retail sales figure have several weaknesses, limiting their usefulness as indicators of both general economic conditions and consumer activity. The compilation methodology used in many countries has not kept abreast with rapid changes occurring in the retail business. Most retail sales figures are based on department store sales whose market shares are eroding in face of aggressive price competition from discount store chains. Considerable analysis must be applied to evaluate distortions caused by this competitive pricing. In fact, Japan has changed its methodology for collecting retail sales data but is having difficulty providing timely information. Retail sales are also reported at current nominal prices with no inflationary adjustment, making it difficult to evaluate true sales volume. Retail sales tend to be volatile because of weather, fashion, and other unpredictable factors. It is not unusual to experience a dip in retail sales for one month because of severe winter storms and than a surge the following month as consumers replenish depleted cupboards. Retail sales figures represent only a segment of economic consumption because they report only the sale of goods. Services and housing, which absorb a large portion of consumer expenditures, are not included in most countries' retail sales.

COMMODITY PRICE INDEX

Commodity prices have long been considered an important indicator of economic activity. Industrial nations consume a wide variety of raw materials in both the manufacturing process and foods so that commodity price trends should be an early indicator of inflationary pressures and the strength of manufacturing output.

Two composite indexes widely followed to monitor commodity price trends are the Commodity Research Bureau (CRB) index of U.S. commodity prices and *The Economist* commodity price index of OECD-imported commodities. Commodities included in these indexes are raw materials important in manufactured and traded goods. Changes in these indexes are expected to indicate corresponding changes in finished goods sold to consumers.

The CRB index is composed of twenty-one commodities most significant to the U.S. economy and is derived from futures contracts traded on U.S. commodity exchanges. *The Economist* commodity price index measures composite prices weighted by the value of imports into OECD countries. The index is periodically revised and rebased. As of the end of 1993, the index was composed of twenty-six commodities rebased on OECD imports in the 1989–1991 net of intra-European Community trade affected by the common agricultural policy, with $1990 = 100$.[2] Table 14.1 provides a list of individual commodities used in the two indexes and their assigned weights.

Unfortunately, these commodity price indexes do not provide indications of future inflationary trends or economic activity more effectively than the indicators used in the international matrix system. Rather, changes in the indexes tend to confirm inflationary and production activity already evident from

Table 14.1
Comparison of *The Economist* **and CRB Commodity Price Indexes**

Economist Commodity Price Index
Revised and Rebased 1990 = 100

Overall Weights

Metals	33.3
Nonfood Agriculturals	19.3
Industrials	52.6
Foods	47.4
All Items	100.0

Individual Item Weights

Metals	Weights	Nonfood Agriculturals	Weights	Foods	Weights
Aluminum	42.2	Wool	28.4	Coffee	29.2
Copper	33.7	Cotton	24.0	Beef	14.8
Nickel	11.9	Timber	18.9	Soybeans	12.7
Zinc	6.8	Rubber	17.3	Sugar	11.2
Tin	3.3	Hides	7.0	Maize	8.8
Lead	2.1	Soybeans	1.5	Cocoa	8.4
		Coconut oil	1.5	Soya meal	7.8
		Palm oil	1.3	Wheat	5.2
		Soybean oil	0.3	Tea	2.7
				Lamb	2.5
				Palm oil	1.6
				Coconut oil	0.6
				Soya oil	0.5

Commodity Research Bureau (CRB) Index
(Equal Weights)

Meats	Cattle, hogs, porkbellies
Metals	Gold, platinum, silver
Imports	Cocoa, coffee, sugar
Energy	Crude oil, heating oil, unleaded gasoline
Grains	Corn, wheat, soybeans, soybean meal, soybean oil
Industrials	Copper, lumber, cotton
Fruit	Orange juice

Source: "Commodity Brief," *The Economist,* January 22, 1994, p. 76; Knight-Ridder Financial/Commodity Research Bureau, *The CRB Yearbook 1994* (New York: John Wiley & Sons, 1994), p. 6T.

other indicators. There are several reasons contributing to this lack of effectiveness. Agricultural commodities are a large part of both indexes, but enormous productivity improvements in the agricultural sector combined with the declining proportion of industrial economic resources devoted to agriculture activity have lessened their price impact in the manufacturing and consumer sectors. Furthermore, government price-support programs, subsidies, and cartels have distorted the relationship between commodity prices and general economic activity.

In contrast, a greater inflationary influence are employee wages and benefits, productivity, and growing government-administered prices through tax and regulatory practices which are not measured by these indexes. For example, the average component cost of manufactured products is estimated to consist of 50 percent labor and labor-related costs and only 10 percent raw material costs. As technology and skilled workers become a larger component of the manufacturing process, commodity prices are likely to have an even smaller impact on prices.

Both indexes are highly regarded but are designed for two different economic systems.[3] With the United States less dependent on raw material imports, the CRB index is composed of commodities important to the overall U.S. economy rather than limited to import trade. Two principal advantages of this index are that it is quoted daily in most American financial news media and that it is included in the CRB's annual yearbook, which contains substantial current and historical information on individual commodities and commodity markets.

Europe's dependence on raw material imports makes *The Economist* commodity price index more important for European country analysis. This index has several other advantages. Though periodically revised, it dates from 1864, giving it a much longer history than the CRB index and making it particularly useful for historical analysis. Its subdivision into industrial metals, nonfood agricultures, and food commodities indexes provides better means for analyzing the relationship between commodity price changes and economic activity. This index and its subdivision are also presented in three different prices—U.S. dollars, pounds sterling, and SDRs—making it more useful for international analysis.

These two indexes also take different approaches in selecting commodities for index inclusion. The CRB index includes the precious metal prices of gold, silver, and platinum, which also perform a dual function as raw material for manufacturing and official reserves in the international monetary system. Accordingly, precious metal prices have fluctuated for reasons other than changes in industrial supply and demand, causing distortions in the CRB index not directly related to economic output or inflationary pressures. In contrast, *The Economist* commodity price index excludes precious metals, reporting gold prices separately. *The Economist* index also excludes oil prices because of its greater sensitivity to political rather than economic conditions, reporting separately the price per barrel of Brent crude oil.

Although commodity prices are a confirming rather than a leading indicator of inflationary trends, following either index may indicate central bank monetary policy changes. It has been reported that the Federal Reserve monitors the relationship of interest rates, money supply, and commodity prices in accordance with an economic theory developed by a highly respected but little-known Swedish economist named Knut Wicksell (1851–1926). Professor Wicksell propounded that when short-term interest rates were below long-term rates and commodity prices were rising, the money supply was too loose and, unless tightened, would lead to inflation. Conversely, if short-term interest rates were above long-term interest rates and commodity prices were declining, the money supply was not sufficiently expanding and, if not loosened, would result in a decline in production.

The Wicksell theory is a variation of the basic monetary theory regarding the relationship between money supply and growth. Professor Wicksell's major contribution was to distill a basic monetary theory into a workable formula for monetary authorities who lacked timely data on money supply and credit. He identified the specific factors of interest rates and commodity prices that could be monitored daily by a central bank anxious to devise a timely and effective monetary policy.

While the Wicksell theory is still applicable today, changes in the overall structure of industrial- and technological-based economies require modification for its application. At the time Professor Wicksell developed his theory, commodities were a far greater component of economic activity; and labor consisted primarily of unskilled and semiskilled individuals. Today, commodities are a less significant factor in the manufacturing process, while skilled labor, productivity, and government activity are far greater cost factors.

SPECIFIC COMMODITIES

Some commentators recommend monitoring the price of certain specific commodities as indicators of future economic trends. The thinking underlying this method is that certain commodities have a significant and consistent relationship to economic activity that is otherwise diluted by a composite commodity price index. Thus, rising demand for the specific commodity emanates from an improving economy causing price increases, reflecting rising demand for the commodity. Likewise, a declining economy will cause declining prices for the specific commodity as its demand slackens.

While the relationship between economic growth and demand for certain commodities has a sound theoretical basis, supply-and-demand forces unrelated to economic output often affect commodity prices. Strikes, natural disasters, embargoes, war, technology, and a host of other events affect supply and demand and, therefore, prices. Consequently, monitoring the price of an individual commodity is of limited use unless it is of great overall economic significance.

One such significant commodity is oil. For the reasons discussed in the preceding chapters, oil supply is critical to all industrial economies, making its price movements an important indicator in the international matrix system. Unlike most other commodities, there are few that are as critical to industrial economies and affect such large segments of a nation's economy as oil; and in the event of shortages or unusually high prices, there are few readily available substitutes.

Nevertheless, monitoring several additional commodity prices can round out an overall understanding of economic trends. Two widely followed commodities are gold and copper. Because of its historic role in the international monetary system, gold is traditionally considered an indicator of economic confidence; but it has less significance with respect to current economic output. A rising price indicates falling confidence, while a falling price indicates rising confidence.

More specifically, since gold does not earn income except from appreciation, a growing economy is expected to open new investment opportunities more attractive than gold, causing its price to decline. On the other hand, a declining economy is fraught with risk so that preservation of capital is more important than earning income; and gold tends to hold its value during a recession. However, central banks are slowly removing gold as an official reserve because it does not earn income compared to other forms of international reserves. In fact, only 14 percent of gold supply is held by central banks, while 61 percent is used in jewelry and 14 percent for industrial purposes.

In contrast, copper is a commodity important solely as a raw material used in the industrial process. While being displaced in many industries by other materials such as fiber optics in the communications industry, copper remains important in general electronics, which is rapidly becoming the mainstay of modern industrial economies. Copper is also widely used in the auto and housing sectors.

In using the price of these two commodities, a limiting factor is their susceptibility to wide fluctuations caused by unstable inventory levels rather than overall economic conditions. Major gold- and copper-producing regions are located in countries with histories of political instability. Russia and South Africa are two of the largest gold producers, while Russia and Chile are principal copper producers.

If used as an indicator of economic trends, some rough benchmarks are helpful. It appears that a gold price of $400 per ounce and a copper price of $1.00 per cathode pound are associated with normal supply-and-demand activity. If the price of gold moves above the $400-per-ounce figure, it is an indication of declining economic confidence, while a price below that figure indicates continuing economic confidence. If the price of copper moves above $1.00 per cathode pound, it is an indication of inflationary pressure or strong demand for the commodity. If the price is below this figure, it is generally an indication of a weak economy.

HOUSING STARTS

Many economists consider new housing start figures a key economic indicator because many industrial countries begin recessionary recoveries with a strong rebound in this sector. For U.S. government statistics, the U.S. Department of Commerce defines a housing start as the commencement of excavation for the structure's footing and foundation, except in the case of public housing, in which case the month of the construction contract award is used. The U.S. housing start number quoted most often in business publications includes both single-unit and multi-unit structures.

For most people, a house purchase is the single largest acquisition with mortgage payments, consuming as much as 40 percent of their annual income. Its greatest impact is in the economic ripple effect. Cities support housing development by building new infrastructures such as roads and sewers, receiving in return new tax revenue sources. Telephones and other utilities are installed, and owners increase purchases of durable goods such as furnishings and household appliances. Expanded population also increases local consumer spending.

A unique characteristic of housing is that 70 to 80 percent of the cost of a new house is generally financed by a mortgage loan. The first ten years of mortgage payments go to pay interest, making housing extremely sensitive to interest rates. Imbalances in the economy, causing changes in long-term interest rates, directly affect the housing market. When interest rates are high, housing starts are often the first segment of the economy to decline, leading the rest of the economy into a recession. Following a recession, housing starts are often the first economic segment to improve as consumers take advantage of lower interest rates to purchase new homes.

Housing start statistics are an important U.S. economic indicator, often indicating changes in the business cycle. U.S. housing starts have varied from 2,000,000 during a strong rebound to 850,000 during an economic downturn. As the American population increases, the average number of housing starts during a normal economic growth period also increases. Under economic conditions of the 1990s, a housing start rate of about 1.2 million indicates a modestly growing U.S. economy. Unfortunately, little international attention is given to housing start data so that there is no uniform international system for reporting such data. In addition, government housing programs vary widely among the industrial countries so that any housing start data would require unique interpretation.

CAPACITY UTILIZATION

A lesser-known economic indicator is the capacity utilization rate which in several respects is a more significant measure of economic trends than the more widely used industrial production index. The rate of change of the industrial production index tells the direction and rate of speed of industrial output but not the level. In contrast, the capacity utilization rate gives the level of activity for the reported month, making it more useful in relationship analysis.

Capacity utilization studies have been pioneered by the U.S. Federal Reserve which has the most reliable data on U.S. utilization levels dating from 1967. It defines *capacity utilization* as the greatest level of output a firm "could reasonably expect to attain using a realistic employee work schedule and the machinery and equipment in place during the time periods covered by the survey." It is reported monthly in the middle of the following month in conjunction with the industrial production index.

While a relatively new economic indicator, a brief discussion of U.S. benchmarks will illustrate its significance in the hopes that more countries will use capacity utilization indexes. Under the Federal Reserve's capacity utilization index, a rate of 83 percent of available capacity is considered full capacity. If the rate goes above this figure, bottlenecks are likely to occur and inflationary pressures build. If the rate falls below 83 percent, the economy is turning downward. A fall in the capacity utilization rate below 80 percent indicates a weak U.S. economy; and if the capacity utilization rate approaches 70 percent, the economy is in serious decline. During the 1978–1991 period, the U.S. capacity utilization rate reached a high of 87.3 percent in March 1979, a period of high inflation, and a low of 71.8 percent in December 1982, the middle of the U.S. recession and a month when U.S. unemployment reached its highest cyclical level of 10.7 percent.

CONFIDENCE INDEX

In many countries, an increasingly popular index is a consumer or business confidence index which some economists believe are indicators of future purchasing or business activity. Some of the most widely followed indexes covering national economies are prepared by the Confederation of British Industry, the U.S. National Association of Purchasing Managers, and the U.S. Conference Board. While confidence indexes are helpful in understanding consumer and business psychology, they are better utilized when incorporated in a sophisticated econometric model. In the short run, employment, inflation, and interest rates are real economic factors that more greatly influence consumer and business purchasing behavior than confidence levels. Consumers tend to maintain buying habits despite dropping confidence levels, while businesses' confidence is a reaction to immediate business activity with no anticipation of future economic conditions. In fact, real economic factors lead the confidence levels rather than vice versa. As long-term indicators, these consumer and business confidence indexes tend to confirm other economic factors such as the rate of unemployment and industrial production.

RATIO OF GOVERNMENT BUDGET BALANCES
TO NOMINAL GDP

Since World War II, most industrial countries have achieved sustained economic growth punctuated by significant business downturns while incurring almost continuous central government budget deficits. This extensive experience indicates certain benchmarks for understanding the impact of budget deficits on the overall economy. Table 14.2 provides a summary of budget balances as a ratio to GDP for the matrix countries during the period 1986 to 1992. A central government budget deficit no greater than –1.5 percent of nominal GDP was manageable because of the continued economic growth in real GDP, which averaged in excess of 2.4 percent per year.

Other than Japan, the matrix countries have incurred budget deficits greater than –1.5 percent, creating economic imbalances and causing a dilemma for monetary policy that exacerbated the problem. To finance the deficits, central governments issued bonds in competition with the private sector, threatening a dislocation of private investment. Expanded foreign imports avoided such dislocation but at the cost of mortgaging future income to pay for the foreign-owned debt. Consequently, matrix countries with large budget deficits also incurred large current account deficits. An alternative approach was money supply expansion which caused inflation and exchange rate depreciation but

Table 14.2
Government Financial Balances, 1986–1992

	1986	1987	1988	1989	1990	1991	1992
	Budget Balances as a Percentage of GDP						
United States	-3.4%	-2.5%	-2.0%	-1.5%	-2.5%	-3.4%	-4.7%
Japan	-0.9%	0.5%	1.5%	2.5%	2.9%	3.0%	1.8%
Germany	-1.3%	-1.9%	-2.2%	0.1%	-2.0%	-3.2%	-2.8%
Britain	-2.4%	-1.3%	1.0%	0.9%	-1.3%	-2.9%	-6.7%
Canada	-5.4%	-3.8%	-2.5%	-3.0%	-4.1%	-6.1%	-6.4%
	Net Public Debt as a Percentage of GDP						
United States	29.4%	30.9%	30.9%	30.4%	33.1%	34.7%	38.0%
Japan	26.4%	21.5%	17.8%	14.9%	9.7%	6.2%	4.2%
Germany	22.1%	23.2%	24.2%	22.7%	22.8%	23.2%	24.4%
Britain	44.7%	42.0%	35.3%	30.1%	28.5%	30.2%	35.8%
Canada	37.0%	38.3%	36.9%	40.3%	43.5%	49.2%	54.7%

Source: OECD Economic Outlook (Paris: Organization for Economic Cooperation and Development, June 1993), pp. 141 and 214.

limited growth in government debt. Through this method, Germany limited its current account deficit arising from the unification with East Germany but at the cost of persistent inflation.

RATIO OF GOVERNMENT DEBT TO NOMINAL GDP

Any analysis of the budget deficit issue also requires an analysis of the national debt. While the terms *deficit* and *debt* are often used interchangeably, the distinction is important. The deficit refers to the amount central government expenses exceed central government revenues collected during the year. A deficit could be eliminated by raising revenue such as taxes or cutting expenditures. The deficit can be financed by borrowing from the public and increasing the central government debt. The total outstanding central government debt is, in essence, the financing of deficits that is cumulative over a period of years.

Budget deficits are manageable if investors are willing to purchase the debt instruments issued to finance it, and a key factor is the country's ability to service its national debt. Through the power to tax, central governments have the capability to raise substantial revenues to pay their debts. However, this power is not unlimited and is subject to the overall economic resources of the country. Accordingly, a common measure of the central government's ability to service the national debt is to calculate the ratio of the outstanding central government debt to nominal GDP.

Table 14.2 presents the ratio of net publicly held central government debt to nominal GDP for the matrix countries. With a debt-to-GDP ratio of 54 percent in 1992, Canada had the highest ratio contributing to a growing current account deficit of sizable proportions. The United States and Britain also have high ratios—38 percent and 36 percent, respectively—contributing to high domestic interest rates and chronic current account deficits. Japan, on the other hand, has a very low debt-to-GDP ratio of 4 percent and generated budget surpluses despite a weak domestic economy in 1991 and 1992. Although criticized for this restrictive budget, Japan has defended its policy by the need to prepare for future budget deficits necessary to support an aging population.

DIVIDEND YIELD ON SHARE INDEXES

In using the stock market as an indicator of economic trends and investor sentiment, it is important to know if the market is undervalued or overvalued relative to overall business earning capacity. Price-to-earnings ratios are one of the favorite techniques for evaluating the reasonableness of stock prices. However, a significant limitation on the price-to-earnings ratio method occurs during recessionary periods when firms incur losses and reduced profits.

During such a period, the price-to-earnings ratio is generally high as the market discounts the earnings decline as being only a temporary phenomenon.

A better indicator of the reasonableness of stock market value is dividend yields. Dividend yields indicate business firms' and investors' judgment of future economic trends. Table 14.3 lists factors influencing corporate dividend policy developed from a survey conducted by the Bank of England. Representing 43 percent in the survey, long-term growth was the most important factor. Firms must analyze economic trends and their own earnings capability within the economic environment to formulate their dividend policy. Dividends are increased in a growth economy. Dividend levels are generally maintained in a downturn if it is believed that the downturn will be short or shallow. Firms will have no choice but to reduce dividends in a serious downturn. In making share investments, investors consider the return from dividend payments and the likelihood of payment in addition to share price appreciation.

Dividend policy varies from company to company. However, a composite dividend yield in relation to the related share index is a good indicator of the reasonableness of overall equity market conditions. Composite dividend yields are prepared for most share indexes by calculating the current composite dividends paid divided by the current share index value.

Historically, dividend yields for U.S. share indexes has been a consistent indicator of market sentiment throughout various phases of the business cycle. During the 1978–1991 period covered by the historical matrix, the dividend yield on the DJIA has fluctuated from a high of 6.1 percent in April 1980 to a low of 2.8 percent in September and November 1987. In a normally healthy economy, the dividend yield has generally been between 3 and 4.5 percent. When the dividend yield falls below 3 percent, U.S. stock prices are unusually high, indicating the presence of speculative sentiment. When the dividend yield rises above 4.5 percent, U.S. stock prices are low, indicating growing

Table 14.3
Factors Influencing Corporate Dividend Policy

Projected long-term earnings growth	43%
Shareholder expectations	19%
Need to retain cash	15%
Historical earnings growth	11%
Need to maintain access to capital markets	10%
Analysts' expectations	2%
	100%

Source: Bank of England, *Quarterly Bulletin* (London: Bank of England, August 1993).

Table 14.4
Dividend Yields, 1990 and 1991

	1990	1991
United States	3.6%	3.3%
Japan	0.5%	0.6%
Germany	3.2%	3.6%
Britain	4.9%	4.8%
Canada	3.7%	3.4%

Source: Basic Statistics of the Community, 29th ed. (Brussels: European
Communities, 1992).

investor pessimism. Table 14.4 presents dividend yields for selected stock
markets in 1990 and 1991.

NOTES

1. The Economist, *Guide to Economic Indicators* (London: Century Business, 1992),
contains a good discussion of many economic indicators commonly used in international
economic analysis. Another helpful but more limited source is Mark Jones and Ken Ferris,
Market Movers (London: McGraw Hill, 1993).

2. "Commodities Brief," *The Economist,* January 22, 1994, p. 76.

3. In comparing the two commodity indexes, see also *The Economist,* March 5, 1994,
p. 92.

CHAPTER 15

Analytical Techniques Using the International Matrix System

Under the international matrix system, key economic indicators and their relationships are presented in a format that paints a vivid picture of current economic conditions and future trends. This format consists of arranging the indicators and relationships into five sections, each section designed to explain specific economic conditions. The first section provides an overview of the country's current economic condition through the monthly government indicators of year-to-year change in industrial production, rate of unemployment, year-to-year change in CPI, year-to-year change in wage index, and year-to-year change in producer prices. The second section indicates the nature of the exchange rate regime and exchange rate stability by showing the trade-weighted exchange rate index, the bilateral exchange rate with the U.S. dollar, and then the rate of change for both exchange rates from the beginning of the current year to the current month. The third section provides an overview of current monetary conditions and monetary policy by showing the year-to-year rate of change in nominal M, nominal broad M, and real broad M; three-month money market yields, government-bond yields, prime interest rates and related real interest rates, and yield spreads. The fourth section provides the most recent annualized balance of trade and balance on current account figures together with their ratios to current-year projections for nominal GDP and the country's foreign exchange reserves. The fifth section monitors additional inflationary pressures indicated by providing changes in the share price indexes and oil prices.

Most government-supplied data are reported monthly, so statistics should be accumulated in the international matrix format monthly. In conformity, weekly reported data such as interest and exchange rates should be accumulated using end-of-month figures from *The Economist*. It is also insightful to accumulate these weekly figures separately to keep abreast of developing trends. The historical matrix data contained in Appendix A use month-end figures for the four quarterly months in the year and are easy to extend into more current periods by reviewing prior issues of *The Economist* found in most public or university libraries.

This format also enables the international matrix to be studied using several different analytical techniques providing not only more precise information on the direction of economic trends but also signals of changing economic direction and relationships to major trading partners.

PRINCIPAL ANALYTICAL APPROACH

At first glance, the international matrix may overwhelm the reader with the volume of data to be analyzed while attempting to understand economic conditions in several countries simultaneously. One approach to discerning economic direction is to integrate key economic and financial indicators into a single master index of leading economic indicators as is done by many industrial countries. An increase in the index of leading economic indicators forecasts an upturn in the economy, while a decrease forecasts a downturn. Usually, three consecutive changes in the same direction is considered a strong indicator of the economy's future direction.

In practice, most leading indicator indexes have been helpful in confirming the direction of economic trends. They have been less helpful in signaling changes in its direction. These indexes are based on data that are usually one or two months old; and thus, during periods of economic turbulence or rapid change, their accuracy and timeliness are questionable. For executives and investors, a more significant weakness is that general indication of economic trends is not sufficient. They need information on specific aspects of economic activity such as interest rate and exchange rate changes, and they need to evaluate the degree and rapidity of economic change. The many component items included in leading indexes are submerged in the composite nature of the index, making it unsuitable for sophisticated analytical use beyond the mere signals derived from the monthly change in the index.

Although requiring more effort, accumulating current data in the international matrix system enables a systematic analytical approach that makes sense of all the data enabling better and more timely business and investment decisions. For the principal analytical approach, a seven-step analytical process should be applied to each of the five matrix countries and to any other country subject to particular study. This analytical approach integrates the benchmark figures and the relationships discussed in this book. In summary, the seven-step process is as follows:

1. What are the current economic conditions in the country?
2. What is the indicated exchange rate regime?
3. What is the current monetary policy, and does it focus on domestic economic conditions or on maintaining the exchange rate regime?
4. If the monetary policy focuses on maintaining the exchange rate regime, can such policy be maintained in light of deteriorating domestic economic conditions?
5. What inflationary pressures are building?
6. How will the government respond?
7. What impact will arise from trading partners' economic conditions?

What Are the Current Economic Conditions?

Begin the seven-step analytical process by reviewing the first section of key economic indicators reported monthly by each country (year-to-year change in the industrial production index, unemployment rate, year-to-year rate of change in the consumer price index, year-to-year rate of change in the wage index, and year-to-year rate of change in producer price index) intended to provide an overview of current economic conditions. Compare the most recent numbers to the respective benchmark figures discussed in the preceding chapters. This analysis will provide a snapshot of the current state of the economy.

What Is the Exchange Rate Regime?

Reviewing the current and preceding year's rate of change in a country's trade-weighted exchange rate index and bilateral exchange rate with the dollar will indicate the exchange rate regime being followed. Generally, a rate of change that is in the range of ±2.5 percent indicates a fixed exchange rate regime, while a change greater than ±5 percent indicates a floating exchange rate regime.

What Is the Monetary Policy?

Next, study the rate of change in narrow M and real broad M for the preceding four months, considering the impact upon current economic trends.

For example, if the economy is weak and real broad M is rising, the economy should strengthen. If the economy is weak and real broad M is trending downward, the economy will remain weak and may contract further. On the other hand, if the economy is strong and the trend for real broad M is rising, inflation may be around the corner. If the economy is strong and real broad M is declining, higher short-term interest rates may be expected. Furthermore, if the year-to-year rate of change in CPI is above 5 percent, imbalances in the economy are growing. The central bank may initiate a tight monetary policy to combat the inflationary trend.

After determining the trend in real broad M, study the key interest rate indicators and their relationships with one another in a manner discussed in greater detail in Chapter 13. This analysis indicates the degree the credit markets are conforming with the trend indicated by narrow M and real broad M. For example, one measure for evaluating the degree of conformity of the credit markets is the spread between the three-month money market and government-bond yield. To the extent that this analysis indicates the credit markets are conforming with the trend indicated by real broad M, the economy will likely move in the same direction in a more rapid and sustained manner. If the credit markets are not in conformity with the trend of real broad M, it is likely that the economy will remain in its current state. For example, where real broad M is declining but the three-month money market yield is below the yield on government bonds, the credit expansion is negated by the decline in real broad M, indicating that economic growth (if any) may be sluggish.

Can Monetary Policy Be Maintained?

Levels of real money market and real government-bond yields indicate monetary policies focusing on exchange rate stability rather than domestic economic conditions. When a country is incurring a current account deficit, real interest rates rise above normal benchmark levels to support stable exchange rates. When a country is incurring a current account surplus, real interest rates fall below normal benchmark levels to counter an increase in the exchange rate. A deteriorating domestic economic condition, however, may require that a new monetary policy be initiated, which may put pressure on the exchange rate. Monetary authorities face a dilemma of concentrating on the deteriorating domestic economic condition or maintaining the exchange rate regime. An evaluation is made as to whether the exchange rate regime can be maintained despite growing pressure.

What Inflationary Pressures Are Building?

An analysis of changes in oil prices, stock exchange indexes, trend in the CPI, monetary policy, wage indexes, and unemployment rate will indicate building inflationary pressures.

How Will the Government Respond?

After answering the previous questions, consider what response, if any, will be initiated by the central government. In particular, if the analysis indicates that the unemployment rate is rising or the rate of change in the CPI is rising, expect a reaction from the central government. The first reaction may commence with remarks by central bank officials or government spokespersons reported in the business press. Typically, several weeks will elapse for sufficient concern to build before the central bank or government arrives at a consensus policy. The next reaction will probably come from some change in central bank monetary policy. A change in rate of growth in real broad M or official interest rates will signal the central bank's response. If the central bank response has insufficient impact on the economic imbalance, a public debate will often begin on the next level of government response.

What Impact Will Arise from Trading Partners?

Changes in domestic economic conditions or government economic policy will quickly translate into changes in domestic interest rates. Such changes may create adjustments in the commercial relationship with major trading partners, reflected by changes in bilateral exchange rates. Comparing the economic condition of a home country with that of its major trading partners will indicate the adjustments, if any, that will be necessary.

This comparison is begun by evaluating step by step each section of key economic indicators of one country with the corresponding section of economic and financial indicators of the principal trading partners. Hence, the first section on current economic conditions often indicates that one country's economy is growing while a trading partner's economy is weak. This imbalance between two major trading partners will be confirmed by other matrix indicators such as different interest rate levels and yield spreads as each country pursues domestic economic policies in accordance with its economic conditions. Where two principal trading partners are experiencing different phases in the business cycle, pursuing different economic policies requires adjustments in their bilateral exchange rates. However, if a country's domestic policy is to maintain fixed exchange rates, then its domestic economic policy will be constrained, exacerbating existing domestic economic conditions. A comparison of the year-to-year rates of change in the CPI indexes also indicates the price competitiveness between trading partners.

In comparing trading partners, two elements are important. First, the United States, Japan, Germany, and several other countries are key currency countries for their respective major trading partners. Accordingly, a key currency country's monetary policy and economic condition will have a great influence on trading partners, compelling them to adopt similar economic policies and conditions if they wish to maintain stable trade-weighted exchange rates. Second, U.S. capital markets remain a key world influence so that U.S. interest rate levels set the international standard.

OTHER ANALYTICAL TECHNIQUES

Economic data are best understood when studied from several different perspectives. Most economists use complex econometric models by which to undertake this process; but such a process is beyond the expertise or, for that matter, the need of most executives and investors. Several other techniques, including the relationship and trend analysis methods previously discussed, are much more helpful. When the indicators are examined utilizing these simple techniques, a fairly good understanding of the global economy and its direction is achieved. The international matrix of key economic and financial indicators presented in this book is in a format that indicates future economic trends using other different analytical techniques:

- Trend analysis
- Relationship analysis
- Historical comparison
- Time sequence analysis
- Economic forecast comparison
- Stimulation checklist
- Input of other economic data

Trend Analysis

Trend analysis is the study of the monthly levels or rates of change in a key indicator to determine the future direction indicated by the prior levels or rates of change. Each indicator is studied separately to determine the indicated trend or in conjunction with the trend of other indicators. A declining industrial production index along with an increase in the unemployment rate indicates a weakening economy. Furthermore, a decline in all the interest rates included in the indicators would also be expected in a declining economy.

For example, study the trend of the British unemployment rate in 1991 as shown in the historical matrix located in Appendix A. The unemployment rate is slowly rising throughout 1991, from 6.5 percent at the end of the preceding year to 9.0 percent at the end of the year. During the same period, year-to-year rates of change in the industrial production index showed deterioration in the first half of the year with slight improvement in the second half. The nature of the decline in these two indicators shows a weak economy. As measured by the year-to-year rate of change in CPI, the rate of inflation is also declining. For most of the year, real broad M is between 1.2 and 2.0 percent, indicating a tight money supply. However, bank lending activity continues but appears to decline in the second half of the year. The bank prime rate declines, and the spread with the government-bond yield narrows from 4.0 percent to 1.9 percent in December. Interest rates are falling as the credit markets contract in light of the weak economy.

Relationship Analysis

Studying the relationships among all the indicators has been discussed at considerable length in previous chapters and is one of the most important analytical functions to be undertaken. This matrix presents all the data on a monthly basis so that the relationships can be easily examined. As discussed in the previous chapter, changes in real broad M will not necessarily affect industrial production unless there is a conforming change in the credit markets as manifested by changes in the relationships between various interest rates. This matrix enables the examination of all the indicators and their relationships to one another.

For example, study the key 1991 economic indicators for Britain. Real broad M is steady throughout the year; and after declining in the first half of the year, the year-to-year change in the industrial production index begins improving in the second half. The three-month money market yield is substantially above the government-bond yield, indicating a tight monetary policy, while during the same period, the bank prime rate is considerably above the government-bond yield. The lack of conformity between tight government monetary policy and continued bank lending indicates that the economy will continue to be sluggish.

Historical Comparison

The reaction of human beings to prior similar situations is the core to our expectation of people's reaction to future events so that a complete understanding of current economic conditions requires an understanding of its historical context. A study of key indicators from previous business cycles will aid in understanding data accumulated for the current business cycle and its probable direction. Presented in Appendix A are key economic and financial indicators for the matrix countries laid out as a matrix on a quarterly basis for the years 1988 to 1993. This period includes the most recent recessionary period for the matrix countries that began in about 1990.

Time Sequence Analysis

Analyzing the time sequence of changes in primary factors and the magnitude of such changes is a vital part of economic trend analysis. The daily fluctuations of the financial markets and commentators' discussions on economic matters often give an impression of the economy's ability to react quickly and efficiently to new events or new policies. However, if a nation's economy did attempt to rapidly change in response to new stimuli, it would disfunction.

Most segments of a nation's economy and most nations do not respond to change with equal ability or alacrity. There are a number of reasons for this apparent rigidity in national economies, making them vulnerable to dislocation. Many industries require long lead times to adjust. Construction of new buildings, training workers with new skills, and product development are only a few of the important economic activities that require considerable planning and investment to achieve ultimate success. For example, the length of time for construction of a new building, from when the architect prepares the plans to when the building is occupied, is generally three years. Still other industries are prevented from timely adjustment because of government regulation or agency rigidity. More fundamental to the problems of rapid economic change is that efficiency and stability are the keys to economic growth and are fostered by long-term commitments embodied in contractual obligations. Based on these contractual obligations, many firms have made substantial investments; and in response to rapid economic change, the obligations cannot be quickly unwound without resulting in their complete ruin and massive worker layoffs.

In most cases, individually and collectively the global economy grows best if the changes in economic factors are steady and orderly, thereby allowing the various segments and nations to adjust without severe disruption. Accordingly, a period of time should elapse before changes in some of the indicators result in the expected change in economic conditions. The international matrix permits a study of all the key economic and financial indicators during a twelve-month period, and each year's set of indicators can be easily studied to understand the economic flow over several years. Using the benchmark figures described for the key indicators, sudden changes in any one of the key indicators can be studied to evaluate the magnitude and likely influence of the change on economic conditions and ultimately on the direction of the overall economy. An economy is prone to dislocation when any of the key matrix indicators exhibits a large change in a short time frame.

Economic Forecast Comparison

For the past several years, economic forecasts have been much derided for their apparent failure to warn of major changes. Considering the complexity of the global economy, the many imponderable chance events, and the fickle nature of human beings, most economic forecasts in the past have generally not been that far off. If properly used in conjunction with the matrix system presented in this book, many published economic forecasts are very valuable even if the forecasts ultimately prove to be "wide of the mark."

The value of these forecasts lies in the professional preparation by skilled and knowledgeable economists. These forecasts are generally based on a forecasting model derived from an extensive data base and mathematical relationships that have been refined and improved over the years. With such extensive information, these forecast models are capable of providing a far more accurate economic analysis than could be achieved by the matrix system in this book, which relies on only seventeen key indicators. The international matrix system presented in this book is not an attempt to replace forecasts or current forecasting techniques. Rather, the matrix system is designed to assist executives and investors in making the best use of available published forecasts.

To use a forecast, it is necessary to understand some of the weaknesses inherent in those published for general public use. The first major weakness is in the nature of the data that constitute the basis of the forecast. Most forecasts rely in part on data supplied by the national governments. Some of these government-supplied data are used in this book as key indicators and were discussed in prior chapters. Such data are often several weeks or months old by the time they are disseminated to the public. Hence, when an economic forecaster begins developing the forecast, the government-supplied data are technically stale. In addition, much of these data are based on surveys and estimates subject to subsequent revisions. Using econometric models and studying past behavior, the forecaster can usually correct for these problems. However, during the forecast preparation period, major events are occurring, creating economic turbulence and uncertainty. Thus, the accuracy of the forecast is obviously questionable.

In addition, all forecasts depend on certain assumptions. Prices of key raw materials such as oil, stability in government policy, and stability in central bank monetary policy are usually some of the more significant assumptions. The dynamics of a changing economy usually results in a change in one or more of the assumptions subsequent to the forecast preparation. Illustrative of the importance of assumptions are those underlying the June 1993 OECD economic forecasts summarized in Table 15.1 using the international matrix format. The forecasters listed three principal assumptions. Exchange rates were expected to remain constant except for those countries with announced exchange rate policies. The price of crude oil was expected to remain the same according to a separate forecast of energy prices. Fiscal and monetary policies for individual countries were based on stated official policies and most recent budgetary statements.

The next major problem of forecasts is the delay from the time the forecaster completes the economic projection to the time it is disseminated to the public. As with most publications, the forecaster's material must be reviewed by others, formatted into the publication style, scheduled for print, and ultimately made available to the readers. It is not unusual for the published forecast to be as much as one month old by the time it reaches the general readership.

Despite the several weaknesses inherent in published economic forecasts, an informative one can be valuable. An economic forecast is like a budget, and

Table 15.1
Comparison of Economic Forecast to Actual Results

	OECD FORECAST JUNE 1993					REPORTED INDICATORS DECEMBER 1993				
	U.S.	Japan	Ger.	Britain	Canada	U.S.	Japan	Ger.	Britain	Canada
Ind. Production	4.0	-1.2		2.8	4.6	4.7	-4.2	-0.1	4.0	4.5
Unemployment	6.9	2.5	10.9	10.7	11.0	6.4	2.9	9.0	9.8	11.2
CPI	2.6	1.6	3.7	2.4	2.2	2.7	1.0	3.6	1.9	1.7
Currency to Dollar		111.0	1.61	0.65	1.27		113.0	1.74	0.67	1.32
Nominal Broad M	0.5/	0.0/	4.5/	0.0/						
(OECD Ranges)	4.5	1.0	6.5	4.0		1.6	1.5	8.1	4.0	2.9
Real Broad M						-1.1	0.5	4.5	2.1	1.2
Short-term Interest	3.0	3.2	6.1	5.8	5.3	3.3	2.0	5.8	5.4	3.8
Government Bond	5.9	5.1	6.3	8.0	7.5	5.7	3.5	5.5	6.3	6.7
Yield Spread	-2.9	-1.9	-0.2	-2.2	-2.2	-2.4	-1.5	0.3	-0.9	-2.9
Real M M Yield	0.4	1.6	2.4	3.4	3.1	0.6	1.0	2.2	3.5	2.1
Real Bond Yield	3.3	3.5	2.6	5.6	5.3	3.0	2.5	1.9	4.4	5.0
Bank Prime Rate	6.0	5.0	8.5	8.0	7.5	6.0	3.0	9.0	6.5	5.5
Spread-MM	3.0	1.8	2.4	2.2	2.2	2.7	1.0	3.2	1.1	1.7
Spread-Bond	0.1	-0.1	2.2	0.0	0.0	0.3	-0.5	3.5	0.2	-1.2
Balance of Trade	-112.0	149.0	31.7	-24.2	8.7	-115.7	141.5	36.0	-20.1	9.1
Current Account	-81.0	139.0	-25.8	-20.9	-23.6	-109.2	131.5	-22.1	-16.0	-19.6
Trade % of GDP	-1.8%	4.1%	1.9%	-2.2%	1.4%	-1.8%	3.8%	2.0%	-1.9%	1.6%
C/A % of GDP	-1.3%	3.9%	-1.5%	-1.9%	-3.7%	-1.7%	3.5%	-1.2%	-1.3%	-3.3%

Sources: OECD Economic Outlook (Paris: Organization for Economic Cooperation and Development, June 1993); "Economic and Financial Indicators," *The Economist,* 1993 and 1994 issues; Schaefer Brothers.

comparing it to the actual data when reported is the best utilization. With the chosen forecast, either keep a copy or plot the forecast into the matrix in such a manner as to be able to compare it to actual reported data. This comparison, combined with a review of the assumptions contained in the original forecast, will provide valuable information of the unfolding variation of the current economy from that of the forecast.

Many economic forecasts limit themselves to only three or four items, consisting of the change in GDP, CPI, and one or two interest rates. This type of forecast is not helpful because the diversity of the global economy requires information on several sectors within the economy. The best economic forecast is one that forecasts each of the international matrix key indicators. Two that meet this criterion are the annual J. P. Morgan international forecast and the semiannual OECD forecast published in June and December of each year. Both forecasts discuss current economic conditions of several industrial countries, including the matrix countries; forecast future economic trends; and discuss other topics of international interest. These are particularly helpful because they usually include forecasts on various other economic factors along with an explanation of the underlying assumptions. Using the international matrix format, Table 15.1 presents a summary of economic indicators forecasted by the OECD in June 1993 together with a comparison of actual indicators for December 1993.

This comparison shows that the U.S. and British economies grew stronger than forecasted while Japan's economy grew weaker. Japan's year-to-year change in its industrial production index was declining at –4.2 percent, compared to the forecast of –1.2 percent. The rate of growth in U.S. real broad M is an unusual –1.1 percent as it brings inflation under control. Despite an economic decline more severe than forecasted, Japan's monetary policy appears more restrictive than necessary as indicated by a rate of growth in real broad M of 0.5 percent and a spread between three-month interest rates and government-bond interest rates of –1.5 percent. The dollar has risen against the Deutsche mark and Canadian dollar more than anticipated, reflecting a stronger U.S. economy and tighter monetary policy.

Stimulation Checklist

In 1986, a brief article in *The Economist* presented a checklist by which a government could determine whether it should adopt an expansionary economic policy to stimulate the domestic economy or a restrictive economic policy to combat inflation.[1] Table 15.2 presents the checklist modified for use with the international matrix system. This checklist focuses on four key economic indicators included in the international matrix system: the year-to-year

Table 15.2
Stimulation Checklist

Stimulate
- Year-to-year change in industrial production index falls below 2.5 percent.
- Trade-weighted exchange rate rises 7 percent.
- Current Account ratio to GDP improves over prior year.
- Year-to-year change in CPI index is below prior year.

Hold Steady
- Year-to-year change in industrial production index rises above 2.5 percent.
- Trade-weighted exchange rate declines 7 percent.
- Current Account ratio to GDP is worse than prior year.
- Year-to-year change in CPI index is above prior year.

Sources: "An ABC for Reflation," *The Economist,* September 6, 1986, p. 65; Schaefer Brothers.

change in the industrial production index, change in the trade-weighted exchange rate, ratio of the current account balance to GDP, and the year-to-year change in the CPI. If a country's current economic indicators show that three or more of the conditions exist, it should undertake the appropriate policy change. However, for any number of reasons, a country may choose not to undertake such indicated policy. Comparing this checklist to a country's key indicators provides another insight into current economic conditions of that country.

Input of Other Economic Data

The economic and financial indicators used in the international matrix constitute some but not all of the more significant indicators monitored by businesses and investors. It was limited to these indicators to provide a timely understanding of economic trends. Many readers may include other economic and financial indicators or may wish to study the relationships of other factors such as those discussed in Chapter 14. With a personal computer and appropriate spreadsheet program, this matrix can be expanded to include such other data.

MATRIX APPLICATION BY EXECUTIVES AND INVESTORS

An understanding of the global economic system opens up new opportunities for enterprising executives and investors. An advantage of the international matrix system is the ability to focus on a specific economic or financial indicator such as bond interest rates or stock prices and individual countries in addition to the matrix countries.[2] Data regarding these specific indicators and other country indicators can be added to the matrix and compared to evaluate economic trends. Several examples of specific use of the matrix system are discussed in the following sections.

Executives

In the global environment, managing export sales, import purchases, overseas subsidiaries, foreign investments, multinational taxation, and multinational finances in a system integrated for overall profitability is a daunting task. The international matrix system is an important prerequisite to any meaningful integrated management system. It provides key executives at the home office and local affiliates a common set of up-to-date figures, economic information, and analytical process, facilitating communication and business decision making.

Most management systems begin with sales forecasts based on an overall expectation of future economic trends. Most firm sales, including those serving a limited region, have some correlation to national economic trends. The international matrix enables a correlation of sales revenue with economic indicators of relevant countries. A historical pattern for firm gross sales can be calculated on a quarterly basis for each country and the relation with economic indicators. Firm sales tend to fluctuate widely from month to month but tend to be more consistent on a quarterly basis. Consequently, it is better to calculate the rate of change in firm sales quarterly and compare the data to the matrix of key indicators to determine the correlation. Such an analysis is particularly helpful if the sales figures can be isolated by product line or division.

In addition, many firms serve only limited regions in a country and sales may not correlate with national economic trends. A special matrix of economic indicators derived from the particular region as well as particular countries is more effective. For example, firms serving the tourist industry often study local hotel occupancy rates and air fares as an indication of industry trends.

Multinational firms can obtain capital from a variety of international financial markets to take advantage of the lowest available interest rates. Since the international matrix is designed to monitor interest rates and economic trends that effect interest rates, it keeps executives abreast of global financial conditions. However, such opportunities also create greater responsibility to maintain the advantageous terms by skillful management of the exchange rate obligations. For example, in November 1993, U.S. corporate-bond yields of 7.1 percent were much higher than Japanese corporate-bond yields of 4.0 percent. However, the Japanese yen had appreciated more than 12 percent against the dollar from the beginning of the year. The interest savings of 3.1 percent per year could be wiped out by the exchange rate loss. To minimize exchange rate fluctuations, companies engage in various hedging strategies. If annual hedging costs can be kept below 2 percent per year, the interest expense saving of 1 percent per annum could be significant for a large loan. However, even hedging strategies incur certain risks because of the dependence on parties to fulfill their part of the hedging agreement. Hence, the economic viability of participants requires maintaining information on global economic trends.

Exchange rate management and forecasting is also critical to publicly held companies. Financial statements must be recast in the exchange rate of principal shareholders and creditors where exchange rate gains and losses can cause a major adjustment to income statements.

Competitive ability is partially a function of the economic environment surrounding a company's principal place of business. A company headquartered in a country experiencing high interest rates is at a competitive disadvantage against companies in foreign countries offering lower rates. Hence, knowledge of the economic environment of competitors is an important aspect of developing competitive strategies. The international matrix system should include economic data of countries where principal competitors are located. Economic trend analysis will help anticipate the future economic environment of competitors and their ability to respond to competitive strategies.

Investors

Global capital markets offer investors expanded opportunities in higher-yielding overseas investments where modern communications have substantially reduced many of the investment risks. The international matrix system enables investors to follow key interest rates, share indexes, and economic conditions in global financial markets and anticipate changes in financial conditions.

However, the benefits of overseas investing can be negated by exchange rate losses or improved by exchange rate gains. Although most countries attempt to maintain stable exchange rates to attract overseas investors, economic conditions may compel modifications or abandonment of its exchange rate policy. Accordingly, the international matrix system provides information to anticipate changes in exchange rates and policies.

More than 75 percent of most individuals' investments are directly associated with an interest-earning investment such as bonds and savings deposits or with an interest-paying obligation such as a mortgage or car loan. Accordingly, monitoring economic trends with a specific view of anticipating changes in interest rates is of primary importance. The international matrix system of key indicators is particularly sensitive to anticipating changes in certain key interest rates. There is a wide variety of interest-earning or fixed income–earning assets and mortgages. Monthly historical data of interest rates of the particular obligation can be compiled. This historical data can be compared to the historical international matrix of key indicators, in particular, the interest rates, to discern a particular pattern or relationship. This relationship can then be incorporated in the international matrix system.

Stock market investors must also pay particular attention to economic trends. As previously discussed, general stock market prices are directly affected by changes in interest rates and anticipated changes in overall company profits. Both factors are directly affected by the business cycle, making economic trend analysis particularly important.

Individual publicly traded companies are affected by the business cycles in each of the countries in which they operate. While some smaller companies can buck general economic trends because of superior products and management, many cannot. Most publicly held companies conduct business throughout the United States and in many foreign countries. Even with the best of products and management, these companies will be impacted by global economic trends. However, the nature of the impact and its timing vary depending on the industry and customers being served and the particular countries.

Companies associated with the housing and construction industry generally have a direct correlation to changes in interest rates, in particular, long-term rates in each of the countries served. Financial institutions such as banks and thrifts are particularly sensitive to changes in short-term interest rates such as the three-month money market yield. On the other hand, utility stocks tend to move in the same direction as the price of bonds; that is, they decline as the yield on government bonds rises and rise in value as government-bond yields fall. Oil company stocks are influenced by the price of oil. Stocks of large consumer-oriented companies such as automobiles and retail stores tend to correlate with the anticipated changes in the business cycle.

After determining the financial condition in each of the countries, the companies must translate the information into the currency of the principal shareholders. Gains or losses from currency translations are an income or expense as the case may be, thereby having a direct impact on financial statements and stock prices.

Supply-and-demand pressures caused by economic trends can also impact commodity prices. Industrial raw materials are particularly sensitive to changes in the business cycle. Agricultural prices tend to be less sensitive to the business cycle because of the stable demand for food. However, American farm products have been an important source of export earnings, causing even agricultural commodities to be impacted by changes in economic and financial conditions such as the trade-weighted value of the dollar.

SOURCES OF ECONOMIC AND FINANCIAL DATA

Current Data

Other than *The Economist,* inexpensive sources of current economic and financial data are limited. The monthly government economic indicators reported in *The Economist* are available directly from the OECD and the IMF but at a higher cost. The London-based *Financial Times* systematically reports some key economic and financial indicators for the industrial countries, but most major financial dailies report international and economic data irregularly.

Historical Data

The Economist publishes an annual yearbook that includes historical figures for its economic and financial indicators, enabling an update of the international matrix system from the data found in Appendix A. For all other historical data including most countries in the world, the best source is *International Financial Statistics,* published monthly by the IMF and found in major public and university libraries. Other good sources for international statistics include *Eurostat*, published annually by the Office for Official Publications of the European Communities (Luxembourg), and the OECD biannual forecasts which include some historical data.

Each country publishes extensive economic and financial data for its own economy. The *Survey of Current Business*, published by the U.S. Department of Commerce, is the principal source for American economic data and provides some statistical data on other major industrial countries. The Commerce Department also publishes annually *The Statistical Abstract of the United States*, which has an international section containing historical international economic data.

NOTES

1. "An ABC for Reflation," *The Economist*, September 6, 1986, p. 65.

2. For a practical and more detailed guide of business and investment issues that arise in day-to-day decision making, see J. Manville Harris, *International Finance* (New York: Barron's, 1992).

CHAPTER 16

Global Economic Trends into the Twenty-First Century

As the world moves into the twenty-first century, a gradual shift from U.S. global economic hegemony to a multipolar one is occurring. How each country responds to this shift will be vital to economic development and will be reflected in the key economic and financial indicators tracked by the international matrix system. Historically, such momentous change in economic power triggers economic and political turbulence. The adjustment process is difficult, often leading to economic depression or wars. By anticipating the general overview of economic conditions generated by this global shift, international economic trend analysis will be more effective.[1]

CHANGING NATIONAL ECONOMIES

Since gaining independence in 1783, the U.S. economy has had a powerful international influence achieving global hegemony through two world wars that crippled much of the industrial world, followed by a cold war that retarded economic growth of many countries through ideological rivalry. Following World War II, the United States assumed international economic leadership promoting free trade, unrestricted capital flow, and stable exchange rates. This highly successful leadership created an economic environment that revived war-torn economies and produced global economic growth for those countries willing to adopt free-market systems.

This unqualified success also launched a new global economic environment of competing economic regions with a political stability and economic size rivaling that of the United States. The seminal event marking this new environment was the end of the Cold War. It eliminated the last vestiges of political tension, ideological differences, and concentration over military security that had prevented worldwide economic development during the twentieth century. Now, if nations so choose, they can devote full attention to economic matters and the new opportunities for growth and development. Clearly, many nations are choosing this path, unleashing economic capabilities that can alter the global economic system.

Since the Cold War's recent end, sufficient economic development has taken place to provide a glimpse of the global economy as it will appear in the first quarter of the twenty-first century and the economic challenges it will confront. As discussed in Chapter 6, there are many structural factors contributing to a nation's growth; and no one can fully predict how a society will utilize them within the context of overall global developments. Furthermore, disastrous events such as war, drought, or poor economic policies can sidetrack even the strongest of economies.

With a population of 250 million, the United States will remain a powerful national economy. Most economic experts believe its economy is capable of averaging 2.4 percent annual growth in real GDP. It could do better, but in the past ten years it has also incurred chronic budget deficits averaging 3 to 4 percent of GDP per year and chronic current account deficits averaging 1 to 2 percent of GDP per year. Thus, despite the size and influence on the global economy, its growth and living standard is being maintained by a combination of domestic credit expansion and cheaper imports rather than from a dynamic domestic economy. Abandonment of the Bretton Woods fixed exchange rate system in 1971 and dependence on a consortium of countries to provide limited financial assistance to countries of the former Soviet Union are two events that did not cause but resulted from the relatively weakened U.S. economic position.

Japan is a formidable economic powerhouse that has developed a social and economic system producing high economic growth. Despite the severity of its 1990–1993 economic recession, Japan's unemployment rate remained no worse than 3 percent, demonstrating its industrial system's ability to cope with wrenching readjustments caused primarily by economic policy mistakes. Nevertheless, it faces limitations on its ability to match past growth levels. Now that the United States and Europe can devote more attention to international economic issues, Japan is likely to witness greater international competition and resistance to its cross-border trading practices. The growth in population over age 65 will absorb greater resources, limiting the savings and purchasing power of younger generations. This concern already weighs heavy on its political leadership, limiting Japan's flexibility in economic policy.

Because of its strong economy, many nations would like Japan to play a greater international role. However, with a population of 124 million that is one-half the size of the United States and one-tenth the size of China, Japan finds itself between a large and growing China economy and a large but slowly growing U.S. economy. Both countries are significant for future trade and investment, but it leaves Japan as a junior partner with less control over its international economic relationship. This situation contributes to a sense of vulnerability that limits its desire to play a global leadership role and focuses energy on protecting the domestic economy.

A population of 1.2 billion combined with the ability and enthusiasm to rapidly transform its economy by adopting Western technology, China is maintaining a rapid growth rate. By the first quarter of the twenty-first century, China is likely to achieve a national GDP approaching that of Japan. This fast economic growth is well understood and discussed in many books and periodicals. However, it raises questions about the ability of any population to absorb such rapid economic growth and technological change in a short time without losing domestic social and political cohesion.[2] Internal social disparity is developing, and it is probable China's leadership will slow the pace of economic growth to protect the hard-won political cohesion developed after so much strife and turbulence. Nevertheless, growing awareness of China's economic potential combined with the self-assuredness of a great historical continuity is eliminating barriers to cross-border commercial activity. Consequently, China is expanding its role in the global economic system by joining international economic organizations. Should its GDP approach the size of Japan, it will likely have a sophisticated financial system and currency market influential in the global economy.

Despite the multiplicity of countries, ethnicities, and historic deadly rivalries, Europe is astounding by its continued vitality. Recognizing that individual European countries are playing a diminishing role in the global economy, union offers to reestablish Europe as a significant economic influence. Although fraught with complexities and uncertainty, the drive toward political and economic union appears to be steadily moving forward. The GDP and population size involved in this endeavor represent in the aggregate the largest concentration of industrial economic strength on the globe that would exceed even that of the United States (see Table 7.1).

Nevertheless, overcoming the national identities to achieve European cooperation, let alone full union, is a daunting task. The centerpiece of union is the EMU. Table 16.1 summarizes the criteria for joining EMU. As of 1993, most European countries did not meet these criteria. EMU also envisions a European central bank which is yet to be formed and, when formed, will require a period of operating experience. European capital markets must also

Table 16.1
Criteria for Membership in European Monetary Union

---

1. Inflation rate must not be more than 1.5 points above the average of the three lowest inflation rates (in 1991, 2.5 percent).

2. General government budget deficit must not be more than 3 percent of GDP, apart from exceptional circumstances (i.e. German unification).

3. General government debt should not exceed 60 percent of GDP. (Exceptions for countries showing steady progress toward level.)

4. Countries must participate in exchange rate band width of EMS.

5. Long-term interest rates must not exceed by more than 2 points those of three lowest-inflation European Community nations.

Source: European Commission.

merge into a uniform but decentralized system. Accordingly, a European Union sufficiently capable of directly influencing global economic conditions will require about twenty years of sustained effort.

Whether the European nations can achieve union depends upon economic conditions as well as political will. A key to this unification process is Germany which could become sidetracked by rivalry with a resurging Russia or the growing opportunities in adjacent Central European countries. Adding to this difficulty is the challenge to sustained European economic growth presented by EMU. The fixed exchange rate regime of EMR is intended to continue under EMU managed by the European central bank. However, disparities in national economic structures and policies together with unrealistic exchange rate levels make it difficult for the member nations to operate under EMU without suffering domestic economic dislocation that will retard economic growth.

Russia and the other countries that formed the Soviet Union are questionable. With all the technological development, industrial infrastructure, and technical capabilities built under the Soviet Union, it would appear that after fully adopting a free-market system, it could become a formidable economic power. Germany and Japan became formidable economic competitors within twenty years following the end of a war when they were far more destitute than today's Russia. Germany went on to become the anchor economic power for the EMS. With a 1990 population of 148 million that is skilled and educated, Russia could, by the first quarter of the twenty-first century, emerge as an industrial power—developing a common market system with its neighboring countries similar to the EEC and with a combined population equal to the United States.

The turn to market-driven economies and privatization of government-owned industries is spreading through Latin America opening the region to an era of dynamic growth. With a population of 86 million located adjacent to the United States, Mexico is in a position to take full advantage of the new opportunities. Through NAFTA, Mexico joined the United States and Canada to develop a more integrated economic system that could be expanded to include other Western Hemisphere nations. However, while Latin American governments are committing themselves to free-market economies, the general population appears less enthusiastic. A history of strong central government economic planning that extends back to the great native civilizations has prevented development of institutions, thinking, and legal systems supportive of individual economic enterprise. Although immigrants into the United States have clearly responded to free-market systems, changing national economic cultures and institutions takes time; and Latin America is just beginning.

Developments in other regions are so new that their direction is still uncertain. With elimination of apartheid in South Africa, perhaps the rest of Africa can resolve the domestic strife that plagues most of the region, preventing effective utilization of the rich natural resources abundantly located there. However, political stability in the face of ethnic rivalries is a long and difficult road; and it is unlikely to be achieved within the next twenty years. The Middle East, North Africa, and other adjacent Islamic countries, comprising what is called the Islamic Crescent, are far better organized and engaged in more extensive economic development; but they, too, suffer from regional rivalries and religious disputes that limit their economic capabilities. In addition, no one country has emerged from the rivalries to exert full cultural and economic leadership for coordinating development of economic resources. However, Egypt is demonstrating a remarkable capability for coalition building that could lead to a dynamic Middle East economy. India is also turning to more market-oriented systems which could make its population of 800 million more productive, although this too will be a slow process, for it must overcome forty-five years of bureaucratic regulation of its economic system. Southeast Asia is benefiting from growing Chinese and Japanese markets and is expected to conform economic policies with these two countries.

IMPLICATIONS FOR THE U.S. ECONOMY

The rise of large economic regions rivaling the United States will challenge its competitive strength and ability to withstand cross-border economic turbulence that it has not faced in over fifty years. These challenges have been successfully met before, but whether the U.S. is prepared to discipline itself again to face these challenges will be determined in the next twenty years.

There are four economic issues facing the United States:

- Developing a stronger domestic political consensus
- Enhancing a globally competitive economy
- Balancing the budget
- Eliminating the current account deficit

The basic problem is the inability to resolve domestic political issues that would enable a balanced budget and concentration on a sustained and coherent approach to economic growth. While campaign rhetoric often discusses economic growth, much of the actual work done by the government accomplishes only shifting of existing economic resources among the population.

Until this problem is solved, budget and current account deficits are likely to continue. In the past, these deficits did not create a serious economic problem because countries were anxious to spur their domestic economies by exporting to the giant U.S. market. To pay for the deficits, export countries willingly accepted U.S. financial assets. As the global economy grows and expands to include other large markets such as China, southeast Asia, the European Union, and Latin America, the U.S. market will need to compete in attracting imports.

Unfortunately, the United States is now the largest global debtor. Table 9.2 shows the growing deficit balance in cross-border bank liabilities, and Appendix C shows the growing cross-border ownership of U.S. government securities. If other economies are growing faster, imports can be financed by financial assets offering higher interest rates, forcing the U.S. financial markets to offer high real interest rates which will be a drag on the U.S. economy. Alternatively, to reduce the current account deficit, the U.S. may refrain from raising interest rates, allowing the dollar exchange rate to steadily decline and causing domestic inflationary pressures which will trigger higher interest rates. This scenario places U.S. economic policy in a discouraging dilemma between interest rates and dollar decline. Following World War II, Britain struggled with the same dilemma as it was unable to balance social programs with economic resources and international competitiveness.

A more hopeful possibility is that the United States will quickly reduce its budget deficit and become more internationally competitive. However, even under this scenario, the United States cannot escape from the competitive pressures of a steadily widening global industrial economy. Following World Wars I and II, Britain experienced a similar challenge; and its economic decline was punctuated by currency crisis and trade friction. The question raised is whether the United States will experience the same conditions. Converting its current account deficits into surpluses will signify a vigorous domestic economy.

In the meantime, while attempting to improve the domestic economy, American policymakers will be providing political and economic leadership to maintain global harmony and guide the global economy through its reorientation. Confronting different growth patterns, trade policies, exchange rate needs, and political processes will tax its economic resources and leadership. Giving up power and prestige gracefully is rarely done; and the United States, as with many other leading nations in the past, will fulfill its leadership responsibilities by undertaking policies and expenditures at the expense of domestic economic growth, thus running the risk of overextending itself. On the other hand, through realistic management of government activities, this imbalance need not occur. An encouraging example is Britain during the nineteenth century and before the enormous cost of World War I, when it maintained strong economic growth despite the economic rivalry and challenges of the United States, Germany, and France.

IMPLICATIONS FOR THE GLOBAL ECONOMY

Adjusting cross-border commercial relationships and domestic economic systems to reflect the rise of new economic regions will also challenge the entire global economic system. Historically, countries have adjusted their cross-border commercial relationships by focusing on trade regulation and exchange rate regime.

Nations are contending with overwhelming internal changes brought about by the technological revolution and reorientation of the global economy. Despite theoretical models favoring free trade, historically, such difficult transition periods caused countries to adopt protectionist policies; and the complexity of modern manufacturing process allows nontrade barriers to effectively achieve protectionist policies. Removing nontrade barriers is a difficult and time-consuming task fraught with international tensions as countries accuse each other of unfair trade practices. Furthermore, if a global fixed exchange rate system is reestablished, the inability of many countries to maintain the system by disciplining their domestic economies will expand implementation of protectionist policies. Countries adhering to a unilateral free-trade policy are likely to incur chronic trade deficits with those countries practicing protectionist policies. To achieve some form of equitable cross-border trade that can approximate free trade while avoiding diplomatic tensions, countries will have no choice but to expand their trade quota policies.

Global economic growth will expand international trade, requiring expansion of the international currency market. Such growth is likely to outstrip the ability of monetary authorities to maintain orderly markets, creating turbulent exchange rates. In reaction, the debate on the benefits of fixed exchange versus floating exchange rates will intensify. Because of the different exchange rate needs in each region, this debate will never be fully resolved. The economic interdependence of Europe causes that region to favor a fixed exchange rate regime. Japan also prefers a fixed exchange rate regime to support its export industries and protect its dependence on imported foods and raw materials.

However, its dynamic growth and current account surpluses make it difficult to maintain a consistent exchange rate level. The rapidly growing areas of China, southeast Asia, and other regions should achieve economic growth that will require periodic upward exchange rate adjustments similar to those experienced by Japan and Germany as they achieved rapid post–World War II growth. Their inclusion in a fixed rate regime would provide a competitive advantage at the expense of more established industrial countries.

At the vortex of all this change will be the United States. To retain international political as well as economic leadership, the U.S. dollar must remain a principal vehicle currency which requires that it either protect the dollar's value through a fixed rate regime or remove the current account deficits. On the other hand, inability to resolve domestic political issues and current account deficits requires adoption of a managed exchange rate regime to provide maximum flexibility in domestic economic policies. It is unclear which direction will be pursued.

From time to time, recommendations are made to restore a fixed exchange rate system either by means of the gold standard or reestablishment of the Bretton Woods system.[3] Adoption of such recommendations would certainly alleviate exchange rate fluctuations and the attendant uncertainty. However, the question remains whether countries are willing to discipline their economies while establishing exchange rate levels that can accommodate dissimilar long-term growth rates and economic conditions. The political will for domestic economic discipline appears lacking in many countries or, if present, is not uniform in the sacrifices willing to be made. A global fixed exchange rate regime will only benefit growing regions while masking slow growth countries from the prolonged adjustment process that their domestic industries must undertake. Even under the gold standard and the Bretton Woods system, countries periodically adjusted exchange rates to reflect domestic economic conditions.

THE CHALLENGE

Under existing economic growth trends, by the first quarter of the twenty-first century it appears that in addition to the large U.S. economy, there could be a unified Europe slightly larger than the United States; a China and Japan with roughly equal national GDP but wide disparities because of population size; and regional areas based on Russia, India, and Latin America with their own significant economies. All this development and growth potential is exciting, but it also moves the global economy into a position rarely seen in the last two hundred years: a global economy with no one nation capable of imposing international economic and financial leadership.

For much of industrial history, the global economic system was led by either Britain or the United States contributing economic theories, practices, concepts, experiences, and expectations built on the premise of one global key currency system led by the preeminent industrial power at the time. Despite the many countries and regions that comprise the global economy, these two countries were such large markets and offered a sophisticated financial system that other countries were compelled to follow their leadership if they wanted the benefits of participation. This leadership faltered following World War I. Britain was financially weakened by the war effort with substantial debts owed to the United States. Economically, the United States had overtaken Britain but had not developed the institutions or political will to exercise global economic leadership. The net result was economic dislocation that was expanded and magnified by the cross-border transmission process.

Concern that history is about to repeat itself with a period of competitive currency devaluations and trade wars is causing experts to search for a new global economic system to achieve growth and stability. Much of the debate focuses on reestablishment of a fixed rate regime. Whether a new exchange rate regime will emerge or whether it will be a formal mechanism similar to Bretton Woods or more informal remains to be seen. However, when the global economy is undergoing so much change, a fixed rate regime will be costly to maintain and ultimately prove ineffective. When several countries or regions are growing faster than others, a rigid fixed exchange rate regime only delays the inevitable readjustment. When adjustment occurs, it can be sudden and devastating, exacerbating economic conditions as it did in the Great Depression. To avoid damaging dislocation, a system of flexible exchange rates and trade flow patterns are necessary to allow all countries and their domestic industries to adjust gradually to the changing global economic environment.

Exchange rate regimes are at the periphery of what should be the central focus of most countries. With the shift in economic power causing economic turbulence, the United States and other countries must be in a position of maximum economic flexibility to absorb the consequences of this turbulence. Reducing current account deficits by dynamic domestic economies is the best means of achieving this flexibility. Countries that wish to resume high economic growth rates to provide better living standards can adopt the necessary economic discipline. Failing that, it is better that the economic decline be gradual rather than swift and devastating.

NOTES

1. In addition to purely economic conditions, there are a number of other forces that will affect the future global economy. The effect of population growth and migration interwoven into their economic consequences is discussed in Paul Kennedy, *Preparing for the Twenty-First Century* (New York: Random House, 1993). Historical and potential global political rivalries facing the new world order are discussed with great insight in Henry Kissinger, *Diplomacy* (New York: Simon & Schuster, 1994). A more detailed analysis of comparative geopolitics is discussed in Gerard Chaliand and Jean-Pierre Rageau, *Strategic Atlas*, 3rd ed. (New York: Harper Perennial, 1992), originally published in France in 1983.

2. A realistic appraisal of China's economic development is found in Richard Hornik, "Bursting China's Bubble," *Foreign Affairs*, New York, May/June 1994, pp. 28–42.

3. For example, a proposal for a fixed rate regime is being considered by a group of experts including former Federal Reserve Chairman Paul Volcker, *Wall Street Journal*, May 9, 1994.

□ □ ■ □ □

Appendixes

Historical International Matrix, 1988–1993

NOTES TO HISTORICAL MATRIX

1. Figures for industrial production index, consumer price index, wage index, narrow M, and broad M are year-to-year rates of change; all other figures are as of the end of the month indicated.

2. German figures are primarily for West Germany only.

3. For the German share index, the DAX index was used after March 1990.

4. Germany was undergoing reunification and did not report narrow M monetary aggregates.

5. Due to space limitations, the price for West Texas Intermediate oil is shown on a separate schedule along with the CRB index and the mark-to-pound exchange rate.

Sources: "Economic and Financial Indicators," *The Economist,* 1988–1994 issues; *International Financial Statistics,* (Washington, D.C.: International Monetary Fund, January 1994); Knight-Ridder Financial/Commodity Research Bureau, *The CRB Commodity Yearbook 1994* (New York: John Wiley & Sons, 1994).

United States	1988 Mar	Jun	Sep	Dec	1989 Mar	Jun	Sep	Dec	1990 Mar	Jun	Sep	Dec
Industrial Production	5.7	5.8	5.5	4.7	4.7	3.4	2.7	1.7	1.0	1.2	2.3	-1.4
Unemployment Rate	5.6	5.3	5.4	5.3	4.9	5.3	5.3	5.3	5.2	5.2	5.7	6.1
Consumer Price Index	3.9	4.0	4.2	4.6	5.0	5.2	5.0	4.6	5.2	4.7	6.2	6.1
Wage Index	2.8	3.2	3.3	3.4	4.8	3.8	3.8	4.1	4.0	4.1	4.0	3.8
Producer Price Index	1.8	2.3	2.7	4.0	5.6	5.9	4.5	4.8	4.4	2.7	4.9	6.3
Weighted Currency	63.7	67.1	68.6	66.5	68.6	71.3	69.9	67.9	68.8	66.4	62.5	61.4
Currency to Dollar												
% from December	-3.2%	2.0%	4.3%	1.1%	3.2%	7.2%	5.1%	2.1%	1.3%	-2.2%	-8.0%	-9.6%
% from December												
Narrow M	4.0	4.6	4.7	4.9	3.0	-0.7	-0.3	0.9	2.4	4.6	5.1	3.9
Broad M	4.7	5.8	5.3	5.7	3.7	2.5	3.9	4.8	6.0	5.8	4.9	3.2
Real Broad M	0.8	1.8	1.1	1.1	-1.3	-2.7	-1.1	0.2	0.8	1.1	-1.3	-2.9
Money Market Yield	6.5	7.6	8.1	9.1	10.1	9.1	8.9	8.3	8.3	8.1	8.0	8.1
Government-Bond Yield	8.7	8.9	9.1	9.1	9.2	8.2	8.3	8.0	8.6	8.5	8.9	8.1
Yield Spread	-2.2	-1.3	-1.0	0.0	0.9	0.9	0.6	0.3	-0.3	-0.4	-0.9	0.0
Real Money Market Yield	2.6	3.6	3.9	4.5	5.1	3.9	3.9	3.7	3.1	3.4	1.8	2.0
Real Govt.-Bond Yield	4.8	4.9	4.9	4.5	4.2	3.0	3.3	3.4	3.4	3.8	2.7	2.0
Bank Prime Rate	8.5	9.0	10.0	10.5	11.5	11.0	10.5	10.5	10.0	10.0	10.0	10.0
Spread - Money Market	2.0	1.4	1.9	1.4	1.4	1.9	1.6	2.2	1.7	1.9	2.0	1.9
Spread - Govt. Bond	-0.2	0.1	0.9	1.4	2.3	2.8	2.2	2.5	1.4	1.5	1.1	1.9
Balance of Trade	-168.0	-155.9	-127.4	-118.7	-114.4	-112.6	-111.0	-108.5	-106.5	-101.9	-102.6	-100.4
Current Account	-151.7	-145.8	-135.1	-135.3	-125.2	-122.4	-113.9	-105.9	-105.9	-97.8	-96.4	-99.3
Foreign Reserves	32.1	30.0	36.7	36.7	38.8	49.2	57.4	63.6	65.2	66.2	69.0	72.3
Balance of Trade % GDP	-3.4%	-3.2%	-2.6%	-2.4%	-2.2%	-2.1%	-2.1%	-2.1%	-1.9%	-1.8%	-1.9%	-1.8%
Current Account % GDP	-3.1%	-3.0%	-2.8%	-2.8%	-2.4%	-2.3%	-2.2%	-2.0%	-1.9%	-1.8%	-1.7%	-1.8%
Share Index	1,980	2,131	2,082	2,193	2,276	2,525	2,755	2,810	2,737	2,912	2,505	2,634
% from December	-2.5%	4.9%	2.5%	8.0%	3.8%	15.1%	25.6%	28.1%	-2.6%	3.6%	-10.9%	-6.3%

United States	1991 Mar	Jun	Sep	Dec	1992 Mar	Jun	Sep	Dec	1993 Mar	Jun	Sep	Dec
Industrial Production	-3.3	-2.9	-2.3	0.6	2.1	0.8	0.2	2.9	4.1	3.9	4.5	4.7
Unemployment Rate	6.8	7.0	6.7	7.1	7.3	7.8	7.5	7.3	7.0	7.0	6.7	6.4
Consumer Price Index	4.9	4.6	3.4	3.1	3.2	3.1	3.0	2.9	3.1	3.0	2.7	2.7
Wage Index	3.9	3.6	2.9	3.2	3.0	2.2	2.3	2.3	2.4	2.3	2.3	2.5
Producer Price Index	3.9	3.2	0.6	-0.1	0.9	1.6	1.7	1.6	2.0	1.4	1.0	0.2
Weighted Currency	65.2	67.8	64.5	60.9	64.9	61.2	60.3	66.7	65.7	65.1	65.0	67.8
Currency to Dollar												
% from December	6.2%	10.4%	5.0%	-0.8%	6.6%	0.5%	-1.0%	9.5%	-1.5%	-2.4%	-2.5%	1.6%
% from December												
Narrow M	4.7	5.8	5.9	8.6	11.5	11.1	13.4	14.1	10.7	12.1	11.9	10.2
Broad M	3.2	3.4	2.2	2.9	2.6	1.5	2.0	1.4	0.1	1.3	1.4	1.6
Real Broad M	-1.7	-1.2	-1.2	-0.2	-0.6	-1.6	-1.0	-1.5	-3.0	-1.7	-1.3	-1.1
Money Market Yield	6.3	6.1	5.5	4.5	4.1	3.8	3.3	3.4	3.2	3.3	3.2	3.3
Government-Bond Yield	8.1	8.3	7.7	7.1	7.5	7.3	6.4	6.8	6.0	6.0	5.4	5.7
Yield Spread	-1.8	-2.2	-2.2	-2.6	-3.4	-3.5	-3.1	-3.4	-2.8	-2.7	-2.2	-2.4
Real Money Market Yield	1.4	1.5	2.1	1.4	0.9	0.7	0.3	0.5	0.1	0.3	0.5	0.6
Real Govt.-Bond Yield	3.2	3.7	4.3	4.0	4.3	4.2	3.4	3.9	2.9	3.0	2.7	3.0
Bank Prime Rate	9.0	8.5	8.0	6.5	6.5	6.5	6.0	6.0	6.0	6.0	6.0	6.0
Spread - Money Market	2.7	2.4	2.5	2.0	2.4	2.7	2.7	2.6	2.8	2.7	2.8	2.7
Spread - Govt. Bond	0.9	0.2	0.3	-0.6	-1.0	-0.8	-0.4	-0.8	0.0	0.0	0.6	0.3
Balance of Trade	-92.7	-83.7	-75.1	-64.3	-63.2	-69.8	-75.7	-84.3	-93.8	-103.2	-110.0	-115.7
Current Account	-62.4	-33.8	-20.5	-20.4	-21.2	-42.0	-45.2	-62.4	-80.6	-90.7	-101.2	-109.2
Foreign Reserves	66.9	63.9	63.7	66.7	63.6	66.0	67.5	60.3	63.2	64.0	64.8	62.4
Balance of Trade % GDP	-1.6%	-1.5%	-1.3%	-1.1%	-1.1%	-1.2%	-1.3%	-1.4%	-1.5%	-1.6%	-1.7%	-1.8%
Current Account % GDP	-1.1%	-0.6%	-0.4%	-0.4%	-0.4%	-0.7%	-0.8%	-1.0%	-1.3%	-1.4%	-1.6%	-1.7%
Share Index	2,945	2,973	3,018	3,169	3,236	3,319	3,267	3,308	3,457	3,519	3,566	3,784
% from December	11.8%	12.9%	14.6%	20.3%	2.1%	4.7%	3.1%	4.4%	4.5%	6.4%	7.8%	14.4%

Japan

Japan	1988 Mar	1988 Jun	1988 Sep	1988 Dec	1989 Mar	1989 Jun	1989 Sep	1989 Dec	1990 Mar	1990 Jun	1990 Sep	1990 Dec
Industrial Production	12.8	9.1	9.2	8.2	9.4	7.4	3.8	3.2	0.2	3.0	5.3	6.0
Unemployment Rate	2.6	2.4	2.5	2.3	2.3	2.2	2.2	2.1	2.0	2.2	2.2	2.1
Consumer Price Index	0.7	0.2	0.6	1.0	1.1	3.0	2.6	2.6	3.5	2.2	3.0	3.8
Wage Index	2.2	7.0	1.7	3.0	7.1	3.0	4.6	7.0	3.3	8.4	4.8	6.3
Producer Price Index	-1.0	-0.6	-0.9	-1.1	0.5	3.7	3.3	3.9	3.9	0.9	0.9	2.2
Weighted Currency	147.5	146.3	145.9	152.2	146.9	141.8	139.0	129.3	117.6	121.1	129.8	129.0
Currency to Dollar	124.0	131.0	134.0	126.0	133.0	141.0	141.0	146.0	159.0	151.0	137.0	136.0
% from December	2.0%	1.2%	0.9%	5.3%	-3.5%	-6.8%	-8.7%	-15.0%	-9.0%	-6.3%	0.4%	-0.2%
% from December	-2.4%	3.1%	5.5%	-0.8%	5.6%	11.9%	11.9%	15.9%	8.9%	3.4%	-6.2%	-6.8%
Narrow M	9.5	9.8	5.9	10.3	8.9	9.4	9.9	10.6	1.1	2.8	3.4	5.6
Broad M	11.8	12.3	10.6	10.4	10.3	9.4	9.9	10.6	11.6	12.6	12.0	8.6
Real Broad M	11.1	12.1	10.0	9.4	9.2	6.4	7.3	8.0	8.1	10.4	9.0	4.8
Money Market Yield	3.8	3.8	4.2	4.2	4.2	4.5	5.0	5.8	6.6	7.0	7.5	7.6
Government-Bond Yield	4.5	4.9	5.1	4.8	5.0	5.4	5.2	5.5	7.3	7.3	8.3	7.1
Yield Spread	-0.7	-1.1	-0.9	-0.6	-0.8	-0.9	-0.2	0.3	-0.7	-0.3	-0.8	0.5
Real Money Market Yield	3.1	3.6	3.6	3.2	3.1	1.5	2.4	3.2	3.1	4.8	4.5	3.8
Real Govt.-Bond Yield	3.8	4.7	4.5	3.8	3.9	2.4	2.6	2.9	3.8	5.1	5.3	3.3
Bank Prime Rate	3.4	3.4	3.4	3.4	3.4	4.9	4.9	4.9	6.3	7.1	7.4	8.0
Spread - Money Market	-0.4	-0.4	-0.8	-0.8	-0.8	0.4	-0.1	-0.9	-0.3	0.1	-0.1	0.4
Spread - Govt. Bond	-1.1	-1.5	-1.7	-1.4	-1.6	-0.5	-0.3	-0.6	-1.0	-0.2	-0.9	0.9
Balance of Trade	92.4	91.8	92.1	95.2	95.2	92.4	86.5	76.9	70.1	64.2	55.9	64.2
Current Account	83.7	81.1	79.0	79.6	77.6	72.3	67.8	56.1	52.7	47.0	41.1	37.6
Foreign Reserves	84.3	86.9	90.3	96.7	98.4	88.1	85.1	84.0	73.5	74.1	76.3	78.5
Balance of Trade % GDP	3.2%	3.2%	3.2%	3.3%	3.3%	3.2%	3.0%	2.7%	2.4%	2.2%	1.9%	2.2%
Current Account % GDP	2.9%	2.8%	2.7%	2.7%	2.7%	2.5%	2.4%	2.0%	1.8%	1.6%	1.4%	1.3%
Share Index	25,623	27,398	27,500	31,007	32,306	34,267	35,366	38,916	28,760	32,415	22,898	23,849
% from December	18.8%	27.0%	27.5%	43.7%	4.2%	10.5%	14.1%	25.5%	-26.1%	-16.7%	-41.2%	-38.7%

Japan	1991				1992				1993			
	Mar	Jun	Sep	Dec	Mar	Jun	Sep	Dec	Mar	Jun	Sep	Dec
Industrial Production	3.0	1.1	0.7	-1.4	-5.3	-4.2	-4.1	-8.2	-2.2	-5.1	-4.4	-4.2
Unemployment Rate	2.2	2.1	2.2	2.2	2.1	2.1	2.2	2.4	2.3	2.5	2.6	2.9
Consumer Price Index	4.0	3.6	2.7	2.7	2.0	2.3	2.0	1.2	1.2	0.9	1.5	1.0
Wage Index	4.2	3.5	2.8	3.5	2.2	3.9	2.1	-1.8	1.4	-1.6	1.4	-2.5
Producer Price Index	1.0	0.6	-0.4	-1.6	-1.4	-1.5	-1.1	-1.4	-2.3	-3.2	-3.7	-3.3
Weighted Currency	133.3	138.4	139.2	140.8	138.5	140.5	146.4	151.9	163.5	180.5	182.6	174.3
Currency to Dollar	138.0	139.0	133.0	126.0	133.0	126.0	120.0	125.0	117.0	107.0	105.0	113.0
% from December	3.3%	7.3%	7.9%	9.1%	-1.6%	-0.2%	4.0%	7.9%	7.6%	18.8%	20.2%	14.7%
% from December	1.5%	2.2%	-2.2%	-7.4%	5.6%	0.0%	-4.8%	-0.8%	-6.4%	-14.4%	-16.0%	-9.6%
Narrow M	1.7	6.1	7.1	8.6	7.1	4.0	2.7	1.2	0.6	2.9	3.6	3.9
Broad M	4.9	3.7	2.2	2.0	1.8	0.9	-0.4	-0.4	-0.3	1.4	2.0	1.5
Real Broad M	0.9	0.1	-0.5	-0.7	-0.2	-1.4	-2.4	-1.6	-1.5	0.5	0.5	0.5
Money Market Yield	7.7	7.4	6.5	5.8	4.8	4.5	3.9	3.8	3.3	3.2	2.5	2.0
Government-Bond Yield	6.6	6.8	6.0	5.4	5.3	5.3	4.8	4.5	4.2	4.4	3.8	3.5
Yield Spread	1.1	0.6	0.5	0.4	-0.5	-0.8	-0.9	-0.7	-0.9	-1.2	-1.3	-1.5
Real Money Market Yield	3.7	3.8	3.8	3.1	2.8	2.2	1.9	2.6	2.1	2.3	1.0	1.0
Real Govt.-Bond Yield	2.6	3.2	3.3	2.7	3.3	3.0	2.8	3.3	3.0	3.5	2.3	2.5
Bank Prime Rate	8.3	7.9	7.4	6.6	5.9	5.3	4.8	4.5	4.0	4.0	3.8	3.0
Spread - Money Market	0.6	0.5	0.9	0.8	1.1	0.8	0.9	0.7	0.7	0.8	1.3	1.0
Spread - Govt. Bond	1.7	1.1	1.4	1.2	0.6	0.0	0.0	0.0	-0.2	-0.4	0.0	-0.5
Balance of Trade	70.0	78.9	89.9	103.0	113.8	121.6	128.6	133.2	137.1	137.8	141.4	141.5
Current Account	34.3	44.6	56.4	72.6	89.8	100.0	109.5	118.2	126.7	128.9	133.0	131.5
Foreign Reserves	72.8	70.7	69.9	72.1	71.2	70.5	72.4	71.6	73.0	85.0	98.8	98.5
Balance of Trade % GDP	2.1%	2.4%	2.7%	3.1%	3.1%	3.3%	3.5%	3.6%	3.7%	3.7%	3.8%	3.8%
Current Account % GDP	1.0%	1.3%	1.7%	2.2%	2.4%	2.7%	3.0%	3.2%	3.4%	3.5%	3.6%	3.5%
Share Index	26,252	23,996	24,377	22,984	19,346	15,952	17,748	16,843	18,963	19,543	20,173	17,370
% from December	10.1%	0.6%	2.2%	-3.6%	-15.8%	-30.6%	-22.8%	-26.7%	12.6%	16.0%	19.8%	3.1%

Germany	1988 Mar	1988 Jun	1988 Sep	1988 Dec	1989 Mar	1989 Jun	1989 Sep	1989 Dec	1990 Mar	1990 Jun	1990 Sep	1990 Dec
Industrial Production	2.3	3.5	3.6	4.2	5.1	2.1	3.3	5.4	3.7	5.0	6.1	5.7
Unemployment Rate	8.8	8.9	8.7	8.3	7.7	7.9	7.8	7.8	7.2	7.3	7.1	6.6
Consumer Price Index	1.0	1.1	1.4	1.6	2.7	3.1	3.1	3.2	2.8	2.3	3.0	2.8
Wage Index	3.0	3.4	3.4	3.4	3.2	3.7	3.8	4.0	6.0	5.6	5.7	6.1
Producer Price Index	0.6	1.6	1.7	2.0	3.5	2.9	3.0	3.1	1.4	1.5	2.1	1.5
Weighted Currency	115.7	113.8	113.5	113.7	112.6	112.5	113.9	119.5	119.0	118.0	119.0	121.0
Currency to Dollar	1.66	1.81	1.88	1.84	1.90	1.96	1.89	1.71	1.70	1.65	1.56	1.49
% from December	0.1%	-1.6%	-1.8%	-1.6%	-1.0%	-1.1%	0.2%	5.1%	-0.4%	-1.3%	-0.4%	1.3%
% from December	1.8%	11.0%	15.3%	12.9%	3.3%	6.5%	2.7%	-7.1%	-0.6%	-3.5%	-8.8%	-12.9%
Narrow M	10.5	10.3	9.2	10.6	8.9	4.5	4.7	5.3	2.1	3.3	5.1	6.9
Broad M	6.1	6.5	6.9	6.8	6.9	5.1	5.1	5.3	4.3	4.3	4.7	5.1
Real Broad M	5.1	5.4	5.5	5.2	4.2	2.0	2.0	2.1	1.5	2.0	1.7	2.3
Money Market Yield	3.5	4.2	4.9	5.5	6.6	7.0	7.5	8.3	8.2	8.2	8.5	9.3
Government-Bond Yield	6.0	6.3	6.4	6.5	7.0	6.9	7.3	7.8	8.7	8.8	9.1	8.9
Yield Spread	-2.5	-2.1	-1.5	-1.0	-0.4	0.1	0.2	0.5	-0.5	-0.6	-0.6	0.4
Real Money Market Yield	2.5	3.1	3.5	3.9	3.9	3.9	4.4	5.1	5.4	5.9	5.5	6.5
Real Govt.-Bond Yield	5.0	5.2	5.0	4.9	4.3	3.8	4.2	4.6	5.9	6.5	6.1	6.1
Bank Prime Rate	5.5	6.0	6.0	6.5	7.3	8.5	8.5	10.5	10.5	10.5	10.5	10.5
Spread - Money Market	2.0	1.8	1.1	1.0	0.7	1.5	1.0	2.2	2.3	2.3	2.0	1.2
Spread - Govt. Bond	-0.5	-0.3	-0.4	0.0	0.3	1.6	1.2	2.7	1.8	1.7	1.4	1.6
Balance of Trade	65.8	70.3	72.0	72.9	77.2	75.1	75.9	71.5	73.8	72.8	70.8	74.3
Current Account	42.6	47.1	47.7	48.4	54.8	53.5	55.2	51.9	54.2	51.9	49.3	44.0
Foreign Reserves	73.0	64.8	58.0	58.5	55.0	55.5	57.7	60.7	61.5	63.5	64.9	67.9
Balance of Trade % GDP	5.5%	5.9%	6.0%	6.1%	6.5%	6.3%	6.4%	6.0%	4.9%	4.9%	4.7%	5.0%
Current Account % GDP	3.6%	3.9%	4.0%	4.1%	4.6%	4.5%	4.7%	4.4%	3.6%	3.5%	3.3%	2.9%
Share Index	1,342	1,422	1,569	1,683	1,633	1,830	2,008	2,204	2,414¡	2,330	1,771	1,701
% from December	4.5%	10.7%	22.2%	31.0%	-3.0%	8.7%	19.3%	30.9%	9.5%¡	Note 3	-24.0%	-27.0%

Germany	1991 Mar	1991 Jun	1991 Sep	1991 Dec	1992 Mar	1992 Jun	1992 Sep	1992 Dec	1993 Mar	1993 Jun	1993 Sep	1993 Dec
Industrial Production	4.0	5.4	-0.3	-0.8	-1.1	-4.5	-3.3	-3.7	-10.5	-8.7	-7.6	-0.9
Unemployment Rate	6.1	6.3	6.4	6.2	6.2	6.6	6.8	7.4	7.8	8.2	8.6	9.0
Consumer Price Index	2.5	3.5	3.9	4.2	4.9	4.3	3.6	3.8	4.3	4.2	4.0	3.6
Wage Index	6.3	6.5	7.0	6.7	5.4	5.2	5.5	5.4	4.2	3.8	5.8	4.0
Producer Price Index	1.8	2.3	2.6	2.6	2.5	2.0	0.8	0.7	0.3	-0.4	-0.5	-0.1
Weighted Currency	117.5	115.6	117.5	120.6	118.7	119.9	125.3	125.3	126.6	121.7	126.0	122.8
Currency to Dollar	1.67	1.80	1.67	1.52	1.65	1.52	1.42	1.63	1.62	1.69	1.62	1.74
% from December	-2.9%	-4.5%	-2.9%	-0.3%	-1.6%	-0.6%	3.9%	3.9%	1.0%	-2.9%	0.6%	-2.0%
% from December	12.1%	20.8%	12.1%	2.0%	8.6%	0.0%	-6.6%	7.2%	-0.6%	3.7%	-0.6%	6.7%
Narrow M			Note 4			Note 4	8.6	11.7	10.0	10.1	9.5	8.4
Broad M	4.4	3.4	4.6	5.7	7.0	8.2	9.1	8.8	7.6	8.6	7.5	8.1
Real Broad M	1.9	-0.1	0.7	1.5	2.1	3.9	5.5	5.0	3.3	4.4	3.5	4.5
Money Market Yield	9.1	8.9	9.2	9.6	9.7	9.7	9.1	8.7	8.0	7.5	6.6	5.8
Government-Bond Yield	8.6	8.7	8.7	8.5	8.2	8.4	8.0	7.2	6.7	6.7	6.1	5.5
Yield Spread	0.5	0.2	0.5	1.1	1.5	1.3	1.1	1.5	1.3	0.8	0.5	0.3
Real Money Market Yield	6.6	5.4	5.3	5.4	4.8	5.4	5.5	4.9	3.7	3.3	2.6	2.2
Real Govt.-Bond Yield	6.1	5.2	4.8	4.3	3.3	4.1	4.4	3.4	2.4	2.5	2.1	1.9
Bank Prime Rate	10.5	10.5	11.5	11.3	11.0	11.0	11.0	11.0	10.5	10.0	9.5	9.0
Spread - Money Market	1.4	1.6	2.3	1.7	1.3	1.3	1.9	2.3	2.5	2.5	2.9	3.2
Spread - Govt. Bond	1.9	1.8	2.8	2.8	2.8	2.6	3.0	3.8	3.8	3.3	3.4	3.5
Balance of Trade	46.8	28.1	16.2	12.9	13.4	17.5	23.2	21.4	22.9	27.5	27.0	36.0
Current Account	21.0	6.0	-11.0	-20.0	-20.0	-20.0	-22.8	-25.3	-26.2	-23.1	-23.5	-22.1
Foreign Reserves	59.1	57.7	61.2	62.5	61.6	64.1	88.4	91.0	70.3	68.2	85.3	77.9
Balance of Trade % GDP	3.0%	1.8%	1.0%	0.8%	0.8%	1.0%	1.3%	1.2%	1.3%	1.5%	1.5%	2.0%
Current Account % GDP	1.3%	0.4%	-0.7%	-1.3%	-1.1%	-1.1%	-1.3%	-1.4%	-1.4%	-1.3%	-1.3%	-1.2%
Share Index	1,862	1,906	1,869	1,578	1,718	1,753	1,476	1,556	1,685	1,708	1,914	2,254
% from December	9.5%	12.0%	9.9%	-7.2%	8.9%	11.1%	-6.4%	-1.4%	8.3%	9.8%	23.0%	44.8%

Britain	1988 Mar	Jun	Sep	Dec	1989 Mar	Jun	Sep	Dec	1990 Mar	Jun	Sep	Dec
Industrial Production	1.6	4.7	3.8	1.5	0.9	-1.9	-0.4	1.6	1.6	5.5	-2.3	-4.2
Unemployment Rate	9.0	8.4	8.0	7.2	6.7	6.3	6.0	5.8	5.6	5.7	5.8	6.5
Consumer Price Index	3.5	4.6	5.9	6.8	7.9	8.3	7.6	7.7	8.1	9.8	10.9	9.3
Wage Index	8.5	8.5	9.3	8.8	9.3	9.0	9.0	9.3	9.5	10.0	10.3	9.8
Producer Price Index	4.1	4.6	5.0	4.9	5.2	4.9	5.0	5.2	5.6	6.2	5.9	5.8
Weighted Currency	96.4	94.0	95.1	97.9	95.6	90.7	91.2	86.8	87.4	92.3	93.5	86.0
Currency to Dollar	0.54	0.58	0.60	0.57	0.59	0.64	0.62	0.62	0.61	0.56	0.53	0.52
% from December	4.7%	2.1%	3.3%	6.3%	-2.3%	-7.4%	-6.8%	-11.3%	0.7%	6.3%	7.7%	-0.9%
% from December	-1.8%	5.5%	9.1%	3.6%	3.5%	12.3%	8.8%	8.8%	-1.6%	-9.7%	-14.5%	-16.1%
Narrow M	20.8	18.6	17.4	14.4	14.3	5.5	4.5	6.0	6.3	6.4	4.6	2.7
Broad M	20.9	20.3	22.6	20.4	22.6	18.6	17.5	18.1	17.5	16.8	14.6	12.0
Real Broad M	17.4	15.7	16.7	13.6	14.7	10.3	9.9	10.4	9.4	7.0	3.7	2.7
Money Market Yield	8.8	9.9	12.1	13.1	13.0	14.1	14.6	15.1	15.2	14.9	14.9	14.0
Government-Bond Yield	9.3	9.6	9.8	9.8	9.5	10.1	10.0	10.0	11.8	11.1	11.5	10.7
Yield Spread	-0.5	0.3	2.3	3.3	3.5	4.0	4.6	5.1	3.4	3.8	3.4	3.3
Real Money Market Yield	5.3	5.3	6.2	6.3	5.1	5.8	7.0	7.4	7.1	5.1	4.0	4.7
Real Govt.-Bond Yield	5.8	5.0	3.9	3.0	1.6	1.8	2.4	2.3	3.7	1.3	0.6	1.4
Bank Prime Rate	9.5	10.5	13.0	14.0	14.0	15.0	15.0	16.0	16.0	16.0	16.0	15.0
Spread - Money Market	0.7	0.6	0.9	0.9	1.0	0.9	0.4	0.9	0.8	1.1	1.1	1.0
Spread - Govt. Bond	0.2	0.9	3.2	4.2	4.5	4.9	5.0	6.0	4.2	4.9	4.5	4.3
Balance of Trade	-20.5	-25.4	-30.4	-36.4	-39.7	-40.8	-42.2	-37.7	-36.5	-34.1	-32.3	-32.0
Current Account	-7.4	-14.1	-20.6	-25.6	-28.8	-31.9	-35.2	-33.4	-36.2	-31.6	-29.7	-28.7
Foreign Reserves	41.4	40.4	41.7	44.1	41.4	37.2	37.5	34.8	34.1	34.2	35.7	35.9
Balance of Trade % GDP	-2.4%	-3.0%	-3.6%	-4.3%	-4.7%	-4.8%	-5.0%	-4.5%	-3.7%	-3.5%	-3.3%	-3.3%
Current Account % GDP	-0.9%	-1.7%	-2.5%	-3.0%	-3.4%	-3.8%	-4.2%	-4.0%	-3.7%	-3.2%	-3.0%	-2.9%
Share Index	1,743	1,857	1,808	1,836	2,071	2,206	2,319	2,434	2,241	2,372	2,059	2,144
% from December	1.7%	8.4%	5.6%	7.2%	12.8%	20.2%	26.3%	32.6%	-7.9%	-2.6%	-15.4%	-11.9%

Britain	1991 Mar	1991 Jun	1991 Sep	1991 Dec	1992 Mar	1992 Jun	1992 Sep	1992 Dec	1993 Mar	1993 Jun	1993 Sep	1993 Dec
Industrial Production	-3.5	-5.6	-1.7	-0.1	-2.2	-2.3	-0.2	0.6	1.5	3.3	2.1	4.0
Unemployment Rate	7.4	8.1	8.7	9.0	9.4	9.6	10.1	10.5	10.5	10.4	10.3	9.8
Consumer Price Index	8.2	5.8	4.1	4.5	4.0	3.9	3.6	2.6	1.9	1.2	1.8	1.9
Wage Index	9.0	8.3	7.8	7.3	7.5	6.0	5.5	4.8	4.0	3.5	3.0	3.0
Producer Price Index	6.3	5.7	5.2	5.0	4.5	3.6	3.2	3.5	3.7	4.0	4.2	4.0
Weighted Currency	92.2	89.9	91.0	91.5	90.2	93.1	83.7	81.2	79.3	80.8	80.1	82.1
Currency to Dollar	0.57	0.61	0.57	0.54	0.58	0.53	0.57	0.65	0.67	0.66	0.66	0.67
% from December	7.2%	4.5%	5.8%	6.4%	-1.4%	1.7%	-8.5%	-11.3%	-2.3%	-0.5%	-1.4%	1.1%
% from December	9.6%	17.3%	9.6%	3.8%	7.4%	-1.9%	5.6%	20.4%	3.1%	1.5%	1.5%	3.1%
Narrow M	2.7	2.0	2.2	2.8	2.2	1.4	2.1	3.0	4.9	4.4	5.3	5.8
Broad M	9.9	7.9	6.4	6.2	5.6	5.1	5.1	3.7	3.6	3.3	3.9	4.0
Real Broad M	1.7	2.1	2.3	1.7	1.6	1.2	1.5	1.1	1.7	2.1	2.1	2.1
Money Market Yield	12.5	11.3	10.3	10.9	10.8	10.1	9.0	7.2	5.9	5.9	5.9	5.4
Government-Bond Yield	10.2	10.4	9.4	9.6	9.7	9.1	9.2	8.7	8.3	8.1	7.3	6.3
Yield Spread	2.3	0.9	0.9	1.3	1.1	1.0	-0.2	-1.5	-2.4	-2.2	-1.4	-0.9
Real Money Market Yield	4.3	5.5	6.2	6.4	6.8	6.2	5.4	4.6	4.0	4.7	4.1	3.5
Real Govt.-Bond Yield	2.0	4.6	5.3	5.1	5.7	5.2	5.6	6.1	6.4	6.9	5.5	4.4
Bank Prime Rate	13.5	12.5	11.5	11.5	11.5	11.0	10.0	8.0	7.0	7.0	7.0	6.5
Spread - Money Market	1.0	1.2	1.2	0.6	0.7	0.9	1.0	0.8	1.1	1.1	1.1	1.1
Spread - Govt. Bond	3.3	2.1	2.1	1.9	1.8	1.9	0.8	-0.7	-1.3	-1.1	-0.3	0.2
Balance of Trade	-27.0	-21.8	-19.1	-17.8	-17.7	-19.5	-22.2	-24.1	-25.4	-23.2	-19.9	-20.1
Current Account	-17.1	-13.5	-12.7	-10.5	-7.4	-13.6	-19.2	-20.7	-21.9	-15.5	-13.6	-16.0
Foreign Reserves	39.1	38.2	40.4	41.9	40.2	42.6	40.2	38.0	36.7	37.1	38.3	38.9
Balance of Trade % GDP	-2.7%	-2.1%	-1.9%	-1.8%	-1.7%	-1.9%	-2.1%	-2.3%	-2.4%	-2.2%	-1.9%	-1.9%
Current Account % GDP	-1.7%	-1.3%	-1.3%	-1.0%	-0.7%	-1.3%	-1.8%	-2.0%	-2.0%	-1.4%	-1.3%	-1.5%
Share Index	2,488	2,460	2,646	2,493	2,440	2,521	2,566	2,834	2,861	3,100	3,037	3,409
% from December	16.1%	14.8%	23.4%	16.3%	-2.1%	1.1%	2.9%	13.7%	1.0%	9.4%	7.2%	20.3%

Canada	1988				1989				1990			
	Mar	Jun	Sep	Dec	Mar	Jun	Sep	Dec	Mar	Jun	Sep	Dec
Industrial Production	6.0	7.3	5.0	2.7	1.0	0.7	0.3	1.0	-1.1	-2.2	-4.2	-6.6
Unemployment Rate	7.8	7.6	7.8	7.6	7.5	7.3	7.3	7.7	7.2	7.5	8.4	9.3
Consumer Price Index	4.1	3.9	4.1	4.0	4.6	5.4	5.2	5.1	5.3	4.3	4.2	5.0
Wage Index	4.6	7.4	5.3	4.9	5.0	4.7	5.0	6.4	5.4	6.4	4.8	6.2
Producer Price Index	4.6	3.8	3.5	3.2	3.6	2.3	1.6	0.2	0.2	0.2	0.6	1.8
Weighted Currency	96.3	100.7	101.1	100.9	102.5	103.7	104.8	105.2	105.0	104.2	103.0	101.8
Currency to Dollar	1.34	1.21	1.22	1.20	1.19	1.19	1.18	1.16	1.17	1.16	1.15	1.16
% from December	1.7%	6.3%	6.8%	6.5%	1.6%	2.8%	3.9%	4.3%	-0.2%	-1.0%	-2.1%	-3.2%
% from December	3.1%	-6.9%	-6.2%	-7.7%	-0.8%	-0.8%	-1.7%	-3.3%	0.9%	0.0%	-0.9%	0.0%
Narrow M	5.9	2.3	4.3	5.3	8.1	5.0	2.5	2.9	-1.6	-1.9	-4.2	-0.2
Broad M	6.7	7.1	8.8	10.2	12.2	10.7	10.1	12.7	10.4	9.8	8.9	8.2
Real Broad M	2.6	3.2	4.7	6.2	7.6	5.3	4.9	7.6	5.1	5.5	4.7	3.2
Money Market Yield	8.7	9.3	10.5	11.1	12.4	12.3	12.3	12.3	13.5	13.7	12.5	12.0
Government-Bond Yield	10.0	9.6	10.1	10.2	10.5	9.5	9.8	9.5	11.1	10.9	11.1	10.3
Yield Spread	-1.3	-0.3	0.4	0.9	1.9	2.8	2.5	2.8	2.4	2.8	1.4	1.7
Real Money Market Yield	4.6	5.4	6.4	7.1	7.8	6.9	7.1	7.2	8.2	9.4	8.3	7.0
Real Govt.-Bond Yield	5.9	5.7	6.0	6.2	5.9	4.1	4.6	4.4	5.8	6.6	6.9	5.3
Bank Prime Rate	9.8	10.8	11.8	12.3	13.5	13.5	13.5	13.5	14.3	14.8	13.8	13.0
Spread - Money Market	1.1	1.5	1.3	1.2	1.1	1.2	1.2	1.2	0.8	1.1	1.3	1.0
Spread - Govt. Bond	-0.2	1.2	1.7	2.1	3.0	4.0	3.7	4.0	3.2	3.9	2.7	2.7
Balance of Trade	7.1	8.1	7.8	7.1	8.7	5.6	5.4	4.0	2.6	5.0	7.7	9.4
Current Account	-7.8	-7.8	-7.3	-9.2	-10.1	-13.1	-14.9	-16.6	-15.8	-15.6	-15.0	-13.7
Foreign Reserves	11.7	15.4	13.9	15.4	15.4	15.1	15.7	16.1	13.8	13.9	17.5	17.8
Balance of Trade % GDP	1.4%	1.6%	1.6%	1.4%	1.6%	1.0%	1.0%	0.7%	0.5%	0.9%	1.3%	1.6%
Current Account % GDP	-1.6%	-1.6%	-1.5%	-1.9%	-1.8%	-2.4%	-2.7%	-3.0%	-2.8%	-2.7%	-2.6%	-2.4%
Share Index	3,270	3,435	3,262	3,444	3,561	3,778	4,012	4,004	3,648	3,560	3,191	3,257
% from December	1.0%	6.1%	0.7%	6.4%	3.4%	9.7%	16.5%	16.3%	-8.9%	-11.1%	-20.3%	-18.7%

Canada	1991				1992				1993			
	Mar	Jun	Sep	Dec	Mar	Jun	Sep	Dec	Mar	Jun	Sep	Dec
Industrial Production	-7.4	-4.5	-1.2	-0.8	1.3	-0.7	0.3	4.3	6.2	5.7	5.1	4.5
Unemployment Rate	10.5	10.5	10.2	10.3	11.1	11.6	11.4	11.5	11.0	11.3	11.2	11.2
Consumer Price Index	6.3	6.3	5.4	3.8	1.6	1.1	1.3	2.1	1.9	1.6	1.9	1.7
Wage Index	6.3	5.5	5.6	4.2	3.9	3.3	3.3	3.3	2.6	2.7	1.9	0.8
Producer Price Index	0.9	-0.7	-2.4	-3.1	-1.4	0.2	2.1	3.5	3.6	2.9	2.7	3.2
Weighted Currency	104.0	107.0	106.0	101.9	101.0	98.4	93.2	94.8	96.4	94.0	90.8	92.4
Currency to Dollar	1.16	1.14	1.13	1.16	1.19	1.20	1.26	1.28	1.25	1.28	1.32	1.32
% from December	2.2%	5.1%	4.1%	0.1%	-0.9%	-3.4%	-8.5%	-7.0%	1.7%	-0.8%	-4.2%	-2.5%
% from December	0.0%	-1.7%	-2.6%	0.0%	2.6%	3.4%	8.6%	10.3%	-2.3%	0.0%	3.1%	3.1%
Narrow M	3.1	5.1	8.0	5.5	5.3	4.8	5.7	6.8	10.6	14.6	8.9	19.0
Broad M	9.0	7.8	5.8	5.7	5.9	5.8	8.1	7.9	6.9	7.2	4.4	2.9
Real Broad M	2.7	1.5	0.4	1.9	4.3	4.7	6.8	5.8	5.0	5.6	2.5	1.2
Money Market Yield	9.8	8.7	8.4	7.3	7.2	5.4	7.6	7.0	5.1	4.5	4.0	3.8
Government-Bond Yield	9.8	10.3	9.6	9.0	9.4	9.0	8.6	8.6	8.3	8.2	7.6	6.7
Yield Spread	0.0	-1.6	-1.2	-1.7	-2.2	-3.6	-1.0	-1.6	-3.2	-3.7	-3.6	-2.9
Real Money Market Yield	3.5	2.4	3.0	3.5	5.6	4.3	6.3	4.9	3.2	2.9	2.1	2.1
Real Govt.-Bond Yield	3.5	4.0	4.2	5.2	7.8	7.9	7.3	6.5	6.4	6.6	5.7	5.0
Bank Prime Rate	11.3	9.8	9.5	8.0	8.3	7.0	6.3	7.3	6.0	6.0	5.8	5.5
Spread - Money Market	1.5	1.1	1.1	0.7	1.1	1.6	-1.3	0.3	0.9	1.5	1.8	1.7
Spread - Govt. Bond	1.5	-0.5	-0.1	-1.0	-1.1	-2.0	-2.3	-1.3	-2.3	-2.2	-1.8	-1.2
Balance of Trade	9.9	9.9	9.9	6.4	6.8	5.2	5.9	7.8	9.1	9.7	9.7	9.1
Current Account	-18.3	-18.4	-20.4	-23.4	-25.9	-26.2	-26.2	-23.7	-21.0	-20.5	-19.8	-19.6
Foreign Reserves	17.0	16.5	18.1	16.3	14.7	14.7	12.3	14.0	12.7	11.7	10.7	12.5
Balance of Trade % GDP	1.7%	1.7%	1.7%	1.1%	1.2%	0.9%	1.0%	1.4%	1.6%	1.7%	1.7%	1.6%
Current Account % GDP	-3.1%	-3.1%	-3.5%	-4.0%	-4.6%	-4.6%	-4.6%	-4.2%	-3.6%	-3.5%	-3.4%	-3.3%
Share Index	3,516	3,505	3,395	3,512	3,412	3,383	3,327	3,354	3,586	3,963	3,979	4,369
% from December	8.0%	7.6%	4.3%	7.8%	-2.9%	-3.7%	-5.3%	-4.5%	6.9%	18.2%	18.6%	30.3%

Other Data	1988				1989				1990			
	Mar	Jun	Sep	Dec	Mar	Jun	Sep	Dec	Mar	Jun	Sep	Dec
Mark/Pound Exchange Rate	3.07	3.12	3.13	3.23	3.22	3.06	3.05	2.76	2.79	2.95	2.94	2.87
% from December	3.7%	5.4%	5.7%	9.1%	-0.3%	-5.3%	-5.6%	-14.6%	1.1%	6.9%	6.5%	4.0%
West Texas Oil per barrel	15.65	16.55	14.90	16.05	19.75	20.70	19.95	20.65	20.05	17.07	31.71	26.53
CRB Index	233.0	265.1	238.8	251.8	242.1	234.4	226.8	229.9	238.2	236.9	239.2	222.6
% from December	0.2%	14.0%	2.7%	8.3%	-3.9%	-6.9%	-9.9%	-8.7%	3.6%	3.0%	4.0%	-3.2%

Other Data	1991				1992				1993			
	Mar	Jun	Sep	Dec	Mar	Jun	Sep	Dec	Mar	Jun	Sep	Dec
Mark/Pound Exchange Rate	2.93	2.95	2.93	2.81	2.84	2.87	2.49	2.51	2.42	2.56	2.45	2.60
% from December	2.1%	2.8%	2.1%	-2.1%	1.1%	2.1%	-11.4%	-10.7%	-3.6%	2.0%	-2.4%	3.6%
West Texas Oil per barrel	19.86	19.65	21.82	19.71	19.09	22.31	21.50	19.30	20.50	18.45	18.80	14.15
CRB Index	218.5	208.4	215.6	208.1	209.8	209.3	200.4	202.8	212.8	209.7	216.1	226.2
% from December	-1.8%	-6.4%	-3.1%	-6.5%	0.8%	0.6%	-3.7%	-2.5%	4.9%	3.4%	6.6%	11.5%

Matrix Comparison	1988				1989				1990			
	Mar	Jun	Sep	Dec	Mar	Jun	Sep	Dec	Mar	Jun	Sep	Dec
Industrial Production												
United States	5.7	5.8	5.5	4.7	4.7	3.4	2.7	1.7	1.0	1.2	2.3	-1.4
Japan	12.8	9.1	9.2	8.2	9.4	7.4	3.8	3.2	0.2	3.0	5.3	6.0
Germany	2.3	3.5	3.6	4.2	5.1	2.1	3.3	5.4	3.7	5.0	6.1	5.7
Britain	1.6	4.7	3.8	1.5	0.9	-1.9	-0.4	1.6	1.6	5.5	-2.3	-4.2
Canada	6.0	7.3	5.0	2.7	1.0	0.7	0.3	1.0	-1.1	-2.2	-4.2	-6.6
Unemployment												
United States	5.6	5.3	5.4	5.3	4.9	5.3	5.3	5.3	5.2	5.2	5.7	6.1
Japan	2.6	2.4	2.5	2.3	2.3	2.2	2.2	2.1	2.0	2.2	2.2	2.1
Germany	8.8	8.9	8.7	8.3	7.7	7.9	7.8	7.8	7.2	7.3	7.1	6.6
Britain	9.0	8.4	8.0	7.2	6.7	6.3	6.0	5.8	5.6	5.7	5.8	6.5
Canada	7.8	7.6	7.8	7.6	7.5	7.3	7.3	7.7	7.2	7.5	8.4	9.3
Consumer Prices												
United States	3.9	4.0	4.2	4.6	5.0	5.2	5.0	4.6	5.2	4.7	6.2	6.1
Japan	0.7	0.2	0.6	1.0	1.1	3.0	2.6	2.6	3.5	2.2	3.0	3.8
Germany	1.0	1.1	1.4	1.6	2.7	3.1	3.1	3.2	2.8	2.3	3.0	2.8
Britain	3.5	4.6	5.9	6.8	7.9	8.3	7.6	7.7	8.1	9.8	10.9	9.3
Canada	4.1	3.9	4.1	4.0	4.6	5.4	5.2	5.1	5.3	4.3	4.2	5.0
Wages												
United States	2.8	3.2	3.3	3.4	4.8	3.8	3.8	4.1	4.0	4.1	4.0	3.8
Japan	2.2	7.0	1.7	3.0	7.1	3.0	4.6	7.0	3.3	8.4	4.8	6.3
Germany	3.0	3.4	3.4	3.4	3.2	3.7	3.8	4.0	6.0	5.6	5.7	6.1
Britain	8.5	8.5	9.3	8.8	9.3	9.0	9.0	9.3	9.5	10.0	10.3	9.8
Canada	4.6	7.4	5.3	4.9	5.0	4.7	5.0	6.4	5.4	6.4	4.8	6.2
Weighted Exchange Rate												
United States	-3.2%	2.0%	4.3%	1.1%	3.2%	7.2%	5.1%	2.1%	1.3%	-2.2%	-8.0%	-9.6%
Japan	2.0%	1.2%	0.9%	5.3%	-3.5%	-6.8%	-8.7%	-15.0%	-9.0%	-6.3%	0.4%	-0.2%
Germany	0.1%	-1.6%	-1.8%	-1.6%	-1.0%	-1.1%	0.2%	5.1%	-0.4%	-1.3%	-0.4%	1.3%
Britain	4.7%	2.1%	3.3%	6.3%	-2.3%	-7.4%	-6.8%	-11.3%	0.7%	6.3%	7.7%	-0.9%
Canada	1.7%	6.3%	6.8%	6.5%	1.6%	2.8%	3.9%	4.3%	-0.2%	-1.0%	-2.1%	-3.2%

Matrix Comparison	1988				1989				1990			
	Mar	Jun	Sep	Dec	Mar	Jun	Sep	Dec	Mar	Jun	Sep	Dec
Real Broad M												
United States	0.8	1.8	1.1	1.1	-1.3	-2.7	-1.1	0.2	0.8	1.1	-1.3	-2.9
Japan	11.1	12.1	10.0	9.4	9.2	6.4	7.3	8.0	8.1	10.4	9.0	4.8
Germany	5.1	5.4	5.5	5.2	4.2	2.0	2.0	2.1	1.5	2.0	1.7	2.3
Britain	17.4	15.7	16.7	13.6	14.7	10.3	9.9	10.4	9.4	7.0	3.7	2.7
Canada	2.6	3.2	4.7	6.2	7.6	5.3	4.9	7.6	5.1	5.5	4.7	3.2
Money Market Yield												
United States	6.5	7.6	8.1	9.1	10.1	9.1	8.9	8.3	8.3	8.1	8.0	8.1
Japan	3.8	3.8	4.2	4.2	4.2	4.5	5.0	5.8	6.6	7.0	7.5	7.6
Germany	3.5	4.2	4.9	5.5	6.6	7.0	7.5	8.3	8.2	8.2	8.5	9.3
Britain	8.8	9.9	12.1	13.1	13.0	14.1	14.6	15.1	15.2	14.9	14.9	14.0
Canada	8.7	9.3	10.5	11.1	12.4	12.3	12.3	12.3	13.5	13.7	12.5	12.0
Government-Bond Yield												
United States	8.7	8.9	9.1	9.1	9.2	8.2	8.3	8.0	8.6	8.5	8.9	8.1
Japan	4.5	4.9	5.1	4.8	5.0	5.4	5.2	5.5	7.3	7.3	8.3	7.1
Germany	6.0	6.3	6.4	6.5	7.0	6.9	7.3	7.8	8.7	8.8	9.1	8.9
Britain	9.3	9.6	9.8	9.8	9.5	10.1	10.0	10.0	11.8	11.1	11.5	10.7
Canada	10.0	9.6	10.1	10.2	10.5	9.5	9.8	9.5	11.1	10.9	11.1	10.3
Yield Spread												
United States	-2.2	-1.3	-1.0	0.0	0.9	0.9	0.6	0.3	-0.3	-0.4	-0.9	0.0
Japan	-0.7	-1.1	-0.9	-0.6	-0.8	-0.9	-0.2	0.3	-0.7	-0.3	-0.8	0.5
Germany	-2.5	-2.1	-1.5	-1.0	-0.4	0.1	0.2	0.5	-0.5	-0.6	-0.6	0.4
Britain	-0.5	0.3	2.3	3.3	3.5	4.0	4.6	5.1	3.4	3.8	3.4	3.3
Canada	-1.3	-0.3	0.4	0.9	1.9	2.8	2.5	2.8	2.4	2.8	1.4	1.7
Real Govt.-Bond Yield												
United States	4.8	4.9	4.9	4.5	4.2	3.0	3.3	3.4	3.4	3.8	2.7	2.0
Japan	3.8	4.7	4.5	3.8	3.9	2.4	2.6	2.9	3.8	5.1	5.3	3.3
Germany	5.0	5.2	5.0	4.9	4.3	3.8	4.2	4.6	5.9	6.5	6.1	6.1
Britain	5.8	5.0	3.9	3.0	1.6	1.8	2.4	2.3	3.7	1.3	0.6	1.4
Canada	5.9	5.7	6.0	6.2	5.9	4.1	4.6	4.4	5.8	6.6	6.9	5.3

Matrix Comparison	1988				1989				1990			
	Mar	*Jun*	*Sep*	*Dec*	*Mar*	*Jun*	*Sep*	*Dec*	*Mar*	*Jun*	*Sep*	*Dec*
Bank Prime												
United States	8.5	9.0	10.0	10.5	11.5	11.0	10.5	10.5	10.0	10.0	10.0	10.0
Japan	3.4	3.4	3.4	3.4	3.4	4.9	4.9	4.9	6.3	7.1	7.4	8.0
Germany	5.5	6.0	6.0	6.5	7.3	8.5	8.5	10.5	10.5	10.5	10.5	10.5
Britain	9.5	10.5	13.0	14.0	14.0	15.0	15.0	16.0	16.0	16.0	16.0	15.0
Canada	9.8	10.8	11.8	12.3	13.5	13.5	13.5	13.5	14.3	14.8	13.8	13.0
Prime and Bond Spread												
United States	-0.2	0.1	0.9	1.4	2.3	2.8	2.2	2.5	1.4	1.5	1.1	1.9
Japan	-1.1	-1.5	-1.7	-1.4	-1.6	-0.5	-0.3	-0.6	-1.0	-0.2	-0.9	0.9
Germany	-0.5	-0.3	-0.4	0.0	0.3	1.6	1.2	2.7	1.8	1.7	1.4	1.6
Britain	0.2	0.9	3.2	4.2	4.5	4.9	5.0	6.0	4.2	4.9	4.5	4.3
Canada	-0.2	1.2	1.7	2.1	3.0	4.0	3.7	4.0	3.2	3.9	2.7	2.7
Trade Balance % of GDP												
United States	-3.4%	-3.2%	-2.6%	-2.4%	-2.2%	-2.1%	-2.1%	-2.1%	-1.9%	-1.8%	-1.9%	-1.8%
Japan	3.2%	3.2%	3.2%	3.3%	3.3%	3.2%	3.0%	2.7%	2.4%	2.2%	1.9%	2.2%
Germany	5.5%	5.9%	6.0%	6.1%	6.5%	6.3%	6.4%	6.0%	4.9%	4.9%	4.7%	5.0%
Britain	-2.4%	-3.0%	-3.6%	-4.3%	-4.7%	-4.8%	-5.0%	-4.5%	-3.7%	-3.5%	-3.3%	-3.3%
Canada	1.4%	1.6%	1.6%	1.4%	1.6%	1.0%	1.0%	0.7%	0.5%	0.9%	1.3%	1.6%
Current Account % of GDP												
United States	-3.1%	-3.0%	-2.8%	-2.8%	-2.4%	-2.3%	-2.2%	-2.0%	-1.9%	-1.8%	-1.7%	-1.8%
Japan	2.9%	2.8%	2.7%	2.7%	2.7%	2.5%	2.4%	2.0%	1.8%	1.6%	1.4%	1.3%
Germany	3.6%	3.9%	4.0%	4.1%	4.6%	4.5%	4.7%	4.4%	3.6%	3.5%	3.3%	2.9%
Britain	-0.9%	-1.7%	-2.5%	-3.0%	-3.4%	-3.8%	-4.2%	-4.0%	-3.7%	-3.2%	-3.0%	-2.9%
Canada	-1.6%	-1.6%	-1.5%	-1.9%	-1.8%	-2.4%	-2.7%	-3.0%	-2.8%	-2.7%	-2.6%	-2.4%
Change in Share Index												
United States	-2.5%	4.9%	2.5%	8.0%	3.8%	15.1%	25.6%	28.1%	-2.6%	3.6%	-10.9%	-6.3%
Japan	18.8%	27.0%	27.5%	43.7%	4.2%	10.5%	14.1%	25.5%	-26.1%	-16.7%	-41.2%	-38.7%
Germany	4.5%	10.7%	22.2%	31.0%	-3.0%	8.7%	19.3%	30.9%	9.5%	Note 3	-24.0%	-27.0%
Britain	1.7%	8.4%	5.6%	7.2%	12.8%	20.2%	26.3%	32.6%	-7.9%	-2.6%	-15.4%	-11.9%
Canada	1.0%	6.1%	0.7%	6.4%	3.4%	9.7%	16.5%	16.3%	-8.9%	-11.1%	-20.3%	-18.7%

273

Matrix Comparison	1988				1989				1990			
	Mar	Jun	Sep	Dec	Mar	Jun	Sep	Dec	Mar	Jun	Sep	Dec
Currency to Dollar												
United States (Weighted)	63.7	67.1	68.6	66.5	68.6	71.3	69.9	67.9	68.8	66.4	62.5	61.4
Japan	124.0	131.0	134.0	126.0	133.0	141.0	141.0	146.0	159.0	151.0	137.0	136.0
Germany	1.66	1.81	1.88	1.84	1.90	1.96	1.89	1.71	1.70	1.65	1.56	1.49
Britain	0.54	0.58	0.60	0.57	0.59	0.64	0.62	0.62	0.61	0.56	0.53	0.52
Canada	1.34	1.21	1.22	1.20	1.19	1.19	1.18	1.16	1.17	1.16	1.15	1.16
Change in Currency												
United States (Weighted)	-3.2%	2.0%	4.3%	1.1%	3.2%	7.2%	5.1%	2.1%	1.3%	-2.2%	-8.0%	-9.6%
Japan	-2.4%	3.1%	5.5%	-0.8%	5.6%	11.9%	11.9%	15.9%	8.9%	3.4%	-6.2%	-6.8%
Germany	1.8%	11.0%	15.3%	12.9%	3.3%	6.5%	2.7%	-7.1%	-0.6%	-3.5%	-8.8%	-12.9%
Britain	-1.8%	5.5%	9.1%	3.6%	3.5%	12.3%	8.8%	8.8%	-1.6%	-9.7%	-14.5%	-16.1%
Canada	3.1%	-6.9%	-6.2%	-7.7%	-0.8%	-0.8%	-1.7%	-3.3%	0.9%	0.0%	-0.9%	0.0%
Real Money Market Yield												
United States	2.6	3.6	3.9	4.5	5.1	3.9	3.9	3.7	3.1	3.4	1.8	2.0
Japan	3.1	3.6	3.6	3.2	3.1	1.5	2.4	3.2	3.1	4.8	4.5	3.8
Germany	2.5	3.1	3.5	3.9	3.9	3.9	4.4	5.1	5.4	5.9	5.5	6.5
Britain	5.3	5.3	6.2	6.3	5.1	5.8	7.0	7.4	7.1	5.1	4.0	4.7
Canada	4.6	5.4	6.4	7.1	7.8	6.9	7.1	7.2	8.2	9.4	8.3	7.0
Prime and MM Spread												
United States	2.0	1.4	1.9	1.4	1.4	1.9	1.6	2.2	1.7	1.9	2.0	1.9
Japan	-0.4	-0.4	-0.8	-0.8	-0.8	0.4	-0.1	-0.9	-0.3	0.1	-0.1	0.4
Germany	2.0	1.8	1.1	1.0	0.7	1.5	1.0	2.2	2.3	2.3	2.0	1.2
Britain	0.7	0.6	0.9	0.9	1.0	0.9	0.4	0.9	0.8	1.1	1.1	1.0
Canada	1.1	1.5	1.3	1.2	1.1	1.2	1.2	1.2	0.8	1.1	1.3	1.0
Share Index												
United States	1,980	2,131	2,082	2,193	2,276	2,525	2,755	2,810	2,737	2,912	2,505	2,634
Japan	25,623	27,398	27,500	31,007	32,306	34,267	35,366	38,916	28,760	32,415	22,898	23,849
Germany	1,342	1,422	1,569	1,683	1,633	1,830	2,008	2,204	2,414	2,330	1,771	1,701
Britain	1,743	1,857	1,808	1,836	2,071	2,206	2,319	2,434	2,241	2,372	2,059	2,144
Canada	3,270	3,435	3,262	3,444	3,561	3,778	4,012	4,004	3,648	3,560	3,191	3,257

Matrix Comparison	1991				1992				1993			
	Mar	Jun	Sep	Dec	Mar	Jun	Sep	Dec	Mar	Jun	Sep	Dec
Industrial Production												
United States	-3.3	-2.9	-2.3	0.6	2.1	0.8	0.2	2.9	4.1	3.9	4.5	4.7
Japan	3.0	1.1	0.7	-1.4	-5.3	-4.2	-4.1	-8.2	-2.2	-5.1	-4.4	-4.2
Germany	4.0	5.4	-0.3	-0.8	-1.1	-4.5	-3.3	-3.7	-10.5	-8.7	-7.6	-0.9
Britain	-3.5	-5.6	-1.7	-0.1	-2.2	-2.3	-0.2	0.6	1.5	3.3	2.1	4.0
Canada	-7.4	-4.5	-1.2	-0.8	1.3	-0.7	0.3	4.3	6.2	5.7	5.1	4.5
Unemployment												
United States	6.8	7.0	6.7	7.1	7.3	7.8	7.5	7.3	7.0	7.0	6.7	6.4
Japan	2.2	2.1	2.2	2.2	2.1	2.1	2.2	2.4	2.3	2.5	2.6	2.9
Germany	6.1	6.3	6.4	6.2	6.2	6.6	6.8	7.4	7.8	8.2	8.6	9.0
Britain	7.4	8.1	8.7	9.0	9.4	9.6	10.1	10.5	10.5	10.4	10.3	9.8
Canada	10.5	10.5	10.2	10.3	11.1	11.6	11.4	11.5	11.0	11.3	11.2	11.2
Consumer Prices												
United States	4.9	4.6	3.4	3.1	3.2	3.1	3.0	2.9	3.1	3.0	2.7	2.7
Japan	4.0	3.6	2.7	2.7	2.0	2.3	2.0	1.2	1.2	0.9	1.5	1.0
Germany	2.5	3.5	3.9	4.2	4.9	4.3	3.6	3.8	4.3	4.2	4.0	3.6
Britain	8.2	5.8	4.1	4.5	4.0	3.9	3.6	2.6	1.9	1.2	1.8	1.9
Canada	6.3	6.3	5.4	3.8	1.6	1.1	1.3	2.1	1.9	1.6	1.9	1.7
Wages												
United States	3.9	3.6	2.9	3.2	3.0	2.2	2.3	2.3	2.4	2.3	2.3	2.5
Japan	4.2	3.5	2.8	3.5	2.2	3.9	2.1	-1.8	1.4	-1.6	1.4	-2.5
Germany	6.3	6.5	7.0	6.7	5.4	5.2	5.5	5.4	4.2	3.8	5.8	4.0
Britain	9.0	8.3	7.8	7.3	7.5	6.0	5.5	4.8	4.0	3.5	3.0	3.0
Canada	6.3	5.5	5.6	4.2	3.9	3.3	3.3	3.3	2.6	2.7	1.9	0.8
Weighted Exchange Rate												
United States	6.2%	10.4%	5.0%	-0.8%	6.6%	0.5%	-1.0%	9.5%	-1.5%	-2.4%	-2.5%	1.6%
Japan	3.3%	7.3%	7.9%	9.1%	-1.6%	-0.2%	4.0%	7.9%	7.6%	18.8%	20.2%	14.7%
Germany	-2.9%	-4.5%	-2.9%	-0.3%	-1.6%	-0.6%	3.9%	3.9%	1.0%	-2.9%	0.6%	-2.0%
Britain	7.2%	4.5%	5.8%	6.4%	-1.4%	1.7%	-8.5%	-11.3%	-2.3%	-0.5%	-1.4%	1.1%
Canada	2.2%	5.1%	4.1%	0.1%	-0.9%	-3.4%	-8.5%	-7.0%	1.7%	-0.8%	-4.2%	-2.5%

Matrix Comparison	1991				1992				1993			
	Mar	Jun	Sep	Dec	Mar	Jun	Sep	Dec	Mar	Jun	Sep	Dec
Real Broad M												
United States	-1.7	-1.2	-1.2	-0.2	-0.6	-1.6	-1.0	-1.5	-3.0	-1.7	-1.3	-1.1
Japan	0.9	0.1	-0.5	-0.7	-0.2	-1.4	-2.4	-1.6	-1.5	0.5	0.5	0.5
Germany	1.9	-0.1	0.7	1.5	2.1	3.9	5.5	5.0	3.3	4.4	3.5	4.5
Britain	1.7	2.1	2.3	1.7	1.6	1.2	1.5	1.1	1.7	2.1	2.1	2.1
Canada	2.7	1.5	0.4	1.9	4.3	4.7	6.8	5.8	5.0	5.6	2.5	1.2
Money Market Yield												
United States	6.3	6.1	5.5	4.5	4.1	3.8	3.3	3.4	3.2	3.3	3.2	3.3
Japan	7.7	7.4	6.5	5.8	4.8	4.5	3.9	3.8	3.3	3.2	2.5	2.0
Germany	9.1	8.9	9.2	9.6	9.7	9.7	9.1	8.7	8.0	7.5	6.6	5.8
Britain	12.5	11.3	10.3	10.9	10.8	10.1	9.0	7.2	5.9	5.9	5.9	5.4
Canada	9.8	8.7	8.4	7.3	7.2	5.4	7.6	7.0	5.1	4.5	4.0	3.8
Government-Bond Yield												
United States	8.1	8.3	7.7	7.1	7.5	7.3	6.4	6.8	6.0	6.0	5.4	5.7
Japan	6.6	6.8	6.0	5.4	5.3	5.3	4.8	4.5	4.2	4.4	3.8	3.5
Germany	8.6	8.7	8.7	8.5	8.2	8.4	8.0	7.2	6.7	6.7	6.1	5.5
Britain	10.2	10.4	9.4	9.6	9.7	9.1	9.2	8.7	8.3	8.1	7.3	6.3
Canada	9.8	10.3	9.6	9.0	9.4	9.0	8.6	8.6	8.3	8.2	7.6	6.7
Yield Spread												
United States	-1.8	-2.2	-2.2	-2.6	-3.4	-3.5	-3.1	-3.4	-2.8	-2.7	-2.2	-2.4
Japan	1.1	0.6	0.5	0.4	-0.5	-0.8	-0.9	-0.7	-0.9	-1.2	-1.3	-1.5
Germany	0.5	0.2	0.5	1.1	1.5	1.3	1.1	1.5	1.3	0.8	0.5	0.3
Britain	2.3	0.9	0.9	1.3	1.1	1.0	-0.2	-1.5	-2.4	-2.2	-1.4	-0.9
Canada	0.0	-1.6	-1.2	-1.7	-2.2	-3.6	-1.0	-1.6	-3.2	-3.7	-3.6	-2.9
Real Govt.-Bond Yield												
United States	3.2	3.7	4.3	4.0	4.3	4.2	3.4	3.9	2.9	3.0	2.7	3.0
Japan	2.6	3.2	3.3	2.7	3.3	3.0	2.8	3.3	3.0	3.5	2.3	2.5
Germany	6.1	5.2	4.8	4.3	3.3	4.1	4.4	3.4	2.4	2.5	2.1	1.9
Britain	2.0	4.6	5.3	5.1	5.7	5.2	5.6	6.1	6.4	6.9	5.5	4.4
Canada	3.5	4.0	4.2	5.2	7.8	7.9	7.3	6.5	6.4	6.6	5.7	5.0

Matrix Comparison	1991				1992				1993			
	Mar	Jun	Sep	Dec	Mar	Jun	Sep	Dec	Mar	Jun	Sep	Dec
Bank Prime												
United States	9.0	8.5	8.0	6.5	6.5	6.5	6.0	6.0	6.0	6.0	6.0	6.0
Japan	8.3	7.9	7.4	6.6	5.9	5.3	4.8	4.5	4.0	4.0	3.8	3.0
Germany	10.5	10.5	11.5	11.3	11.0	11.0	11.0	11.0	10.5	10.0	9.5	9.0
Britain	13.5	12.5	11.5	11.5	11.5	11.0	10.0	8.0	7.0	7.0	7.0	6.5
Canada	11.3	9.8	9.5	8.0	8.3	7.0	6.3	7.3	6.0	6.0	5.8	5.5
Prime and Bond Spread												
United States	0.9	0.2	0.3	-0.6	-1.0	-0.8	-0.4	-0.8	0.0	0.0	0.6	0.3
Japan	1.7	1.1	1.4	1.2	0.6	0.0	0.0	0.0	-0.2	-0.4	0.0	-0.5
Germany	1.9	1.8	2.8	2.8	2.8	2.6	3.0	3.8	3.8	3.3	3.4	3.5
Britain	3.3	2.1	2.1	1.9	1.8	1.9	0.8	-0.7	-1.3	-1.1	-0.3	0.2
Canada	1.5	-0.5	-0.1	-1.0	-1.1	-2.0	-2.3	-1.3	-2.3	-2.2	-1.8	-1.2
Trade Balance % of GDP												
United States	-1.6%	-1.5%	-1.3%	-1.1%	-1.1%	-1.2%	-1.3%	-1.4%	-1.5%	-1.6%	-1.7%	-1.8%
Japan	2.1%	2.4%	2.7%	3.1%	3.1%	3.3%	3.5%	3.6%	3.7%	3.7%	3.8%	3.8%
Germany	3.0%	1.8%	1.0%	0.8%	0.8%	1.0%	1.3%	1.2%	1.3%	1.5%	1.5%	2.0%
Britain	-2.7%	-2.1%	-1.9%	-1.8%	-1.7%	-1.9%	-2.1%	-2.3%	-2.4%	-2.2%	-1.9%	-1.9%
Canada	1.7%	1.7%	1.7%	1.1%	1.2%	0.9%	1.0%	1.4%	1.6%	1.7%	1.7%	1.6%
Current Account % of GDP												
United States	-1.1%	-0.6%	-0.4%	-0.4%	-0.4%	-0.7%	-0.8%	-1.0%	-1.3%	-1.4%	-1.6%	-1.7%
Japan	1.0%	1.3%	1.7%	2.2%	2.4%	2.7%	3.0%	3.2%	3.4%	3.5%	3.6%	3.5%
Germany	1.3%	0.4%	-0.7%	-1.3%	-1.1%	-1.1%	-1.3%	-1.4%	-1.4%	-1.3%	-1.3%	-1.2%
Britain	-1.7%	-1.3%	-1.3%	-1.0%	-0.7%	-1.3%	-1.8%	-2.0%	-2.0%	-1.4%	-1.3%	-1.5%
Canada	-3.1%	-3.1%	-3.5%	-4.0%	-4.6%	-4.6%	-4.6%	-4.2%	-3.6%	-3.5%	-3.4%	-3.3%
Change in Share Index												
United States	11.8%	12.9%	14.6%	20.3%	2.1%	4.7%	3.1%	4.4%	4.5%	6.4%	7.8%	14.4%
Japan	10.1%	0.6%	2.2%	-3.6%	-15.8%	-30.6%	-22.8%	-26.7%	12.6%	16.0%	19.8%	3.1%
Germany	9.5%	12.0%	9.9%	-7.2%	8.9%	11.1%	-6.4%	-1.4%	8.3%	9.8%	23.0%	44.8%
Britain	16.1%	14.8%	23.4%	16.3%	-2.1%	1.1%	2.9%	13.7%	1.0%	9.4%	7.2%	20.3%
Canada	8.0%	7.6%	4.3%	7.8%	-2.9%	-3.7%	-5.3%	-4.5%	6.9%	18.2%	18.6%	30.3%

Matrix Comparison	1991				1992				1993			
	Mar	Jun	Sep	Dec	Mar	Jun	Sep	Dec	Mar	Jun	Sep	Dec
Currency to Dollar												
United States (Weighted)	65.2	67.8	64.5	60.9	64.9	61.2	60.3	66.7	65.7	65.1	65.0	67.8
Japan	138.0	139.0	133.0	126.0	133.0	126.0	120.0	125.0	117.0	107.0	105.0	113.0
Germany	1.67	1.80	1.67	1.52	1.65	1.52	1.42	1.63	1.62	1.69	1.62	1.74
Britain	0.57	0.61	0.57	0.54	0.58	0.53	0.57	0.65	0.67	0.66	0.66	0.67
Canada	1.16	1.14	1.13	1.16	1.19	1.20	1.26	1.28	1.25	1.28	1.32	1.32
Change in Currency												
United States (Weighted)	6.2%	10.4%	5.0%	-0.8%	6.6%	0.5%	-1.0%	9.5%	-1.5%	-2.4%	-2.5%	1.6%
Japan	1.5%	2.2%	-2.2%	-7.4%	5.6%	0.0%	-4.8%	-0.8%	-6.4%	-14.4%	-16.0%	-9.6%
Germany	12.1%	20.8%	12.1%	2.0%	8.6%	0.0%	-6.6%	7.2%	-0.6%	3.7%	-0.6%	6.7%
Britain	9.6%	17.3%	9.6%	3.8%	7.4%	-1.9%	5.6%	20.4%	3.1%	1.5%	1.5%	3.1%
Canada	0.0%	-1.7%	-2.6%	0.0%	2.6%	3.4%	8.6%	10.3%	-2.3%	0.0%	3.1%	3.1%
Real Money Market Yield												
United States	1.4	1.5	2.1	1.4	0.9	0.7	0.3	0.5	0.1	0.3	0.5	0.6
Japan	3.7	3.8	3.8	3.1	2.8	2.2	1.9	2.6	2.1	2.3	1.0	1.0
Germany	6.6	5.4	5.3	5.4	4.8	5.4	5.5	4.9	3.7	3.3	2.6	2.2
Britain	4.3	5.5	6.2	6.4	6.8	6.2	5.4	4.6	4.0	4.7	4.1	3.5
Canada	3.5	2.4	3.0	3.5	5.6	4.3	6.3	4.9	3.2	2.9	2.1	2.1
Prime and MM Spread												
United States	2.7	2.4	2.5	2.0	2.4	2.7	2.7	2.6	2.8	2.7	2.8	2.7
Japan	0.6	0.5	0.9	0.8	1.1	0.8	0.9	0.7	0.7	0.8	1.3	1.0
Germany	1.4	1.6	2.3	1.7	1.3	1.3	1.9	2.3	2.5	2.5	2.9	3.2
Britain	1.0	1.2	1.2	0.6	0.7	0.9	1.0	0.8	1.1	1.1	1.1	1.1
Canada	1.5	1.1	1.1	0.7	1.1	1.6	-1.3	0.3	0.9	1.5	1.8	1.7
Share Index												
United States	2,945	2,973	3,018	3,169	3,236	3,319	3,267	3,308	3,457	3,519	3,566	3,784
Japan	26,252	23,996	24,377	22,984	19,346	15,952	17,748	16,843	18,963	19,543	20,173	17,370
Germany	1,862	1,906	1,869	1,578	1,718	1,753	1,476	1,556	1,685	1,708	1,914	2,254
Britain	2,488	2,460	2,646	2,493	2,440	2,521	2,566	2,834	2,861	3,100	3,037	3,409
Canada	3,516	3,505	3,395	3,512	3,412	3,383	3,327	3,354	3,586	3,963	3,979	4,369

Balance of Payments for Matrix Countries, France, Switzerland, and Mexico, 1988–1992

Source: International Financial Statistics (Washington, D.C.: International Monetary Fund, January 1994).

United States	1988	1989	1990	1991	1992
Trade Exports	320	362	389	417	440
Trade Imports	-447	-477	-498	-491	-536
Trade Balance	*-127*	*-115*	*-109*	*-74*	*-96*
Service Exports	99	114	132	146	159
Service Imports	-94	-98	-112	-113	-117
Service Balance	*5*	*16*	*20*	*33*	*42*
Investment Receipts	131	154	160	146	131
Investment Payments	-111	-130	-129	-120	-111
Investment Balance	*20*	*24*	*31*	*26*	*20*
Summary Balance					
Commercial Exports	550	630	681	709	730
Commercial Imports	-652	-705	-739	-724	-764
Commercial Balance	*-102*	*-75*	*-58*	*-15*	*-34*
Private Transfers	-12	-13	-12	-14	-14
Official Transfers	-13	-13	-21	21	-18
Transfer Balance	*-25*	*-26*	*-33*	*7*	*-32*
Current Account	*-127*	*-101*	*-91*	*-8*	*-66*
Direct Investment	42	39	12	-5	-32
Portfolio Investment	40	44	-33	9	14
Short-Term Capital	8	33	34	-2	55
Total Identified Flows	*90*	*116*	*13*	*2*	*37*
Net Errors and Omissions	0	2	47	-15	-12
Total Private Capital	*90*	*118*	*60*	*-13*	*25*
Change in Reserves	-3	-25	-2	6	4
Liability to Foreign Auth.	40	8	32	16	38
Other Financing	0	0	0	0	0
Total Reserve Changes	*37*	*-17*	*30*	*22*	*42*

Japan	1988	1989	1990	1991	1992
Trade Exports	260	270	280	307	331
Trade Imports	-165	-193	-217	-204	-198
Trade Balance	*95*	*77*	*63*	*103*	*133*
Service Exports	35	40	41	45	48
Service Imports	-64	-75	-82	-85	-90
Service Balance	*-29*	*-35*	*-41*	*-40*	*-42*
Investment Receipts	77	104	125	144	146
Investment Payments	-59	-85	-106	-121	-115
Investment Balance	*18*	*19*	*19*	*23*	*31*
Summary Balance					
Commercial Exports	372	414	446	496	525
Commercial Imports	-288	-353	-405	-410	-403
Commercial Balance	*84*	*61*	*41*	*86*	*122*
Private Transfers	-1	-1	-1	-1	-1
Official Transfers	-3	-3	-4	-12	-3
Transfer Balance	*-4*	*-4*	*-5*	*-13*	*-4*
Current Account	*80*	*57*	*36*	*73*	*118*
Direct Investment	-35	-45	-46	-29	-15
Portfolio Investment	-53	-33	-14	35	-28
Short-Term Capital	21	30	39	-78	-64
Total Identified Flows	*-67*	*-48*	*-21*	*-72*	*-107*
Net Errors and Omissions	3	-22	-21	-8	-10
Total Private Capital	*-64*	*-70*	*-42*	*-80*	*-117*
Change in Reserves	-17	13	7	7	-1
Liability to Foreign Auth.	0	0	0	0	0
Other Financing	0	0	0	0	0
Total Reserve Changes	*-17*	*13*	*7*	*7*	*-1*

Germany	1988	1989	1990	1991	1992
Trade Exports	309	325	391	379	407
Trade Imports	-229	-247	-319	-355	-374
Trade Balance	*80*	*78*	*72*	*24*	*33*
Service Exports	52	56	69	70	74
Service Imports	-66	-67	-86	-92	-107
Service Balance	*-14*	*-11*	*-17*	*-22*	*-33*
Investment Receipts	36	45	64	73	83
Investment Payments	-33	-36	-50	-58	-76
Investment Balance	*3*	*9*	*14*	*15*	*7*
Summary Balance					
Commercial Exports	397	426	524	522	564
Commercial Imports	-328	-350	-455	-505	-557
Commercial Balance	*69*	*76*	*69*	*17*	*7*
Private Transfers	-6	-6	-7	-7	-8
Official Transfers	-12	-12	-16	-29	-24
Transfer Balance	*-18*	*-18*	*-23*	*-36*	*-32*
Current Account	*51*	*58*	*46*	*-19*	*-25*
Direct Investment	-12	-8	-20	-15	-9
Portfolio Investment	-44	-5	-2	24	50
Short-Term Capital	-16	-61	-34	3	28
Total Identified Flows	*-72*	*-74*	*-56*	*12*	*69*
Net Errors and Omissions	2	5	15	10	0
Total Private Capital	*-70*	*-69*	*-41*	*22*	*69*
Change in Reserves	15	-3	-7	6	-37
Liability to Foreign Auth.	3	13	2	-8	-6
Other Financing	0	0	0	0	0
Total Reserve Changes	*18*	*10*	*-5*	*-2*	*-43*

Britain	1988	1989	1990	1991	1992
Trade Exports	143	151	182	183	187
Trade Imports	-181	-191	-215	-201	-212
Trade Balance	*-38*	*-40*	*-33*	*-18*	*-25*
Service Exports	46	47	54	52	55
Service Imports	-39	-40	-46	-45	-49
Service Balance	*7*	*7*	*8*	*7*	*6*
Investment Receipts	103	123	145	139	121
Investment Payments	-95	-118	-141	-137	-114
Investment Balance	*8*	*5*	*4*	*2*	*7*
Summary Balance					
Commercial Exports	292	321	381	374	363
Commercial Imports	-315	-349	-402	-383	-375
Commercial Balance	*-23*	*-28*	*-21*	*-9*	*-12*
Private Transfers	0	0	-1	0	-1
Official Transfers	-6	-7	-8	-2	-8
Transfer Balance	*-6*	*-7*	*-9*	*-2*	*-9*
Current Account	*-29*	*-35*	*-30*	*-11*	*-21*
Direct Investment	-16	-5	15	0	3
Portfolio Investment	6	-32	-19	-24	-24
Short-Term Capital	25	55	22	48	38
Total Identified Flows	*15*	*18*	*18*	*24*	*17*
Net Errors and Omissions	12	3	10	2	1
Total Private Capital	*27*	*21*	*28*	*26*	*18*
Change in Reserves	-5	9	0	-5	3
Liability to Foreign Auth.	7	7	2	-9	0
Other Financing	0	-2	0	0	0
Total Reserve Changes	*2*	*14*	*2*	*-14*	*3*

France	1988	1989	1990	1991	1992
Trade Exports	160	171	207	207	225
Trade Imports	-169	-181	-220	-217	-223
Trade Balance	*-9*	*-10*	*-13*	*-10*	*2*
Service Exports	54	61	77	81	99
Service Imports	-42	-46	-61	-63	-79
Service Balance	*12*	*15*	*16*	*18*	*20*
Investment Receipts	35	42	57	71	82
Investment Payments	-37	-43	-62	-78	-92
Investment Balance	*-2*	*-1*	*-5*	*-7*	*-10*
Summary Balance					
Commercial Exports	249	274	341	359	406
Commercial Imports	-248	-270	-343	-358	-394
Commercial Balance	*1*	*4*	*-2*	*1*	*12*
Private Transfers	-2	-3	-4	-3	-3
Official Transfers	-4	-6	-9	-5	-6
Transfer Balance	*-6*	*-9*	*-13*	*-8*	*-9*
Current Account	*-5*	*-5*	*-15*	*-7*	*3*
Direct Investment	-6	-9	-21	-9	-9
Portfolio Investment	8	22	35	14	34
Short-Term Capital	2	-8	12	-11	-44
Total Identified Flows	*4*	*5*	*26*	*-6*	*-19*
Net Errors and Omissions	1	-2	1	7	2
Total Private Capital	*5*	*3*	*27*	*1*	*-17*
Change in Reserves	5	1	-11	5	2
Liability to Foreign Auth.	-5	1	-1	1	12
Other Financing	0	0	0	0	0
Total Reserve Changes	*0*	*2*	*-12*	*6*	*14*

Switzerland	1988	1989	1990	1991	1992
Trade Exports	63	65	77	74	79
Trade Imports	-67	-69	-84	-78	-79
Trade Balance	*-4*	*-4*	*-7*	*-4*	*0*
Service Exports	14	14	17	18	19
Service Imports	-9	-9	-11	-11	-12
Service Balance	*5*	*5*	*6*	*7*	*7*
Investment Receipts	22	24	30	29	28
Investment Payments	-12	-15	-20	-19	-19
Investment Balance	*10*	*9*	*10*	*10*	*9*
Summary Balance					
Commercial Exports	99	103	124	121	126
Commercial Imports	-88	-93	-115	-108	-110
Commercial Balance	*11*	*10*	*9*	*13*	*16*
Private Transfers	-2	-2	-2	-2	-2
Official Transfers	0	0	0	0	-1
Transfer Balance	*-2*	*-2*	*-2*	*-2*	*-3*
Current Account	*9*	*8*	*7*	*11*	*13*
Direct Investment	-8	-5	-1	-3	-4
Portfolio Investment	-7	-3	-1	-12	-3
Short-Term Capital	1	0	-9	4	-2
Total Identified Flows	*-14*	*-8*	*-11*	*-11*	*-9*
Net Errors and Omissions	3	1	6	2	0
Total Private Capital	*-11*	*-7*	*-5*	*-9*	*-9*
Change in Reserves	2	-1	-1	-1	-4
Liability to Foreign Auth.	0	0	0	0	0
Other Financing	0	0	0	0	0
Total Reserve Changes	*2*	*-1*	*-1*	*-1*	*-4*

Canada

Canada	1988	1989	1990	1991	1992
Trade Exports	115	123	129	127	133
Trade Imports	-107	-117	-120	-122	-125
Trade Balance	*8*	*6*	*9*	*5*	*8*
Service Exports	14	15	16	17	17
Service Imports	-20	-23	-27	-28	-29
Service Balance	*-6*	*-8*	*-11*	*-11*	*-12*
Investment Receipts	10	9	9	9	7
Investment Payments	-25	-27	-29	-28	-27
Investment Balance	*-15*	*-18*	*-20*	*-19*	*-20*
Summary Balance					
Commercial Exports	139	147	154	153	157
Commercial Imports	-152	-167	-176	-178	-181
Commercial Balance	*-13*	*-20*	*-22*	*-25*	*-24*
Private Transfers	1	1	1	1	1
Official Transfers	-1	-1	-1	0	-1
Transfer Balance	*0*	*0*	*0*	*0*	*0*
Current Account	*-13*	*-20*	*-22*	*-25*	*-24*
Direct Investment	-2	-3	3	0	2
Portfolio Investment	8	15	8	15	8
Short-Term Capital	14	7	12	12	4
Total Identified Flows	*20*	*19*	*23*	*27*	*14*
Net Errors and Omissions	-1	0	-1	-4	3
Total Private Capital	*19*	*19*	*22*	*23*	*17*
Change in Reserves	-7	0	-1	2	6
Liability to Foreign Auth.	0	0	0	0	0
Other Financing	0	0	0	0	0
Total Reserve Changes	*-7*	*0*	*-1*	*2*	*6*

Mexico

Mexico	1988	1989	1990	1991	1992
Trade Exports	21	23	27	27	27
Trade Imports	-19	-23	-31	-38	-48
Trade Balance	*2*	*0*	*-4*	*-11*	*-21*
Service Exports	8	10	12	13	14
Service Imports	-6	-8	-10	-11	-11
Service Balance	*2*	*2*	*2*	*2*	*3*
Investment Receipts	3	3	3	3	3
Investment Payments	-10	-11	-11	-10	-10
Investment Balance	*-7*	*-8*	*-8*	*-7*	*-7*
Summary Balance					
Commercial Exports	32	36	42	43	44
Commercial Imports	-35	-42	-52	-59	-69
Commercial Balance	*-3*	*-6*	*-10*	*-16*	*-25*
Private Transfers	0	2	2	2	2
Official Transfers	0	0	1	0	0
Transfer Balance	*0*	*2*	*3*	*2*	*2*
Current Account	*-3*	*-4*	*-7*	*-14*	*-23*
Direct Investment	1	3	3	5	5
Portfolio Investment	-1	0	-5	9	14
Short-Term Capital	-6	-2	11	10	7
Total Identified Flows	*-6*	*1*	*9*	*24*	*26*
Net Errors and Omissions	-3	3	1	-3	-2
Total Private Capital	*-9*	*4*	*10*	*21*	*24*
Change in Reserves	7	-1	-3	-8	-1
Liability to Foreign Auth.	0	0	0	0	0
Other Financing	5	1	1	0	-1
Total Reserve Changes	*12*	*0*	*-2*	*-8*	*-2*

International Investment Position of the United States, 1987–1992

Source: Economic Report of the President (Washington, D.C.: U.S. Government Printing Office, February 1994), p. 385.

	Billions of U.S. Dollars					
	1987	1988	1989	1990	1991	1992
ASSETS						
U.S. Official Assets						
SDRs and IMF Reserve	21	19	19	20	20	20
Gold	128	107	105	102	93	90
Foreign Currencies	13	18	45	52	46	40
Other	89	86	84	83	79	81
Total Official Assets	251	230	253	257	238	231
Private Assets						
Bank Claims	550	653	714	696	692	667
Nonbank Claims	109	122	114	120	119	112
Foreign Bonds	84	91	96	119	135	149
Foreign Stocks	70	86	120	110	159	178
Direct Investment (market value)	577	679	818	716	810	776
Total Private Assets	1,390	1,631	1,862	1,761	1,915	1,882
Total Assets	1,641	1,861	2,115	2,018	2,153	2,113
LIABILITIES						
Foreign Official Assets						
Bank Liabilities	32	32	36	40	38	55
U.S. Government Securities	220	261	264	295	316	336
Other	31	29	42	41	48	52
Total Foreign Official Assets	283	322	342	376	402	443
Foreign Private Assets						
U.S. Bank Liabilities	540	614	677	693	682	701
U.S. Nonbank Liabilities	30	35	40	48	46	46
U.S. Treasury Securities	83	101	167	162	190	225
Corporate Bonds	166	191	232	247	284	317
Corporate Stocks	176	201	251	222	272	300
Direct Investment (market value)	316	392	535	540	673	693
Total Foreign Private Assets	1,311	1,534	1,902	1,912	2,147	2,282
Total Foreign-Owned Assets	1,594	1,856	2,244	2,288	2,549	2,725
Net Investment Position	47	5	-129	-270	-396	-612

Monetary Aggregate Classifications for Selected Countries

FEDERAL RESERVE
(PRINCIPAL MONETARY AGGREGATE TARGET: M2)

- M1
  1. Currency in circulation and bank vaults
  2. Travelers' checks
  3. Demand (checkable) deposits at commercial banks, excluding deposits held by the U.S. government, foreign commercial banks, and foreign central banks
  4. Interest-bearing demand deposits (NOW accounts), automatic transfer services, and certain other demand deposits held at credit unions and thrift institutions

- M2
  1. M1 items
  2. Repurchase agreements
  3. Money market deposit accounts
  4. Savings and small-denomination time deposits with balances of less than $100,000
  5. Broker–dealer money market accounts

- M3
  1. M2 items
  2. Large-denomination time deposits in excess of $100,000

3. Term repurchase agreements
4. Term Eurodollar deposits held by U.S. residents at foreign branches of U.S. banks worldwide

- L
  1. M3 items
  2. Nonbank public holdings of U.S. savings bonds
  3. Short-term Treasury securities
  4. Commercial paper
  5. Banker's acceptances

BANK OF JAPAN (PRINCIPAL MONETARY AGGREGATE TARGET: M2 + CDS)

- M1
  1. Currency in circulation and bank vaults
  2. Demand deposits with the Bank of Japan
  3. Demand deposits with commercial banks and other depository institutions

- M1'
  1. M1 items
  2. Nondemand deposits held by corporate businesses

- M1'+ CDs
  1. M1' items
  2. CDs issued by commercial banks and other depository institutions

- M2
  1. M1' items
  2. Nondemand deposits with the Bank of Japan
  3. Nondemand deposits with commercial banks and other depository institutions

- M2 + CDs
  1. M2 items
  2. CDs issued by commercial banks and other depository institutions

- M3
  1. M2 items
  2. Total deposits credit associations and Postal Savings Service

- M3 + CDs
  1. M3 items
  2. CDs issued by credit associations and Postal Savings Service

BUNDESBANK (PRINCIPAL MONETARY AGGREGATE TARGET: M3)

Uses monetary aggregate classifications similar to Federal Reserve except that M1 includes interest earning commercial bank deposits that can be withdrawn on up to one month's notice.

BANK OF ENGLAND (PRINCIPAL MONETARY
AGGREGATE TARGET: M0)

- M0
  1. Currency in circulation and bank vaults
  2. Operating balances at Bank of England

- M1
  1. Currency in circulation and bank vaults
  2. Demand deposits in clearing banks and other financial institutions
  3. Interest-bearing demand deposits in clearing banks and other financial institutions

- M2
  1. Currency in circulation and bank vaults
  2. Demand deposits at commercial banks and other financial institutions
  3. Interest-bearing time deposits below £100,000 and less than 30 days at commercial banks and building societies
  4. Building society deposits

- M3
  1. M1 items
  2. Interest-bearing time deposits and CDs at all financial institutions

- M4
  1. M3 items
  2. Other demand and time deposits at commercial banks and building societies
  3. Building society vault cash, deposits, and certificates of deposits

- M5
  1. M4 items
  2. Money market instruments of bank, treasury, and local authority bills
  3. Certificates of tax deposit
  4. National savings instruments (excluding certificates and other long-term deposits)

Capitalization of Country Bond and Equity Markets, 1992

Source: Quality of Markets Review (London: London Stock Exchange, Spring 1993), pp. 90 and 91.

Exchange	Fixed Interest				Equities			
	Company	Govt.	Overseas	Total	Domestic	Overseas	Total	GrandTotal
Europe								
Amsterdam	47	147	7	201	174	0	174	375
Athens	4	30	0	34	10	0	10	43
Barcelona	19	9	1	28	94	12	106	134
Bilbao	15	7	0	22	97	0	97	119
Brussels	2	167	208	377	65	0	65	442
Copenhagen	81	139	43	263	33	4	37	300
Germany	721	529	163	1,413	335	0	335	1,748
Helsinki	10	8	0	18	12	0	12	30
Lisbon	0	0	0	0	9	0	9	9
Luxembourg	3	0	1,224	1,227	12	202	215	1,442
Madrid	20	18	0	38	118	18	136	174
Milan	5	19	1	25	117	0	117	143
Oporto	5	19	1	25	9	0	9	34
Oslo	17	21	0	38	18	0	18	57
Paris	103	483	0	586	334	0	334	920
Stockholm	51	47	0	98	77	0	77	176
Switzerland	0	0	0	0	199	0	199	199
Britain	139	280	199	619	961	2,389	3,349	3,968
Vienna	37	46	3	85	19	375	394	479
Warsaw	0	1	0	1	0	0	0	1
Total Europe	1,278	1,970	1,850	5,099	2,694	3,000	5,695	10,793
North America								
United States	246	1,826	25	2,097	4,602	478	5,080	7,177
Canada	0	567	0	567	447	74	520	1,087
Total N. America	246	2,393	25	2,664	5,049	551	5,600	8,264
Far East								
Hong Kong	0	0	0	0	175	0	175	175
Indonesia	0	0	0	0	12	0	12	12
Japan	233	2,298	32	2,562	4,872	1	4,873	7,435
Korea	42	42	0	84	109	0	109	194
Malaysia	2	0	0	2	14	0	14	16
Singapore	0	103	0	103	48	0	48	151
Taiwan	1	21	1	22	102	0	102	124
Thailand	0	5	0	5	58	0	58	64
Total Far East	278	2,469	33	2,780	5,390	1	5,391	8,170
Australasia								
Australia	2	48	0	50	136	135	271	320
New Zealand	0	0	0	0	8	24	31	31
Total Australasia	2	48	0	50	144	158	302	352
Latin America								
Argentina	1	9	0	10	19	0	19	28
Brazil	0	0	0	0	92	0	92	92
Chile	0	0	0	0	30	0	30	30
Colmbia	0	0	0	0	7	0	7	7
Ecuador	0	0	0	0	75	0	75	75
Mexico	7	20	0	28	141	0	141	169
Trinidad and Tobago	0	0	0	0	3	0	3	3
Total Latin America	8	29	0	37	368	0	368	405
Africa								
South Africa	0	61	0	61	151	0	151	212
Zimbabwe	0	2	0	2	1	0	1	2
Total Africa	0	62	0	63	152	0	152	214
Middle East and Asia								
India	0	0	0	0	169	0	169	169
Iran	0	0	0	0	30	0	30	30
Israel	4	27	0	31	28	0	28	60
Jordan	0	0	0	0	4	0	4	4
Kuwait	0	0	0	0	0	0	0	0
Mauritius	0	0	0	0	0	0	0	0
Turkey	0	0	0	0	10	0	10	10
Total Middle East	4	27	0	32	241	0	241	273
Total	1,817	6,998	1,908	10,724	14,037	3,711	17,748	28,472

Influential International Organizations

Since the creation of the League of Nations in 1920, technological advances in travel and communications have enabled national government and central banks to expand consultation on international economic and financial matters. Several attempts have been made to develop international organizations that would have the financial ability to regulate international commerce in a manner similar to a central bank or government commission. Most countries are unwilling to part with their sovereignty so that such movements have had limited success. Nevertheless, a number of formal and informal organizations have grown to develop a cadre of professionals experienced in international commerce and a source of great insight and information essential to national governments and central banks in the formulation and implementation of international economic policy. A brief review of these important organizations is helpful.

The Bank for International Settlement (BIS)

One of the oldest international organizations devoted to international financial matters, the BIS was founded in Basle, Switzerland, in 1930 to coordinate Germany's World War I reparation payments. Today, its principal functions are (1) accept deposits from and make loans on behalf of its member central banks, (2) supervise information on Euromarket finances, and (3) act as a trade organization representing central bank views on domestic and international economic issues. Its board is composed of representatives of thirteen leading central banks.

The General Agreement on Trade and Tariffs (GATT) (Name to Be Changed to the World Trade Organization [WTO])

GATT was begun in 1947 as an institutionalized means of promoting free trade by multilateral negotiations to reduce trade restrictions. By 1991, there were 103 members and it began extending its free-trade charter to include reducing restrictions on services and developing an international approach to copyright protection.

Group of Seven (G-7)

Following the abandonment of the Bretton Woods system and its formal arrangement for maintaining a fixed exchange rate regime, the United States commenced periodic informal gatherings of a small working group of finance ministers representing countries important to global economic cooperation, hence the designation *G* for government. The number of countries invited has varied as indicated by the number. In 1986, and as of this writing, seven countries are deemed most important for international economic cooperation: the United States, Japan, Germany, France, Italy, Britain, and Canada.

The International Monetary Fund (IMF)

Established by the Bretton Woods agreement of 1944, the IMF was intended to promote international monetary cooperation, stable exchange rates, elimination of exchange controls, and provide short-term funds for countries experiencing balance-of-payment problems jeopardizing the fixed exchange rate regime. In contrast to the BIS, the IMF was authorized to manage an international payments and fixed rate regime created by the Bretton Woods agreement. It was created separate and apart from the BIS in order to incorporate the political and economic realignments resulting from World War II. With the demise of the fixed exchange rate regime, the IMF is still responsible for managing the payments system created by Bretton Woods and has assisted countries in coordinating exchange rate management consistent with the present floating exchange rate system.

The Organization for Economic Cooperation and Development (OECD)

Originally begun as the Organization for European Economic Cooperation to assist in implementing the Marshall Plan, its name was changed to the present form in 1961. Based in Paris, its twenty-four members constitute the principal Western industrial nations of the world and will be expanded to include Mexico. Its principal function is to provide statistical data, information, and advice to improve international economic growth and cooperation.

The World Bank (International Bank for Reconstruction and Development)

Along with the IMF, the World Bank (International Bank for Reconstruction and Development) was established by the Bretton Woods agreement and began operation in 1946. As indicated in its original title, its purpose was to provide financing for war reconstruction, and most of the lending facilities were directed toward Europe. Following Europe's revival, the bank issued bonds and expanded its operations to assist all countries and now is one of the largest lenders to developing countries. In contrast to the IMF, the World Bank provides primarily long-term financing for large projects designed to improve a nation's infrastructure such as power plants and dams. Its lending practices have been subject to considerable criticism.[1]

NOTE

1. Cheryl Payer, *The World Bank: A Critical Analysis* (New York: Monthly Review Press, 1982).

□　□　■　□　□

Selected Bibliography

Berlin, Howard M. *The Handbook of Financial Markets, Indexes, Averages, and Indicators*. Homewood, Ill.: Dow Jones–Irwin, 1990.

Blackman, W. *Swiss Banking in an International Context*. London: Macmillan, 1989.

Brown, Brendan. *The Flight of International Capital*. London: Routledge, 1987.

Chaliand, Gerard, and Rageau, Jean-Pierre. *Strategic Atlas*. 3rd ed. New York: Harper Perennial, 1992.

Chalmin, Philip. *International Commodity Markets Handbook, 1993*. New York: Woodhead-Faulkner, 1992.

Cohen, Benjamin. *American Foreign Economic Policy: Essays and Comments*. New York: Harper & Row, 1968.

Dermine, Jean. *European Banking in the 1990s*. Oxford: Blackwell, 1990.

Dore, Ronald, and Sinha, Radha. *Japan and World Depression*. New York: Macmillan, 1985.

Douch, Nick. *The Economics of Foreign Exchange*. Westport, Conn.: Quorum Books, 1989.

The Economist. *The Economist Book of Vital World Statistics*. New York: Times Books, 1990.

The Economist. *Guide to Economic Indicators*. London: Century Business, 1992.

Ely, Richard T. *Outlines of Economics*. New York: Macmillan, 1926.

Faulkner, Harold Underwood. *American Economic History*. New York: Harper & Brothers, 1943.

Floyd, John E. *World Monetary Equilibrium*. Oxford: Philip Allan Publishers, 1985.

Friedman, Milton. *Essays in Positive Economics*. Chicago: University of Chicago Press, 1953.

Friedman, Milton, and Schwartz, Anna. *A Monetary History of the United States, 1867–1960*. Princeton: Princeton University Press, 1963.

Goldstein, Morris, et al. *International Capital Markets*, Part I. Washington, D.C.: International Monetary Fund, 1993.

Gordon, Robert Aaron. *Business Fluctuations*. New York: Harper & Brothers, 1952.

Greider, William. *Secrets of the Temple*. New York: Simon & Schuster, 1987.

Hallwood, Paul, and MacDonald, Ronald. *International Money*. Oxford: Basil Blackwell, 1986.

Harris, J. Manville. *International Finance*. New York: Barron's, 1992.

Hayek, Friedrich A. *Monetary Theory and the Trade Cycle*. 1937. Reprint. New York: Augustus M. Kelley, 1966.

Homer, Sidney. *A History of Interest Rates*. 2nd ed. New Brunswick: Rutgers University Press, 1977.

Honeygold, Derek. *International Financial Markets*. New York: Nichols Publishing Company, 1989.

Inoguchi, Takashi, and Okimoto, Daniel I. *The Political Economy of Japan*. Stanford: Stanford University Press, 1988.

International Monetary Fund. *International Financial Statistics*. Washington, D.C.: International Monetary Fund, 1993 and 1994 issues.

Kaufman, George F. *Banking Structures in Major Countries*. London: Kluwer Academic Publishers, 1992.

Kennedy, Paul. *Preparing for the Twenty-First Century*. New York: Random House, 1993.

Kennedy, Paul, *The Realities behind Diplomacy*. London: Fontana Press, 1981.

Kindleberger, Charles P. *Economic Response*. Cambridge: Harvard University Press, 1978.

Kissinger, Henry. *Diplomacy*. New York: Simon & Schuster, 1994.

Klein, Philip A., and Moore, Geoffrey H. *Monitoring Growth Cycles in Market-Oriented Countries*, National Bureau of Economic Research Studies in Business Cycles No. 26. Cambridge, Mass.: Ballinger, 1985.

Lewis, W. Arthur. *Economic Survey, 1919–1939*. New York: Harper & Row, 1949.

Lewis, W. Arthur. *Growth and Fluctuations, 1870–1913*. London: George Allen & Unwin, 1978.

Marsh, David. *The Bundesbank*. London: Heinemann, 1992.

Mason, Mark. *American Multinationals and Japan: The Political Economy of Japanese Capital Controls, 1899–1980*. Cambridge: Harvard University Press, 1992.

McKibbin, Warwick J., and Sachs, Jeffrey D. *Global Linkages*. Washington, D.C.: The Brookings Institution, 1991.

Munn, Glenn G. *Encyclopedia of Banking and Finance*. Pasadena, Calif.: Salem Press, 1991.

Murphy, John J. *Intermarket Technical Analysis*. New York: John Wiley & Sons, 1991.

Newman, Peter. *The New Palgrave Dictionary of Money and Finance*. London: Macmillan, 1992.

Park, Yoon S., and Essayyad, Musa. *International Banking and Financial Centers*. London: Kluwer Academic Publishers, 1989.

Prindl, Andreas R. *Japanese Finance*. New York: John Wiley & Sons, 1981.

Pring, Martin J. *How to Forecast Interest Rates*. New York: McGraw Hill, 1981.

Rivera-Batiz, Francisco L., and Rivera-Batiz, Luis. *International Finance and Open Economy Macroeconomics*. New York: Macmillan, 1985.

Schaefer, Howard G. *Economic Trend Analysis for Executives and Investors*. Westport, Conn.: Quorum Books, 1993.

Slichter, Sumner H. *Economic Growth in the United States*. New York: The Free Press, 1961.

Triffin, Robert. *Gold and the Dollar Crisis*. New Haven: Yale University Press, 1960.

Triffin, Robert. *Our International Monetary System*. New York: Random House, 1968.

U.S. Department of Commerce. *Statistical Abstract of the United States: 1992*. Washington, D.C.: U.S. Government Printing Office, 1992.

Volcker, Paul, and Gyohten, Toyoo. *Changing Fortunes*. New York: Times Books, 1992.

World Bank. *World Tables 1992*. Baltimore: Johns Hopkins University Press, 1992.

Index

ABOUT THE AUTHOR

HOWARD G. SCHAEFER is managing partner of Schaefer Brothers, Ltd., a Los Angeles investment banking firm. He has practiced corporate and tax law, with a specialty in international business, and is a frequent lecturer and writer on business and economic issues. His first book, *Economic Trend Analysis for Executives and Investors* (Quorum, 1993), concentrates on the U.S. economy and provides important background for this, his second Quorum book.

ISBN 0-89930-956-9

EAN

9 780899 309569

90000>

HARDCOVER BAR CODE